Wingshooter's Guide to

IOWA

Upland Birds and Waterfowl

Wingshooter's Guide to
IOWA
Upland Birds and Waterfowl

Larry Brown

Wilderness Adventures Press

Gallatin Gateway, Montana

This book was manufactured with an easy-open, lay-flat binding.

Published by Wilderness Adventures Press
P.O. Box 627
Gallatin Gateway, MT 59730
800-925-3339

10 9 8 7 6 5 4 3 2 1

Printed in the United States of America

Library of Congress Cataloging-in-Publication Data:

Brown, Larry, 1945–
    Wingshooter's guide to Iowa: upland birds and waterfowl / Larry Brown.
        p.   cm.
    Includes index.
    ISBN 1-885106-45-9
    1. Upland game bird shooting—Iowa.   2. Waterfowl shooting—Iowa.
I. Title.
SK323.B76   1998
799.2'4'09777—dc21   98–16417
                                                                          CIP

Table of Contents

Foreword

I am tempted to say that I have known Larry Brown since high school. We did, in fact, live across the street from one another and maintained a nodding acquaintance. But it was in 1974, when we were both graduate students of the "nontraditional" type, that we began a hunting partnership that continues to this day. It wasn't until we pulled into the very first woodcock cover we ever hunted together, that I can say with certainty that I began to know Larry. As we stood on opposite sides of his old Ford station wagon, he uncased a prewar Sauer 16-gauge, and I pulled my aging Winchester 101 out of its case. We looked at the guns for a moment and then at each other. As I recall, nothing was said, but we suddenly knew a great deal about one another.

This fall, on a logging road in Michigan, we began our twenty-fourth season. Over that stretch of years, an unspoken understanding has grown up between us that has survived marriages, divorces, children, deaths, and the demands of various occupations. Through those years I have watched the development of an expert. Not the self-proclaimed type who holds forth at any opportunity, but the quiet, efficient type who has no need to expound on his qualifications.

As professional literary men are wont to do, I have come to connect Larry's development as a hunter with William Faulkner's wonderful short story, "The Bear." In it the central character says: "There was a boy who wished to learn humility…in order to become skillful and worthy in the woods, who suddenly found himself becoming so skillful so rapidly that he feared he would never become worthy because he had not learned humility…"[1] Down the years, I had often thought that if there were a failing to which Larry was prone it would be this: that his skill would outstrip his respect for the game he so efficiently sought. It has not happened. Just as the bear lived always in that boy's mind, so have pheasants lived in Larry's. His love and respect for upland birds, and in particular pheasants, has not diminished as his skill in bringing them to bag has increased.

In the pages that follow, I invite you to share not only in that expertise but in that abiding respect and love.

Michael James Carroll
November 1997

---

1 William Faulkner. "The Bear." Kneer, Leo B, ed., The United States in Literature. (Glenview, IL: Scott Foresman and Company, 1973).

Introduction

I saw my first pheasant from the back seat of a 1948 Dodge. My mother had spotted the rooster from the passenger seat up front. Dad slid to a halt on the gravel road, backed up, uncased and loaded his ancient .410 single shot, rolled down the window, and shot it. While my ears rang, he retrieved the bird from the ditch, tossed it in the trunk, and we headed on down the road to continue our hunt.

Dad got married and started a family during the Depression, when a pheasant meant meat on the table to a lot of hard-up Iowans. He never owned a bird dog, although he boarded a couple of mine at different times. But when he finally saw some good dog work, near the end of his hunting career, he began to appreciate ring-necks as sporting targets, not just the main course for dinner.

I started hunting in Iowa with my father and older brother when I was big enough and responsible enough for Dad to allow me to carry a gun. That was back in the late 1950s, and since then, I've only left the state for one extended period of time. Part of that was spent in Washington, DC, where I suffered through about three bird-less seasons. To atone for that, Uncle Sam was kind enough to send me to Morocco, where I hunted native chukar and migratory (coturnix) quail, with a realistic bag limit of 50 a day! It was in Morocco that I acquired my first bird dog and my first side-by-side shotgun—the true beginnings of a passion that continues to this day.

Upon my return, I started hunting birds my dad had never seen, let alone pursued: ruffed grouse and woodcock. Later in the fall, I'd head to southern Iowa to hunt bobwhite quail, birds Dad remembered from his youth in that part of the state but which had long disappeared from the fields around my home farther north.

But then and now, first, last, and always, there were pheasants. This gaudy Oriental immigrant has adapted marvelously to Iowa's modern, intensive agriculture which is a good thing, because the flocks of prairie chickens that greeted the first pioneers to settle the state had disappeared years before Iowa's first pheasant season took place, back in 1925.

Since then, with the exception of a brief downward trend in the late '70s and early '80s, Iowa's pheasant population has fared quite well. Through much of the 1990s, South Dakota's claim of being the nation's pheasant capital aside, bird hunters in Iowa have harvested more ringnecks than in any other state. Most nonresidents who come here with shotgun and bird dog are after pheasants.

But that's far from all Iowa has to offer. Waterfowl hunting has been on a strong recovery in recent years, and with the current trend favoring protection rather than destruction of wetlands, the future for ducks and geese looks very bright. Currently, western Iowa has so many snow geese that the Iowa Department of Natural Resources (DNR) has opened a spring season.

Since the mid-70s, the reintroduction of the Eastern wild turkey in Iowa has been one of the great success stories of modern wildlife management. Twenty years ago, the state turkey biologist told me that our harvest would probably peak at about 1,000 birds per year. We've now passed 10,000, and virtually every sizeable tract of timber in the state has turkeys. While there are states with more birds, Iowa's cornfed gobblers are huge, and nonresidents are starting to come here in search of a feathered trophy.

Although there are now more Iowans who live in cities than on farms—a result of farms growing ever larger, not a change in the agricultural orientation of the state —Iowa retains its rural character and relatively low population. With the exception of the first week or so of the pheasant season, bird hunting in Iowa is not crowded. If you want to pursue one of the "lesser" species, you may find it almost lonely. For example, Iowa hosts a good population of woodcock during the migration. I do all my hunting on public land and seldom encounter another bird hunter. In a typical year, the wings I send in to the federal woodcock research project constitute about half the total for the entire state.

Although you'll often find no more than a couple of inhabited farms per square mile in rural Iowa, almost all the land remains private, and you must have permission to hunt. However, I have found that if my party is small—no more than two or three hunters—landowners will say "yes" to a polite request for permission far more often than not, especially after the hubbub of the pheasant opener is history. Hunting leases, once almost unheard of in Iowa, are still a relative rarity. Stopping to say thanks and offering to share your bag is a good way to get yourself invited back.

So welcome to Iowa, where hunting and bird hunters are part of a long tradition. You'll find churches, volunteer fire departments, and Lions Clubs hosting hunters' breakfasts on the opening morning of pheasant season. As you drive the rural roads, you'll be greeted by friendly waves from passing pickups—people you've never met before. Enjoy the hospitality and enjoy the birds!

Larry Brown
Randall, Iowa

Tips on Using This Book

- The state of Iowa is roughly divided into thirds, each with a different area code. They are: eastern, 319; central, 515; western, 712.

- For the purpose of organization, the state has been divided into the five former DNR regions, based on the primary agricultural activity in that region.

- Statewide distribution information for pheasant, gray partridge, and quail was provided by the DNR prior to the 1997 season. Pheasant distribution in particular can vary significantly from year to year, depending on habitat, farming practices, and weather. Furthermore, the DNR does not prepare distribution maps for ruffed grouse and wild turkey. Those maps are based on our own observations and experience.

- Note that information on local facilities and services (hotels, restaurants, veterinarians, etc.) is current only for 1997. Their inclusion in this book is not a guarantee of the quality of goods and services they provide.

- Because license fees, season dates, and regulations change from year to year, always check with the Iowa DNR for the most current information.

- Most of Iowa's best wingshooting, especially for upland birds, is found on privately owned property. You must have permission to hunt on any private land. Without advance arrangements, finding a place to hunt on opening weekend of pheasant season is virtually impossible. The good news is that hunting pressure drops off sharply after the second weekend of the season, and access to good private ground becomes relatively easy to secure.

- Motel Cost Key: $—less than $40 per night
  $$—between $40 and $60 per night
  $$$—over $60 per night

Major Roads and Rivers of Iowa

Iowa Facts

25th largest state in the nation
56,275 square miles
315 miles east to west
205 miles north to south
33 million acres in farms and CRP lands
Average farm = 332 acres

Elevation: 480 to 1,670 feet
Counties: 99
Towns and Cities: 1,175
Population (1994): 2,800,000 (30th in nation)

Attractions:
1 National Monument
4 State Forests
7 State Recreation Areas
97 State Parks and Preserves

Nicknames: "Hawkeye State," "Tall Corn State"
Primary Industries: Agriculture and agriculture-related
Capital: Des Moines
State Bird: Eastern goldfinch
State Flower: Wild rose
State Tree: Oak
State Stone: Geode

Temperature and Precipitation:
Average temperature and precipitation are quite uniform across the state of Iowa, varying only 5 or 6 degrees from warmest to coldest counties, and only 3 or 4 inches from wettest to driest. The following averages are given for Ames, located near the center of the state:

Average Annual Precipitation: 33 inches
Average Temperature (November): 38 degrees

The Future

This chapter is quite different than it would have been had I written it only a couple of years ago. But things change—sometimes for the better, but not always.

First, the bright side. For waterfowlers, habitat conditions, as well as duck and goose numbers, haven't looked this good in a long time. Prairie potholes and private wetlands are being protected or restored. The result is that for the first time since white settlers came to Iowa, we are gaining rather than losing waterfowl habitat. We actually have too many snow geese, and giant Canadas are also becoming a nuisance in certain urban areas. Numbers of most duck species are also on the increase, mainly in response to the end of a long drought in northern breeding areas and to an improvement in adjacent cover—mainly CRP acres—surrounding Midwestern potholes.

Iowa turkeys are also in excellent shape. Hunters in Iowa kill far more birds every year than biologists ever thought possible when the turkey restoration program began back in the 1970s. Virtually all suitable habitat holds good numbers of turkeys. There will be ups and downs depending on annual nesting success, but the future for turkey hunters looks very good.

Upland birds are another story. Quail numbers have fallen to an all-time low, and while they have recovered slightly, no one is optimistic enough to see the day when Iowa's bobwhite harvest will once more approach a million birds a year. Changes to farming practices in the southern part of the state are the main reason, and unless there are major habitat modifications, quail will remain a very secondary species for Iowa hunters.

Although Hun numbers fluctuate significantly in Iowa, it is unlikely that these birds will ever be of major importance here. Iowa springs tend to be too wet for these dryland birds. Also, the heavy emphasis on corn and soybean farming means that Huns will be hidden in standing crops and mostly unhuntable at the time of year when they would otherwise be most available to hunters.

Ruffed grouse have a very restricted range in northeast Iowa. They will always provide a challenge for a small but dedicated group of hunters. However, Iowa's forests are aging, and without a fairly significant amount of cutting, our habitat will remain far less than ideal for grouse.

Iowa has a relatively low population of native woodcock. Although these little birds can be quite plentiful in the state during their migration, in much of the state this period coincides with the early part of pheasant season, when the attention of Iowa hunters is obviously elsewhere.

But the real future of bird hunting in Iowa, especially for those nonresidents who visit the state, is tied very closely to the fate of the ring-necked pheasant. This fact is truer for Iowa than it is even for the other major pheasant states: South Dakota also has good hunting for sharptails, prairie chickens, and Huns; Nebraska for sharpies and chickens; and Kansas for quail and chickens. Here in Iowa, outside of waterfowl and turkeys, all other gamebirds are minor considerations in comparison to pheasants.

Unfortunately, over the past few years, habitat conditions for pheasants in Iowa have deteriorated significantly. The major reason is loss of CRP acres. We have gone from over two million acres in the 10-year set-aside program to about 1.4 million acres. Most of what we have left is in southern Iowa, which is not the state's prime pheasant range, and where, if anything, there is too much nonproductive land and not enough corn and soybeans.

The impact will not be felt immediately. I'm writing this at the end of the 1997 season, and although we lost a lot of CRP this year and last, we still had very good hunting. But there is bound to be a longterm decline, due to a loss of critical nesting habitat and, to a lesser extent, winter cover. The impact will be most noticeable, in general, the farther north you go in the state. The terrain is flatter in the north, and outside of creeks and wetlands, without CRP there will be very little good habitat left. In general, from about the middle of the state on south—below US Highway 30—the terrain is more rolling and not as intensively farmed. But even there, the loss of CRP will be felt. Some counties have had 20,000 or more acres taken out of CRP and put back into row crop production. With this shift in management causing the loss of that much tall grass acreage, changes are bound to show up.

Also, during the "boom" years of CRP when Iowa farmers were working less ground, many were busy taking out some of those small pieces of cover that were also productive for pheasants. Fencerows have been ripped out, waterways tiled out of existence, and timber cleared from stream banks.

The one glimmer of hope is that Iowa farmers will embrace those elements of the current CRP that allow for the establishment of what is essentially "permanent" set-aside. The one clause in the program that could benefit Iowa bird hunters the most permits the establishment of buffer strips, 100 feet wide, on either side of permanent waterways. Although even large-scale acceptance of this program would result in far fewer acres than the two million we had at the peak of the CRP enrollment, it is about the best we can expect. And with the renewed emphasis on water quality and erosion control, together with the lucrative payments farmers receive for establishing buffer strips, we will almost certainly see more of them in the future.

Although our harvest will probably fall below a million birds sometime in the next two to three years, Iowa will always have good pheasanat hunting in comparison to most states. We may recover as farmers adjust their land-use practices to the new government regulations. However, without some really major habitat changes, such as the two million acres of set-aside we had as recently as 1995, our days of one-and-a-half million annual bird bags are probably at an end.

Hunting Regulations

Waterfowl Highlights

Waterfowl seasons and bag limits are published on a flyer available in late September at DNR offices, county recorders' offices, and many retail outlets where licenses are sold.

If you bag a banded duck or goose, you are to report the band number to the U.S. Fish and Wildlife Service promptly. Simply call this toll free number: 1-800-327-BAND (2263). This number is also written on each band. Band return analysis is an important part of waterfowl management programs and is critical to setting hunting seasons for future years.

Waterfowl Stamps Required

If you are 16 years of age or older, you need valid **state** ($5.00) and **federal** ($15) migratory waterfowl stamps (duck stamps) to hunt or take any migratory waterfowl within Iowa. These stamps must be in your possession while hunting and must bear your signature in ink, written across the face of the stamps.

Nontoxic Shot

Nontoxic shot is required for hunting all migratory gamebirds (except wood-cock) in Iowa. When hunting migratory gamebirds, except woodcock, you may not have in your possession any shells loaded with other than nontoxic shot.

Canada Goose Hunting

Canada goose hunting is closed in posted portions of 21 counties. These are listed in the Iowa Hunting and Trapping Regulations. For maps of individual closed areas, call the DNR at 515-281-4687.

North and South Waterfowl Zones

The state is divided into two zones for waterfowl hunting (see map on next page). Seasons and limits are published in a flyer separate from other current hunting regulations. The flyer is available from the DNR in mid- to late September.

Regulations

For waterfowl hunting, regulations are the same for residents and nonresidents. There are no special restrictions, seasons, or limits which apply to nonresidents only.

Blinds and Decoys

You may construct a blind on a game management area, but you must use only natural vegetation found in that area. Trees (except willows) may not be cut for that purpose. You cannot drive nails into trees on game management areas to build a blind. Portable blinds are prohibited on game management areas from one-half hour after sunset until midnight. When attached to a boat, a portable blind is considered to be removed from the area when the boat is moored at an approved access site. Decoys are also prohibited on game management areas from one-half hour after sunset to midnight.

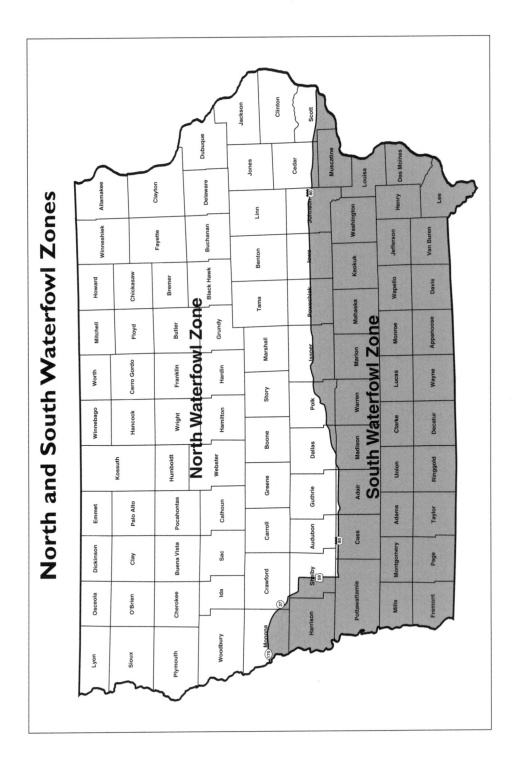

North and South Waterfowl Zones

North Waterfowl Zone

South Waterfowl Zone

Upland Game Highlights

Identification
You cannot transport a pheasant without a foot, fully feathered wing or head attached to the body.

Hunter Orange
Iowa requires hunter orange only for gun deer hunting. However, it is strongly recommended for upland bird hunting.

Use of Radios
You cannot use a mobile radio transmitter to communicate the location or direction of game or to coordinate the movement of hunters. You may use a tracking collar to locate a hunting dog.

Game from Outside the State
You may possess game that has been lawfully taken outside Iowa, but you must be able to prove that it was legally killed and legally brought into the state.

Trespass
It is illegal to hunt on all private land in Iowa, posted or not, without permission. You may hunt in road ditches, up to the fenceline, and you may pursue wounded or dead game onto private property without permission, but you cannot carry a gun when you do so.

Hunting Near Buildings
You may not shoot within 200 yards of a building occupied by people or livestock without the permission of the owner of that building.

Shooting Near Roads
While you may not shoot a rifle, handgun, or shotgun with a slug across a public roadway or railroad right of way, you may shoot a shotgun loaded with shot across roads and railroads.

Guns in Vehicle
Iowa has a cased gun law. When in a vehicle, a gun must be unloaded and fully cased (closed with a zipper or tie), or it must be completely broken down.

Number of Shells in the Gun
When hunting upland game, there is no restriction on the number of shells you may have in your gun. A waterfowl plug is not required.

Nontoxic Shot for Upland Game on Public Hunting Areas
Beginning in 1998, the Iowa DNR will require that nontoxic shot be used for all hunting—including upland birds—on many of its public areas, in general those which are specifically managed for waterfowl. Those areas requiring nontoxic shot for upland hunting will be listed in the 1998 hunting regulations. Be sure to check this list carefully.

Iowa Tentative Bird Hunting Dates

Species	Season	Daily Limit	Possession
Waterfowl	Varies season to season		
Mourning Dove	Closed		
Rooster Pheasant	Oct 31-Jan 10	3	12
Bobwhite Quail	Oct 31-Jan 31	8	16
Gray Partridge	Oct 10-Jan 31	8	16
Ruffed Grouse	Oct 3-Jan 31	3	6
Woodcock	Oct 3-Nov 16	3	6
Rail (sora and Virginia)	Sept 5-Nov 13	12	24
Snipe	Sept 5-Nov 30	8	16
Turkey	Fall—closed to nonresidents Spring—4 seasons, typically early April through mid-May		

Note: Shooting hours on pheasants, quail, and partridge are 8AM–4:30PM. Hours on turkey, snipe, and rail are one-half hour before sunrise to sunset. Hours on grouse and woodcock are sunrise to sunset.

1997–1998 Nonresident License Availability and Fees

Nonresident licenses are available at the recorder's office in all county courthouses, DNR offices, and other license vendors, including most sporting goods stores, and the sporting goods departments of all Wal Mart and K-Mart Stores. Most Casey's General Stores, located in many small towns in Iowa, also sell licenses. Nonresident license applications, for use in purchasing licenses through the mail, are available from the Iowa DNR Headquarters:

Iowa Department of Natural Resources
Wallace State Office Building
Des Moines, IA 50319-0034
515-281-5145
www.state.ia.us/dnr

Nonresident Fees
Hunting $60.50
Wildlife Habitat Stamp 5.00
Iowa Waterfowl Stamp 5.00
Nonresident Turkey License 55.00

Note: A hunting license and Wildlife Habitat Stamp are required to hunt all upland gamebirds. Only a nonresident turkey license and habitat stamp are required of nonresidents who hunt wild turkeys. Nonresident waterfowl hunters need a hunting license, Wildlife Habitat Stamp, and both federal and Iowa waterfowl stamps.

Hunter Education Requirement

Persons born after January 1, 1967, must satisfactorily complete a hunter education course in order to buy a hunting license. A certificate issued by another state will meet the requirement.

Period Covered by Hunting License

A hunting license and habitat stamp, resident or nonresident, are valid from the date of purchase until January 10 (last day of the pheasant season) of the following year.

Exception: a license and habitat stamp purchased on or after December 15 are valid for the remainder of the current season, plus all of the following season.

Turkey Hunting Regulations

The only legal weapons permitted for turkey hunting are: shotguns and muzzle-loading shotguns not smaller than 20-gauge and shooting 4, 5, 6, 7½ or 8 shot only, and longbow, recurve, or compound bows with broadhead or blunthead (with a minimum diameter of 9/16 inch) arrows.

Spring Turkey Zones

Hunters having a valid spring turkey hunting license for Zone 1, Zone 2, or Zone 3 may also hunt in Zone 4. Hunters who have a spring turkey hunting license valid solely for Zone 4 may hunt only in Zone 4.

Fall Turkey Zones

- **Zone 1** is all units of Stephens State Forest west of U.S. 65 in Lucas and Clarke Counties.
- **Zone 2** is all units of Shimek State Forest in Lee and Van Buren Counties.
- **Zone 3** is units of Yellow River Forest in Allamakee County.

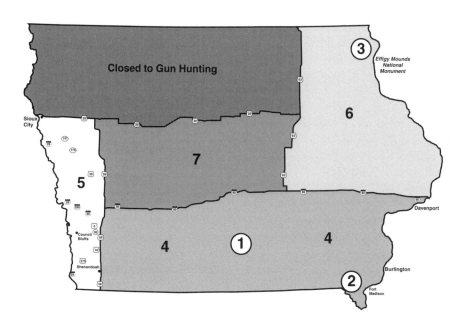

Ruffed Grouse Hunting Zone

The map below shows the area available for ruffed grouse hunting in Iowa.

Harvest Information Program (HIP)

Starting in 1998, federal regulations require all hunters who plan to hunt migratory birds (waterfowl, snipe, rails, woodcock, or mourning doves) to register with the federal government when they buy a 1998 hunting license. Hunters who do not hunt these species will not be affected.

When registering, affected hunters will be asked their names, addresses, and the number of each species bagged in 1997. Hunters will be given a code number to write on their hunting licenses to verify that they have registered. If checked by a Conservation Officer while hunting, hunters who have not registered will be subject to a citation for failure to comply with HIP.

The U.S. Fish and Wildlife Service will select a sample of hunters from those registered. Selected hunters will be contacted by the USFWS before the season and asked to record the number of each species they bag in 1998. HIP will allow more accurate harvest estimates for these species. HIP will replace the Waterfowl Harvest Survey that a sample of hunters currently participate in when they purchase their federal duck stamps at post offices.

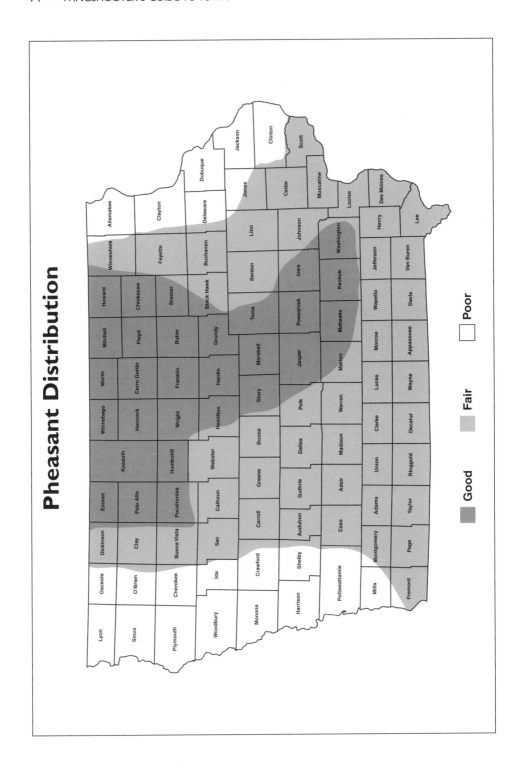

Pheasant Distribution

Pheasant

Phasianus colchicus

FIELD FACTS

Local Names
Ringneck, ring-necked pheasant

Size
An adult rooster will weigh from 2.5 to 3 pounds, and from the tip of his beak to the tip of his tail, he will have an overall length of about 2.5 to 3 feet. More than half of this total can be taken up by a rooster's long tail, which, in exceptional cases, can measure over 2 feet in length. Hens are smaller, weighing around 2 pounds. With a much shorter tail, they seldom exceed 2 feet in length.

Identification in Flight
It is critical that hunters be able to distinguish a legal rooster from an illegal hen. Although this may seem a simple task, it can be particularly difficult with young roosters. Fully colored, mature cocks are usually not a problem with their long tails and bright hues. The white neck ring is often obvious and makes a good aiming point as well as an identification mark. Against a bright sun, or in other situations where clear vision is hampered, roosters will appear much darker. Also, look for the long, streaming tail. Early in the season, one of the first signs of color on a young rooster will be his red eye patch. Also, a bird that cackles when it flushes is always a rooster. Unfortunately, many take wing without sounding off. Always call "rooster" or "hen" for your partners—you may have a clearer view than they do. But in no case should you shoot without being certain that your target is a rooster.

- Since the mid-1980s, Iowa and South Dakota have vied for the largest pheasant bag in the nation. For the past several seasons, Iowa has retained the title with an annual harvest averaging between 1.2 and 1.5 million birds.
- The Conservation Reserve Program (CRP) has done much to improve pheasant hunting in Iowa. At the peak of the program, over 2 million acres of Iowa farmland was taken out of row crop production and planted to pheasant friendly fields of grass. Although CRP acreage has declined somewhat since 1996, the program continues to provide high quality nesting habitat crucial to the future well-being of Iowa's pheasant population.
- Pheasants Forever, a conservation organization formed in Minnesota in the early 1980s, has been popular in Iowa since its inception. Virtually every county has a Pheasants Forever chapter, and Iowa has more members than

any other state. Unlike other conservation organizations, funds are raised and spent locally by individual chapters, with technical advice and assistance from the parent organization. Many annual banquets are held in Iowa during pheasant season, and attending one while visiting the state on a hunting trip is an enjoyable way to spend an evening. If you are not a member of the organization, you can contact them at P.O. Box 75473, St. Paul, Minnesota 55175, telephone 612-773-2000.

- The pheasant has been Iowa's most popular gamebird for most of this century. First brought to Iowa in the late 1800s, pheasants reportedly got a jump start when a storm—together with help from some neighbors—tore down the fences at a game farm near Cedar Falls in 1900, releasing large numbers of birds. Iowa's first pheasant season was held in the northern part of the state in 1925. During the war year of 1943, with both hunters and ammunition in short supply, hens were included in the bag limit. The following year, hunters were allowed a daily bag of 6 roosters. In 1976, the last "closed" region of the state, in southeast Iowa, was opened to pheasant hunting. The entire state has been open ever since.

Color

The ringneck we shoot today in Iowa is a hybrid, the result of the introduction of many different strains of pheasants into this country. In spite of all the mingling of these strains, Iowa roosters tend to look fairly uniform in their multihued plumage. However, there are exceptions. I have seen at least two true albinos in the wild, and in 1996, I shot a rooster that was about two-thirds white.

The rooster pheasant has an iridescent, blue-green head, with a white spot on top, white neck ring, and red patches around the eyes. Body feathers are mostly a burnished copper hue with black highlights. Outer wing feathers are brown and barred with white, while the brown tail is barred with black. Legs will vary in color from gray to yellow and will almost always feature a characteristic spur—short, light-colored, and dull in young birds; long, black, sharp, and shiny in old survivors.

The smaller hen is mostly light brown to tan in color, blending in extremely well with surrounding dead grass. Her tail is significantly shorter than a rooster's, and her legs are spurless.

Sound and Flight Pattern

On the ground, pheasants are mostly silent during hunting season. Roosters crow often during the spring mating season and occasionally in the fall, a ringneck will announce his presence with a raucous, two-note crow, long followed by short. When taking flight, roosters will occasionally let go with a string of avian profanity—a series of short notes quite different from their mating crow. I have never heard a hen pheasant utter any vocal sound whatsoever.

Author swings on a flushing rooster.

Pheasants are large birds, and roosters in particular can be a bit slow getting off the ground. However, once airborne—and especially with the wind at their tails—they can maintain impressive flight speed for distances up to a mile or so. Once they have attained full speed, they can set their wings and glide a surprising distance. In my pickup, I once clocked a gliding hen at between 45–50 miles per hour.

Similar Gamebirds

There are no other gamebirds in Iowa that can be confused with pheasants. The Iowa DNR is attempting to reintroduce both prairie chickens and sharptails, but the chances of encountering either are extremely remote. From a practical standpoint, the Iowa ringneck hunter's only problem is distinguishing cocks from hens.

Flock or Covey Habits

Pheasants are not covey birds, and early in the hunting season, even in those areas with the highest pheasant density, they are found scattered rather than in flocks. Opportunities for shooting a double on roosters are fairly rare.

Late in the season, severe winter weather can push the birds into heavy cover, where the hunter may encounter flocks of up to 100 birds or more in a fairly small

Great weather and a flushing pheasant make a memorable hunt.

area. With that many eyes and ears, these late season flocks tend to be very difficult to approach.

There also seems to be some tendency for the birds to segregate by sex in the late season. After encountering a dozen or more hens without sighting a single rooster, you may suddenly find three or four cocks in close proximity to each other.

Reproduction and Life Span

Pheasants are ground nesting birds that nest in grassy cover such as hayfields, ditches, along streams, or in CRP fields. Depending on weather, the peak of the nesting season in Iowa is from mid-May to mid-June. The hens will lay a dozen or more eggs, while the roosters, which mate with multiple partners, play no part at all in tending the nests or the newly hatched young.

Hen pheasants are persistent renesters. If a hen loses her first clutch before they hatch, she will make a second or even a third attempt. However, once a hen successfully hatches a brood, there is no evidence that she will lay a second clutch. Generally, hens lay fewer eggs each time they renest. Therefore, the best hunting seasons tend to follow those years when a high percentage of hens are successful in their first attempts.

Renesting may continue well into August. In 1993, when Iowa suffered its worst ever floods, much of the best nesting habitat was under water through the end of July. The DNR's August roadside counts noted few chicks. However, the 1993 season actually turned out to be quite good, with many young birds—born well into August —appearing in early season bags.

Most pheasants don't survive their first year. The Iowa DNR estimates that about 60–70 percent of the roosters will be taken by hunters, with weather and predators accounting for more. Many hens die on the nest, victims either of predators or farm machinery. Some are accidentally shot during the hunting season. Most never live to bring off a brood.

Two-year-old roosters are relatively common in hunters' bags. While the birds may live several years in captivity, estimating age—other than distinguishing a two-year-old from a bird of the year by weight as well as length of spur and tail—is difficult beyond the second year.

Feeding Habits and Patterns

Shortly after hatching, pheasant chicks consume insects as a high percentage of their diets. Later on, as adults, they become mostly vegetarian, although even grown birds will eat insects on occasion.

Adult pheasants do establish a feeding pattern. Normally, they will eat shortly after sunup and again in the late afternoon before roosting. They will also gather grit —readily available along Iowa's many gravel roads—before moving to roosting cover.

However, once hunting season starts, these feeding patterns are disturbed. After a few encounters with hunters and dogs, pheasants eat pretty much whenever they can without being disturbed. Due to hunting pressure, they may also move farther away from their prime food sources than they do during the off-season. In winter, severe weather also results in changes in their feeding patterns.

Iowa pheasants are extremely fortunate in that they seldom have to look far for high quality food. The state's major crops are corn and soybeans, and both provide excellent sources of nutrition. Enough waste grain remains available, even throughout the winter, so that the birds virtually never starve. However, harsh weather can force them to travel farther to food, to feed in places where they are more vulnerable to predators, or to feed along roads where they may be killed by cars.

Along with the need for winter cover, the importance of readily available food to pheasants cannot be overemphasized. South-central Iowa, which once had a very good pheasant population, has some of the highest CRP enrollments in the state. Unfortunately, much of the rest of the land is in pasture or woods, and in some places you have to drive several miles to find a cornfield. Pheasant numbers have dropped dramatically.

In my 40-plus years of performing "autopsies" on Iowa pheasants, I've found that they either have empty crops or the crops are filled with corn or soybeans. Those two food sources are obviously key to the welfare of Iowa pheasants.

Heidi makes a point on pheasant.

Preferred Habitat and Cover

Other than roosting, Iowa pheasants can spend nearly all their time in crop fields from about July until harvest. These areas provide food and cover from predators.

The harvest results in a drastic change. A combined soybean field is nothing but bare ground. Even picked corn, however—if it also includes some grass or weeds—will still provide some cover in addition to food.

The Iowa pheasant season traditionally opens on the last Saturday in October. When that date finds much of the corn crop still standing, the birds quickly learn that cornfields are the places to hide. Until then, CRP fields provide excellent hunting opportunities, as do smaller pieces of cover, such as ditches, waterways, and overgrown fencerows.

Hunting standing corn can be extremely productive if you have enough hunters to organize what essentially becomes a Midwest version of a driven birdshoot. One group spaces itself out a dozen or so rows apart and simply walks through the corn. They are the beaters, or drivers. The people who would be referred to as the guns on a fancy English estate are usually called blockers in Iowa. They are posted at the opposite end of the field and count on the drivers flushing birds their way. To work well, these operations must have an almost military precision, with discipline (spacing, speed of advance, safety in taking shots) enforced in both groups. If dogs are used at all, they must be under perfect control.

If the corn is harvested late, hunting the fringes of just picked fields can be very productive for smaller groups, such as a couple of hunters and a dog. The birds, which will have been hiding out in the corn in relative safety, won't have had time to adjust to their new surroundings. They may simply move into edge cover where they can be pretty easy pickings because they have had little contact with gunners and dogs.

Personally, I prefer the more challenging hunting offered by large fields of grass, such as those created by the CRP or found on public hunting areas. If located near food, these areas will almost always hold birds. But because of all the cover, you won't find these pheasants without a good dog, and even then the birds stand a good chance of giving you the slip.

Wetlands can also be very productive, although I prefer to focus on them later in the season. Marshes usually offer very heavy cover, where the birds will take refuge from the snow and cold. Also, chasing swamp dwelling roosters is much easier on both hunter and dog when the ground is frozen and footing is better.

Depending on the weather, a pheasant is likely to hide anywhere not too far from food and where he has become conditioned to feel safe from hunters. That may be in a 200-acre field of switchgrass or in a clump of weeds out behind an old, collapsing barn. Hunting season forces them to adapt, and the fact that pheasants are thriving in Iowa is proof that they do this very well.

Locating Hunting Areas

Remember that food and cover are the two essentials. Likely spots to find pheasants include:

1. Large blocks of cover, such as public hunting areas and CRP fields.
2. Long, narrow "strip" cover, such as ditches, waterways, and fencerows.
3. Standing corn, as long as you have enough people to hunt it properly.
4. Picked corn, if there is enough stubble left in which the birds can hide.
5. Farm groves or other timber areas where the birds must seek shelter from bitter cold and heavy snow.

Looking for Sign

Pheasants leave olive-green and white, pellet sized droppings. You are likely to find several of these in matted down spots in the grass where the birds roost. In snow or mud, the birds leave telltale large, three-toed tracks.

Hunting Methods

The pheasant is a true "blue collar" bird, hunted by farm kids toting worn single shots as well as by well-heeled urban dwellers dressed by Orvis and armed with fancy superposeds.

Some of Iowa's excellent pheasant cover being worked by Heidi.

There are still many hunters who pursue pheasants without a dog. Because of the abundance of birds in many parts of Iowa, this method can be quite effective. Lone hunters or small parties of two or three should confine their hunting to small patches of cover, such as ditches, waterways, and fencerows. If they try hunting larger parcels of cover, they will very likely walk right by tight sitting birds. Although a pheasant in plain sight is a large and gaudy bird, roosters can hide quite effectively even in fairly short grass.

Larger groups of gunners working without dogs, say a dozen or more, can take on standing corn using the driving-blocking method discussed earlier.

Hunters without dogs should walk slowly, zigzag through the cover, and stop often for periods of 10 or 15 seconds. These pauses will often convince a hiding rooster that he has been detected and will result in a high percentage of the dogless hunter's flushes.

Especially since the birth of the CRP program in the mid-1980s, dogs have become increasingly important in helping hunters locate birds. Pheasants will run at least as often as they will hide, and they will do both of those more often than take wing. In a field of 80 acres or more of tall grass, it takes a sharp canine nose to home in on the birds.

Owners of pointing dogs and hard charging spaniels favor larger tracts of cover, such as CRP fields. In such places, the best advice is to turn the dog loose and follow its lead. Usually, it is a good idea to work the edges of large fields first. Dogs will often pick up the scent trail of birds moving back and forth from cover to food. Also, pushing the birds toward an edge where the cover ends will give the hunter a far better chance at a flush and an open shot.

Retrievers, such as Labs and goldens, are better suited to smaller, heavier cover. Working slowly and within gun range, they will root out those birds that have buried themselves in the thick stuff.

Because of a pheasant's tendency to run, the block and drive technique discussed earlier in relation to cornfield hunting can be applied very effectively elsewhere, both with and without dogs. If you can work cover toward where it ends—where a ditch intersects with a road or where a draw peters out in the middle of a field—posting a blocker at the likely exit will often result in a bagged bird.

Although, as mentioned earlier, hunting pressure tends to disturb the pheasant's normal daily routine, certain types of cover are likely to be more productive, depending on the time of day and the weather. At the beginning and end of legal shooting hours, especially on a cold, dark day, the birds often stay on the roost late and return to it early. Hunt heavy cover for the first and last hours under those conditions. On a mild, clear day, the birds will usually be out feeding by 8 AM. Look for them in and around picked corn.

Many pheasant hunters feel that some of the best sport comes after winter snows have arrived. Although I prefer to hunt in conditions of little or no snow, it is true that hunting can be extremely productive right after a heavy snowfall. The morning following a storm, if you're hunting without a dog, you may be convinced that the birds have disappeared. You may not see a single track. However, if accompanied by a dog, pay attention when Rover starts making game. Especially in cover such as heavy grass, the birds will allow themselves to be buried, the snow forming a protective roof and extra insulation from the cold. These snowbound roosters sit extremely tight. I've had many come right out from between my legs! Others will be so reluctant to leave their warm hiding places that they may actually be caught by a persistent dog.

Hunting With Dogs

The old advice used to be that pheasants would ruin pointing dogs. That advice came from hunters used to pursuing birds such as bobwhite quail, which generally hold for the dogs. A dog trained not to move a muscle until released by his owner, especially if he runs fairly wide, is indeed likely to be frustrated by pheasants. However, most pheasant hunters stick with closer-working breeds—the so-called versatiles, such as German shorthairs, wirehairs, and Brittanies—and if allowed to trail until the bird stops before establishing point, these dogs can be very effective. The trailing ability will also pay large dividends when it comes to running down cripples.

Retrievers, as their name implies, specialize in locating dead or crippled game. No matter how proficient you are with a shotgun, you will not kill all your pheasants cleanly. They are big and tough, and of all our most popular gamebirds, they are certainly the hardest to kill. Once a rooster is down and running, a Lab hot on its trail is almost certainly your best chance of recovering it.

Like retrievers, spaniels also work within gun range and flush rather than point their birds. Springers in particular have a well earned reputation as proficient pheasant dogs, and, like the retrievers, tend to be very good at locating cripples.

Dogs help the pheasant hunter find birds, put them to wing, and put them in his game bag. Even if they did nothing but retrieve, they would be very important to any hunter who believes in conservation. The Iowa DNR estimates that dogless hunters lose 1 of every 3 birds they knock down, while those with dogs lose only 1 in 10. Experienced dogs can do even better. During the 1996 season, my cripple losses amounted to 1 in 40. That's reason enough to convince me that I wouldn't want to hunt pheasants without a dog.

Table Preparations

If it is a warm day, drawing your birds in the field is a good idea. I finish the cleaning job when I get home, and then soak the birds overnight in cold saltwater. This is an especially good method on badly shot birds.

Although pheasants can be plucked, most hunters skin them. This does leave some risk that the birds may dry out when cooked. To prevent this, cover them with foil if roasting, or cook them in liquid or with an orange in the body cavity. Bacon strips across the breast will also keep this delicate white meat from drying out.

When dressing pheasants shot in Iowa for transportation, remember that you must leave a body part attached that will allow identification as a rooster. The easiest part to leave is one leg. When you get home and prepare to cook the bird, spur length will tell you if he is a bird of the year or an oldtimer. In the case of old birds, you may want to use a slow cooking method, such as a crockpot, to tenderize the meat.

Shot and Choke Suggestions

No. 6 shot is the best all around choice and will serve under nearly all circumstances. No. 7½ works well if you are mixed-bag hunting for pheasants and quail, especially early in the year when shots will be close and the birds less heavily feathered. You need at least an ounce of shot for pheasants, and loads of 1⅛–1¼ ounce are even more popular.

Hunters with pointing dogs often get closer shots and can probably take most of their chances with improved cylinder choke or modified at the tightest. For dogless hunters or those with flushing dogs, modified or full choke are better choices.

Switch to heavier loads and tighter chokes later in the season. No. 5 shot in loads of 1¼ ounce or more is a good choice for late season birds.

From Start to Finish

Opening day of pheasant season in Iowa is usually a group affair: a time to get together with old friends and relatives, a time to see if the old dog can still do the job, and a time to see if the pup with all the promise has what it takes.

Mike Carroll, my hunting partner for 25 years, and Gene Kroupa, an old friend from Wisconsin, would come in along one branch of the creek. Dana Dinnes, a former student of mine at Iowa State, would join me in covering the other branch. The partnerships were logical: Gene and I had the dogs, giving each team canine assistance. The strategy was to push any runners towards where the two forks met. There, the cover got heavy and, we hoped, the birds would feel secure. Those that survived would be wiser upon their next encounter with hunters and dogs.

"Surprised we haven't put up any birds," Dana said, as we neared the creek junction and spotted Gene and Mike, who hadn't shot, either, coming up the other branch.

"Yeah, and old Heidi doesn't act like they're running on her, either," I remarked, keeping an eye on my battle tested old shorthair who was vacuuming the cover along the waterway.

"No luck?" asked Gene from the far side of the stream, as he and Mike moved up to join us.

"Not even a hen," I replied.

"Point!" called Dana from my left, where a fence formed the boundary between streamside grass cover and picked corn. The others couldn't cross. Dana and I moved in on the rock steady, gray muzzled shorthair.

Instead of the ringneck explosion we were anticipating, a covey of bobwhites, a dozen or more strong, came buzzing out of the grass. Out of the corner of my eye, I saw Dana drop one in the corn. I shot a hole in the sky as a pair swung back across me. A delayed "pop" came from across the creek, and I saw a bird drop in front of Gene.

"Most of them went down in the corn," said Dana, as I took his bird from Heidi, who will seldom retrieve to anyone else.

"Small birds," I said. "Probably a late hatch. I don't see a covey down here all that often. Let's leave them alone and find the roosters." Everyone agreed.

The next 15 minutes were punctuated by several nice points and close flushes, but no shots—every bird we saw carried the dull, brown plumage of a hen.

"It's your fault, Carroll," I called over to Mike, on whom I always heap blame for every bad hunt. "If you weren't along, we wouldn't have blundered into this meeting of the pheasant Ladies' Aid Society."

Then things changed rapidly. In the last 200 yards or so of creekside cover, before we hit our boundary fence, we collected four roosters. Two gave me perfect shots, and I redeemed myself for the bobwhite miss by taking them both without dirtying the left barrel. Feeling overly cocky, I wasn't paying enough attention when Heidi doubled back over the lip of the creek. The clever old rooster gave me an avian cussing as he boiled up behind me. I spun and shot but never touched a feather.

As we followed a decent fence line back in the direction from which we'd come, Heidi peeled off to check out a draw leading into picked corn. Two points later, I had my third bird and Dana his first.

By lunchtime, the temperature had finally cleared 50—chilly for a late October weekend in Iowa. The cloudy skies and hint of dampness in the air made it comfortable weather for both two-legged and four-legged hunters..

Moving to our second farm that afternoon, we passed several tractors pulling wagons filled with just harvested corn. Huge combines cut multirow slashes through fields of dry, golden brown stalks, raising clouds of dust and debris all around them. This was a reminder that, while the pheasant opener is a major recreational weekend for perhaps a quarter of a million resident and nonresident hunters in Iowa every year, for farmers it's the busy season. A few who are dedicated hunters themselves will take time out to grab the shotgun and hunt for at least a couple of hours. Most, however, understand the capricious nature of Midwestern weather. I've seen snow and ice storms late in October and cursed how the elements had upset my bird hunting plans. But for farmers, snowed in crops mean lost income, maybe the difference between a profitable year and one where they have to rely on a sympathetic banker to continue in business. I understood their devotion to their livelihood and silently bade them a trouble-free harvest. Besides, once all the corn is out of the fields, pheasants have fewer places to hide, and, unlike in standing corn where they can run me and my dogs ragged, we can handle most other situations quite well.

Mike, with other obligations, had headed for home early. With the cover on the second farm consisting mostly of draws, creeks, and fence lines, we divided forces again. Gene and Heidi's son, Duke, headed one direction. Dana, Heidi, and I went the other.

Although "party shooting" is accepted among most pheasant hunting groups in Iowa, especially on opening day, it is not legal. Nor do I and the people I shoot with consider it ethical. I had three roosters and was done for the day where pheasants were concerned. I dropped quail loads into my old 16 and hoped for a covey.

Heidi found the first bird, a runner, in a little field of head high weeds. Unfortunately, the bird was able to move through the cover better than we could and beat it out the far side. Dana missed on a tough shot.

Half an hour later, bird number two of the afternoon ran out the far end of a terrace—out of range and on the ground anyhow—just as we were hitting the near end.

"You'll get a chance yet," I encouraged Dana.

Working along a brushy creek, our luck finally changed. Heidi locked up in the thick stuff. "I'll go in to flush if you want to stay out in the open," I offered.

"No, I might as well go in myself," Dana replied. "If the bird goes into the woods instead of coming out, I might never see it."

"Remember the grouse hunter's rule," I told him. "Forget about the branches. If you can see the bird, shoot." He nodded and plunged into the brush.

The rooster hadn't quite cleared the treetops when Dana fired, tumbling the big bird cleanly. "Nice shot!" I praised him. "I'll have to take you grouse hunting next fall."

Almost out of cover, we headed back to rendezvous with Gene. Along the way, Heidi pointed and then pounced on a crippled rooster. "Well, that's six," I told Dana. "Three for me, two for you, one for her. A good opener."

Gene, who'd collected two more birds for his efforts, agreed with that assessment. We also agreed that opening day ringnecks aren't quite as easy as some make them out to be. Heidi, stretched out in the grass after a long drink of water and a couple of Gaines Burgers, would have made it unanimous if she'd had a voice.

❖ ❖ ❖ ❖ ❖

Ten weeks later, I was still hunting pheasants. A nasty cold I'd picked up over the holidays had put me out of action temporarily, but I wasn't about to let the season end with a whimper instead of a bang. Heidi and her junior kennel-mate, an eager Gordon setter named Gwen, were ready to go. The temperature was above 20, not bad for early January. However, the 8 inches of new snow apparently prevented my partner for the day from making the trek to our meeting place. This would be one for just me and the dogs—in many ways, a fitting end to the season.

Now the farm fields were silent. The combines were long done with their job, the grain hauled to the elevators or safely in the bins. In many cases, corn fields had been fall plowed, making it harder for a surviving pheasant to get a square meal. However, finding a place to hunt—an impossibility on opening weekend unless you've made arrangements weeks, if not months, in advance—was now a simple matter of asking. The answer, with a certain look of amazement that anyone would still want to chase birds in deep snow, would almost certainly be yes—especially if the request was coupled with the gift of a dressed bird or two from an earlier trip. I've found that while many farmers don't have the time to hunt, or simply don't care to, most are more than happy to accept a

Gwen, a Gordon setter, likes late season pheasant hunting.

bird ready for the oven. They provide most of the bird's food, as well as a place for me to hunt. It's only fair that they should share in my bag.

With the new snow, I knew right where I wanted to go: a CRP field with some especially heavy cover, right next to corn. I'd found birds there in past years under similar conditions, and I did again on this late season effort. Unfortunately, they were flocked up. While those hunting without dogs may appreciate the fact that heavy snow will concentrate the birds, those of us who run dogs would rather deal with them in ones and twos. When you encounter them in 20s, 30s, and 40s, as I did in this case, the chances of getting close enough for a shot are poor. All Heidi and I managed to do was scatter the flock.

Once scattered, however, your luck may change. Ours did. Fifteen minutes after we'd seen a cloud of pheasants flying every which way, Heidi was pointing into a clump of heavy grass next to an old fence. The rooster had picked a bad place to hide.

By the time we got back to the pickup, after an hour of trudging through the drifts, Heidi had made half a dozen more nice points, any one of which would have been an easy chance had they only been roosters.

I gave myself a break by driving around to the other side of the farm, where I knew I'd find more heavy cover, almost certainly harboring a few birds. In fact, at least three bailed out of the road ditch before I could get myself, my gun, and Gwen together and ready to hunt.

While my shorthairs will hunt in subzero weather, they don't necessarily like it. After an hour in snow that at times brushed her belly, Heidi was ready for the warmth and comfort of her kennel. Gwen, on the other hand, looks at snow like a 5-year-old kid—something in which to play. But after a bit of romping around, she picked up the scent of birds, and she was down to business..

Circling up through a draw with heavy cover, nicely protected from the wind, Gwen started to make game. She froze at the end of the cover, where the bird was out of options. I dumped the rooster wing-busted, and he hit running. Gwen was on him quickly and made a grab that looked like a defensive back nailing a dodging wide receiver during a winter game at Green Bay. She delivered the still live bird to me proudly.

All the desire to play was gone now. Crossing the road to the field on the far side, Gwen quartered the cover nicely. She made five nice points, and in each case, I had to kick the cover in an effort to roust the hiding birds—all of which were hens. Twice my efforts weren't enough, and Gwen felt called upon to dive in and capture them herself. Soft-mouthed as she is, however, the quite startled birds were only minus a few feathers each as they flew off to safety. I hoped they had learned a lesson that might save them if the next hunter were to be a hungry fox or coyote.

My stomach told me it was nearing noon, and my watch confirmed it. A couple of hours plowing through nearly a foot of powder for a brace of birds, one over each dog, seemed just right to me. Some food and water for the dogs, a bowl of chili and a sandwich at the local cafe for me, and we'd call it a day and a season.

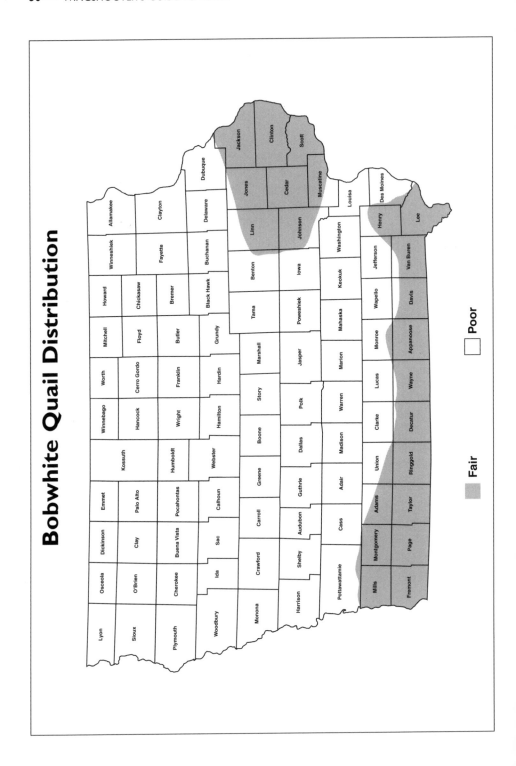

Bobwhite Quail Distribution

Fair

Poor

Bobwhite Quail

Colinus virginianus

FIELD FACTS

Local Name
Quail, bobwhite, bob

Size
An adult bobwhite measures about 10–11 inches in length and has a 14- to 15-inch wingspan. It weighs about 6–7 ounces.

Identification in Flight
Bobwhites flush with significant commotion for a bird of such small size, with the noise being magnified by the mass wingbeats of a dozen or more birds in a covey. Although the covey rise is perhaps the easiest way to identify quail in flight, single birds can also be recognized readily by anyone who has much experience around quail.

- Iowa is on the northern edge of bobwhite range. Harsh winter weather and a lack of suitable habitat limit the bird's primary range to the southern third or so of the state.
- The bobwhite is the only native bird that has been legal game in Iowa ever since white settlers first arrived in the state.
- Bobwhite quail are "edge" birds whose ideal habitat consists of numerous small fields of grass or weeds interspersed with crops. Modern farming, with emphasis on larger fields and fewer brushy, weedy spots, has hurt quail numbers almost everywhere, including Iowa.
- Research by the Iowa DNR has established that, unlike almost all other upland species, a female bobwhite will actually raise a second brood of chicks even after a successful first nesting. Thus, under ideal conditions, quail populations can recover quite quickly from lows.

Color
The bobwhite's back and wings, as well as the top of its head and neck, are mostly a rich, reddish brown, with some black and gray highlights. The bird's underside is off-white, with black edges to the feathers. Male bobwhites have a white throat and patch across the eyes. On females, these parts are buff colored—the only visible distinction between the sexes.

Matt Brown, author's son, with a bobwhite quail.

Sound and Flight Pattern

Bobwhite quail are quite vocal. The male's familiar, three-note whistle of bob-bob-white, rising on the third note, is perhaps their best known call. During fall and winter, the birds will also call to locate each other when a covey has been dispersed. Although quail are probably the most vocal during the spring mating season and through the summer, it is possible to locate coveys during hunting season by driving the back roads and stopping often to listen for their calls. Like many gamebird species, they call more often right around sunrise than at any other time of day.

Although quail usually do not fly far when flushed—200–300 yards is probably about average—they have extremely rapid acceleration and can reach their top speed of about 50 mph quite quickly from a standing start. Once they have put some distance between themselves and whatever startled them into the air, they will set their wings and glide.

Similar Gamebirds

The gray partridge is about the only other gamebird that might be mistaken for quail in Iowa. However, partridge are much larger, coveys are usually smaller, and the birds almost always squawk when flushed. In contrast, the only sound a flushing quail makes is the roar of his wings.

Heidi poses proudly with a bobwhite. Quail and dogs are a perfect match—don't try hunting these birds without one.

Flock or Covey Habits

Especially in the fall and winter, quail are extremely social and only stray from the company of their covey mates when the bunch is startled into flight and scattered. Then they will reassemble quite quickly. "Coveying up" is particularly crucial to their survival during cold winter nights in Iowa. The covey forms a circle, tails pointed inward, which provides the collective warmth needed to weather a subzero night. A covey roost can easily be identified by the large pile of droppings left where the birds spent the night.

Reproduction and Life Span

Bobwhite quail are somewhat atypical among upland gamebirds in that they are monogamous—the male takes only one mate. The male bobwhite is also much more domestic than most of his gamebird cousins. He both builds the nest—usually a simple hollowed out spot in an area of fairly tall grass, often with some sort of roof over it—and helps to rear the young. A female bobwhite's clutch will usually have from 12–15 eggs.

While the hen is incubating the eggs, the male remains fairly close, but not so close as to attract the attention of predators. If a predator does threaten the nest, the male will attempt to lure it away. When a female is killed during incubation, male bobwhites have been known to take over her duties.

In addition to predators, weather poses a significant threat to nesting success and chick survival. Heavy rains can flood the nest, and sustained cold, wet periods after the chicks are hatched can kill them.

A bobwhite quail that lives into its second year has beaten the odds. Natural mortality rates of over 80 percent are not unusual. The bird's large brood size is nature's way of compensating for this problem.

Feeding Habits and Patterns

Bobwhites eat a wide variety of foods: weed seeds of almost every variety, as well as grains such as corn, soybeans, and sorghum. During hunting season sorghum, which is relatively uncommon in Iowa, seems to be a particular favorite of quail. I seldom fail to find a covey somewhere in the vicinity of sorghum. Local chapters of the conservation group Pheasants Forever often assist in the establishment of sorghum plots as winter food sources. This is a particularly good choice in the southern part of the state, where pheasant and quail ranges overlap.

Quail start out their lives as insect eaters, switching over to vegetable matter as they mature through the summer and into the fall. However, even adult bobwhites will consume insects. Quail require grit to aid in digestion. Typical sources are along streams and gravel roads.

Because of the heavy agricultural emphasis in Iowa, quail are seldom far from a wide variety of foods. However, heavy snows or ice storms will occasionally put most of their food sources out of reach. Long periods of subzero cold will also require the birds to consume more food, making them increasingly vulnerable to predators. For those reasons, an especially hard winter—or even one severe blizzard—can result in a sharp population decline.

A quail's natural tendency during much of the year is to feed shortly after first light, move back into resting cover, and to feed again before going to roost. Hunting pressure and weather conditions, however, will often disrupt this pattern during hunting season.

Preferred Habitat and Cover

Bobwhite populations in America boomed as settlers moved west, principally because early farming practices resulted in small fields with lots of edge and numerous pockets of brushy cover. Farms were also diversified, with virtually all landowners raising livestock as well as grain. Unfortunately, that kind of farming is a thing of the past. Large farms growing only one or two row crops—usually corn and soybeans in Iowa—are not nearly as attractive to quail.

Large CRP fields of tall grass, which are quite attractive to pheasants, are of much less value to quail, which cannot move around well in such tall, thick cover. Much of southern Iowa now consists of pasture, woods, and CRP. This mix has resulted in a continued decline in Iowa's bobwhite numbers.

In Iowa, you will usually find quail somewhere near grain fields. Sorghum is the best choice, but corn ranks a good second. Bobwhite can hide quite effectively even

Danny Redding and a mixed bag—quail and pheasant.

in cut cornfields. If brushy draws or streams border the field and if the woody areas contain low, dense cover such as multiflora rose, you're in good quail habitat. Fencerows and stream courses with Osage orange trees, once fairly common in southern Iowa but now much less so as farmers convert to larger fields, are also good spots to seek quail.

Locating Hunting Areas

1. Rolling terrain, featuring hills, draws, and valleys, is more likely to hold quail than flat, open farmland.

2. Quail will use fairly large blocks of timber as long as there are occasional openings, especially if these are grain, grass, or weed fields.

3. The more edge cover there is, the better. A field broken up by draws or a creek and bordered in good, brushy fencerows is much more likely to be productive than 80 acres of nothing but corn.

4. Hunt low, thick, brushy cover, such as stream bottoms and woody draws, in the winter. The birds will be seeking shelter from the cold, snow, and wind. If such cover is adjacent to food, it is almost certain to hold birds.

Looking for Sign

If you locate droppings left at a covey's roost sight, it is a sure sign that quail are not far away. Compared to pheasants, quail do not move far on the ground. If you find fresh tracks in the snow, you'll be into birds very soon.

Hunting Methods

The bobwhite quail is the champion "homebody" of the upland gamebird world. These birds do not wander far. If you find sign or if you have previously encountered a covey in a particular spot, the birds will almost certainly be within a quarter-mile radius. Working edge cover first is usually the easiest way to locate a covey. They prefer to walk from cover to food, and hunting the edge will give your dog the best opportunity to pick up their scent trail.

Hunters unaccustomed to covey birds will initially find quail to be difficult targets. The tendency is to flock shoot rather than to pick out a single bird, and this almost always results in a miss. Remain alert after you've fired at a departing covey. Often there will be two or three stragglers that will flush after the main covey rise. Reload quickly if you're empty.

Mark the covey's flight path. Some of the very best quail shooting can come when the covey has been scattered and you can work the singles. But be careful not to take too many birds from any single covey. The birds may well not make it through the winter if a covey is shot down below about 8 birds. Also, if you break a covey late in the afternoon on a cold winter day, you should not pursue singles. The covey will need to regroup before dark in order to huddle up for the night.

Hunting Dogs

Chasing quail without a dog is just about futile. And because they hold tighter than any other Iowa gamebird, with the possible exception of woodcock, quail and dogs—especially the pointing breeds—are a perfect match. Flushers and retrievers can also be a big help, especially for hunters familiar with local birds. However, to find quail in unfamiliar territory, bigger going pointers are the best bet.

Hunters who specialize in bobwhites often run two distinctly different dogs in a brace. The first will be a wide ranging covey dog, whose job it is to cover as much territory as possible. The second is a singles dog, working much closer and specializing in locating birds once the covey has been scattered. Usually, the singles dog will be a better retriever as well.

Once introduced to these birds, most dogs love to hunt quail. The covey puts out a strong scent, and unlike birds such as pheasants and gray partridge, bobwhites are generally not runners. Without a dog, downed birds can be very hard to find because of their small size and protective coloration. However, cripples seldom run far, and a dog that will hunt diligently won't lose many.

Table Preparations

Most Iowa bird hunters rank quail, along with ruffed grouse, as their favorite table fare. Bobwhite meat is light and delicate, and care should be taken not to overcook it. Although quail can be plucked, most hunters skin them.

Shot and Choke Suggestions

Improved cylinder is the best all-around choice for bobwhites, although a skeet choke is not too open, especially when shooting over points.

Because most Iowa quail are taken as part of a mixed-bag hunt along with pheasants, 7½ is a good compromise shot size. Once a covey is broken and you know you're working quail rather than ringnecks, 8s are an even better choice. For quail shooting, there is no need for any load heavier than an ounce of shot.

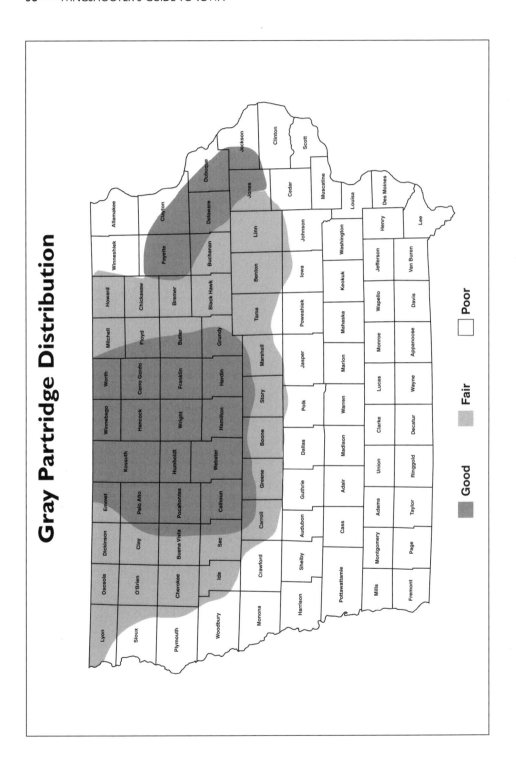

Gray Partridge Distribution

Good Fair Poor

Gray Partridge

Perdix perdix

FIELD FACTS

Local Name
Partridge, Hungarian partridge, Hun

Size
The gray partridge averages about 12–14 inches in length, has a wingspan of 15–16 inches, and weighs slightly less than a pound.

Identification in Flight
Unless the covey has already been scattered, gray partridge almost always flush as a group. They squawk loudly when flushed and have a russet-colored, rounded tail that shows up clearly on the wing.
- Like pheasant, the gray partridge is an immigrant, having come from Europe, where it has been that continent's favorite wingshooting target for many years.
- The first introduction of gray partridge in Iowa occurred in 1910, and the first open season was held in 1963.
- The major limiting factor on partridge populations in Iowa appears to be wet weather during nesting seasons. A dryland bird, gray partridge numbers in Iowa had increased fairly steadily throughout the 1980s but then fell sharply when the state experienced a succession of wet springs in the early 1990s.
- Huns are covey birds, like bobwhites, and do not stray far from their home range. Coveys spotted during the summer will probably be somewhere close by once hunting season opens.

Color
As their name indicates, Huns are mostly gray in color, with light brown markings on the face and throat. The bird's back also has some brown feathers, especially the tail, which is almost russet in color. Wings are also mostly brown, flecked with some white. Their legs and feet are almost black.

Sound and Flight Pattern
Gray partridge normally flush as a covey, in one noisy rise. When taking wing, the birds squawk, making a sound that has been compared to the hinge of a rusty gate. They will fly fairly far, up to a quarter-mile or more, when flushed. Unlike bobwhites, Huns normally land as a covey after having been flushed.

Miles Tratchel's drahthaar brings a Hun to hand.

Similar Gamebirds

The bobwhite quail is the only other covey bird found in Iowa, and it is much smaller and quite different in appearance from a Hun. Also, the two birds are seldom found together. The primary Hun range is in the northern half of the state, while quail are largely confined to the southern third of Iowa.

Flock or Covey Habits

Huns stick together even more tenaciously than bobwhites, usually landing together after having been flushed. If scattered, a covey will reform quickly. Like bobwhites, Huns roost for the night as a covey. One reason the covey is so important to Huns is that they spend much more of their time in relatively open cover than do quail. Safety from predators comes in the form of 10 or 12 pairs of eyes and ears on the alert for danger.

Reproduction and Life Span

Like bobwhites, male gray partridge are monogamous. Early in the spring, when breeding territories are being established, males will fight each other quite vigorously.

A partridge nest is a fairly simple affair: a hollow in the earth lined with grass, looking somewhat like a smaller version of a pheasant nest. Females may lay 20 eggs or more, but the average is about 15. Incubation lasts for about three-and-a-half weeks, and although the male probably does not assist in brooding the eggs, he does remain in the vicinity to help guard against predators. Once the chicks have been hatched, the male does play an active role in raising them. Young partridge are able to fly fairly well by the time they are two-weeks-old.

The brood will remain together throughout the summer and will be the covey that hunters encounter in the fall. While a covey is normally a family group, partridge will adopt orphaned chicks from other broods. Also, unmated birds may join up with a covey in the fall.

Like most gamebirds, partridge have a high mortality rate—up to 70 percent or more. In Iowa, hunting does not play a significant role in Hun mortality. At least 90 percent of the gray partridge bagged in Iowa are taken incidental to pheasants, and there are very few hunters who pursue Huns specifically. Although Huns have the potential of living far longer, a bird over the age of two is a relatively rare exception. Mortality of adult birds in Iowa is mostly due to predators, although nesting hens are frequently killed by farm machinery in hay fields.

Feeding Habits and Patterns

As with many other species of gamebirds, young gray partridge consume mostly insects in the first few weeks after hatching. Gradually, as the summer wears on, they switch over to a mainly vegetarian diet of grain (primarily corn in Iowa), seeds, and greens.

During hunting season, Huns will feed primarily on corn. A field that has not been plowed before the snow falls is an excellent place to look for birds. They will scratch large, bare spots in the snow in their efforts to dig down for food.

Huns will often start feeding well before first light. After they have eaten, they can often be spotted along gravel roads gathering grit. They will repeat this pattern in the evening before going to roost.

Preferred Habitat and Cover

Huns do not require the heavy cover favored by other Iowa gamebirds, such as pheasants and quail. They like grass that is short enough to see over the top of but tall enough so they can duck down and conceal themselves. Back when most Iowa farms had at least some land in the annual set-aside (ACR) program, these shortgrass areas were prime Hun cover. Much of our CRP is too tall and thick for gray partridge. The kind of shorter grass cover they prefer is mostly found in cutover hay fields and road ditches.

When Hun season opens, in early to mid-October, the birds will still be spending much of their time in unharvested grain fields, especially corn. They can be quite difficult to hunt until most of the corn has been harvested.

Huns will often stay in or immediately around a picked cornfield throughout the winter. They can hide quite effectively under stalk stubble. On windy days, look for them just on the downwind side of a hill.

Locating Hunting Areas

Across the Hun's primary range, in northern Iowa, there are several key factors to look for when hunting partridge:

1. Early in the season, look for shortgrass near grain.
2. Hunt cornfields after they have been combined but before they are plowed.
3. In the winter, when there is snow cover, drive back roads slowly. Coveys are often quite easy to spot against the snow.
4. When pheasant hunting, stay alert as you walk from one area of "good" (that is, thick) cover to the next. Huns will hide in places you wouldn't expect to find pheasants and often escape by taking ringneck hunters by surprise.

Looking for Sign

Droppings, which are two-tone green, are often found in large bunches where a covey has roosted for the night. While Huns are not the long distance walkers that pheasants are, they can leave quite a collection of tracks when feeding in snow-covered corn.

Hunting Methods

Very few Iowans can tell you much about hunting Huns. They usually encounter the birds by blundering into them on a pheasant hunt.

Early in the season, Huns are quite predictable and can be found in fields of shortgrass when not out feeding in the corn. For several years, I had a covey within a quarter-mile of my house. They spent most of their time in a patch of short, set-aside grass, and they made great dog training birds. I told myself that I'd be conservative and not take more than one or two because it seemed so easy. As it turned out, that's about all I could take in a season, because once I'd shot my one or two, the covey quickly grew smart and moved into the adjacent unharvested corn.

After the corn is down, walking the cutover grain fields is a good way to find birds. However, you either need a dog or else a good bit of luck. Huns can hide under the stalks and normally won't flush unless you almost step on them.

When bird numbers are up and there is a snowy background against which the birds stand out clearly, you may be surprised by the number of coveys you can spot driving the roads in winter. Unfortunately, approaching Huns in the open is usually an exercise in futility. If you have more than a couple of hunters, you can come at them from several directions and hope they give someone a shot as they flush. If you are alone, you're unlikely to get within range. However, flush them anyhow and mark them down. They may head for heavier cover where they will hold for a second approach.

While Huns in the open seldom hang around to be shot at, those that drop into heavier cover often sit very tight. Mark them down well and hunt their landing spot thoroughly, especially if you are without a dog.

Hunting Dogs

There are some very different schools of thought about dogs and Huns. Early in the season, when the birds are in relatively short grass, a dog can be a big help. Likewise, as mentioned previously, hunting picked corn with a dog can be very effective.

*A brace of Huns
and a pheasant.*

On the other hand, when the birds are sitting out in the open against the snow, you're much better off leaving the dog behind as you attempt a stealthy approach.

Huns will hold relatively well for pointing dogs when they are using cover that is fairly heavy by Hun standards. Because they are covey birds, the group puts out quite a bit of scent that will attract a hunting dog.

Flushing breeds can also work well and are a far better choice than a wide ranging pointer if you expect to find birds in areas with little or no cover. A dog which will walk reliably at heel on command is best when the birds are wary and in the open.

Huns do not have a great deal of tenacity and are not difficult to knock down. Once on the ground, cripples do not generally run. Because they are usually in somewhat open cover, most downed birds are not hard for a dog to find.

Shot and Choke Suggestions

Early in the season: At least an ounce of No. 7½ shot through an improved cylinder or modified choke.

Late in the season: An ounce or more of No. 6 shot, modified or full choke.

Table Preparations

Unlike Iowa's other popular upland birds, the Hun is mostly dark meat. However, the birds are very tasty. They should be field dressed if taken on a warm, early season day. Most hunters skin rather than pluck the birds.

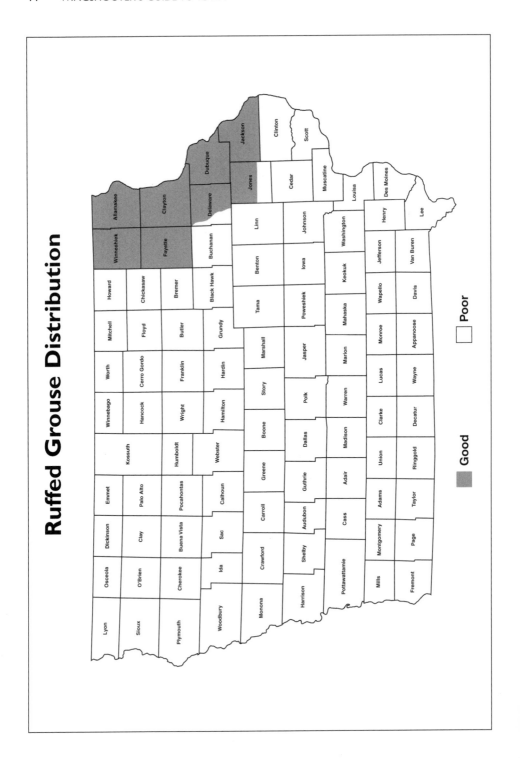

Ruffed Grouse Distribution

Good

Poor

Ruffed Grouse

Bonasa umbellus

FIELD FACTS

Local Names
   Partridge, Pat, Ruff

Size
   Ruffed grouse average about 17 inches in length and have a 2-foot wingspan. Average weight is 1.5 to 2 pounds, with males a bit larger and weighing slightly more than females.

Identification in Flight
   Ruffed grouse are nearly always heard before they are seen, exploding from the forest floor in a roar of wings. The squarish fan tail is easy to spot in flight.
- Pioneers arriving in Iowa found ruffed grouse in wooded areas. Because of declining populations, the grouse season was closed in the 1920s and not reopened until 1968.
- Although ruffed grouse hunting is currently limited to northeast Iowa, the DNR is attempting to reestablish huntable populations in the southern part of the state.
- The Ruffed Grouse Society, a conservation organization which seeks to increase grouse and woodcock numbers through habitat preservation and improvement, has established a chapter in Iowa. The RGS is providing money and labor to assist the DNR in habitat management projects for grouse and woodcock. All grouse and woodcock hunters should belong to this organization. Contact the RGS at 451 McCormick Road, Coraopolis, PA 15108-9327, or call 412-262-4044.

Color

   Ruffed grouse vary greatly in color, from the so-called gray phase birds more typical of northern regions to the reddish brown grouse common to the eastern United States. Iowa has both. In fact, on one hunt several years ago, I bagged a large, gray male and a small, reddish brown female, contrasts in size as well as color. However, other than color differences, all grouse—both males and females—tend to look very similar. There is a large black ruff, or collar, around the neck, somewhat more prominent on males than females. The birds are either mottled brown and white or gray and white. The large fan tail, of the same general color as the rest of the body feathers, will end in a black band. A bird with an uninterrupted band is a male. The band on a female's tail will be broken. However, this is not a completely accurate method of determining sex, because some males will also have a broken band.

The underside of the bird is an off white to light gray color. A grouse's legs are feathered, and the feet have hairlike projections in winter which allow the birds to walk on top of the snow without sinking.

Sound and Flight Pattern

Ruffed grouse usually flush with great commotion, somewhat like giant bobwhites, and are capable of attaining their top speed of about 50 mph very quickly. Occasionally though—especially when flushing from a tree—grouse will ghost off through the woods without a sound. They do not vocalize when flushed, although at times an alarmed grouse will utter a soft "putt-putt-putt" just before flushing. Grouse are quite adept at high speed maneuvers but are also more inclined to fly through leafy cover and small branches rather than around them. In the spring, the male makes a drumming sound by beating his wings rapidly while perched on a log or stump. This sound is part of the bird's mating ritual, and once it has been heard, it will never be mistaken for anything else. Male grouse occasionally drum during hunting season as well, most often on warm, sunny days.

Similar Gamebirds

Grouse spend most of their time in the woods, occasionally venturing into adjacent farm fields to feed. Pheasants prefer more open country but do use woody cover from time to time. Because grouse do not give the hunter much time to think, more than a few Iowans have nearly unloaded on hen pheasants, especially along the forest edge, because the birds are about the same size and roughly the same color. Look for the hen pheasant's pointed tail. Also, an experienced grouse hunter shouldn't have too much trouble distinguishing the two simply by the different sound their wings make as they flush. Finally, pheasants almost always flush out of the woods and into the open, while grouse will nearly always dodge their way deeper into the timber.

Flock or Covey Habits

In general, the grouse is not a covey bird. However, early season hunters will sometimes encounter groups of birds that will almost always flush one or two at a time rather than all together. This is a family group which has not yet dispersed for the fall. In winter, especially in areas where good cover or food are in short supply, several grouse may be found in the same relatively small area, such as a dense stand of evergreens.

Reproduction and Life Span

Male grouse will drum in the spring to attract females. Once a female appears, the male will fluff out his ruff and fan his tail in a further attempt to impress his would-be mate. Grouse are polygamous, and a dominant male who puts on a good spring performance may mate with several females.

Author with grouse and woodcock.

A ruffed grouse nest is not very elaborate, but rather a simple depression in the leaves, almost always positioned against a tree or stump. There the female will lay an average of 9–12 eggs. The golf ball-sized chicks are quite precocious and start foraging for insects almost as soon as they are born. The attentive mother keeps her eye on her brood, attempting to fool predators by feigning a broken wing and leading them away from her chicks.

In the fall, when grouse broods disperse, mortality rates are quite high. Birds may move into areas with inadequate cover. Juveniles also fly into buildings and power lines and get hit by cars during this "fall shuffle."

Unlike with most other gamebirds, too much snow does not bother grouse. As mentioned above, their feet are virtual snowshoes, allowing them to walk on even fluffy powder with ease. In fact, winters of heavy snowfalls are actually favorable to grouse survival, becasue the birds will burrow in the drifts to conserve energy. Iowa grouse, however, seldom have the advantage of that much snow. Ice storms can be fatal if the birds fail to find adequate shelter in cover such as dense evergreens. But perhaps the largest portion of winter mortality comes when the birds must spend too much time away from good cover in search of food, making themselves overly vulnerable to predators.

Especially in the northern states, grouse populations seem to follow a 10-year, boom or bust cycle. Researchers have suggested that this may be tied to a similar cycle in the nutritional value of aspen buds, the bird's major winter food source in that region. Another possible explanation is a similar cycle in the snowshoe hare population, which results in a southward migration of hawks and owls that shift their attention from hares to grouse. Bird numbers in Iowa do appear to follow a similar cycle, although the difference between highs and lows is not as pronounced as in states to our north.

Although grouse can attain the age of 4 or 5, a bird that makes it to its second hunting season has beaten the odds.

Feeding Habits and Patterns

Veteran grouse hunters suggest checking the crop of the first bird you shoot to see what they're feeding on. Although this is an interesting idea, the fact is that grouse will eat just about any kind of vegetable matter—leaves, berries, nuts, buds— and they will also take insects when available. Because much of Iowa's grouse cover is fairly near farm fields, our birds can and do eat corn. I've observed that corn seems to be a particular favorite late in the season, perhaps because other food sources are less available then.

Other than in the dead of winter, grouse don't need to move far to find food. Like most upland birds, their natural tendency is to feed just after leaving the roost and again late in the day. However, this pattern can be disturbed by hunting pressure or by weather.

Preferred Habitat and Cover

Ruffed grouse are birds of the young forest. Mature woods with little underbrush are unsuitable for them. One problem we have in Iowa is a lack of habitat. To have young forest you must cut old trees, and there simply is not enough logging going on to create new cover. Or in some cases, when trees are removed they are replaced with grain fields or pasture.

Because sunlight stimulates plant growth, the cover on the edge of the forest tends to be denser and more attractive to grouse than what you will likely find deeper in the woods. A tract of woods consisting of mixed evergreens and hardwoods, with heavy brush along the edges, is typical Iowa grouse habitat.

Locating Hunting Areas

In general, the farther north and east you go in Iowa, the better the grouse population.
1. Nearly all the Public Hunting Areas in the four counties in the northeastern corner of the state—Winneshiek, Allamakee, Fayette, and Clayton—have ruffed grouse.
2. Focus on edge cover—along trails, roads, streams, and fields.
3. Mark recently logged areas on a map. As new growth begins to appear, they will be good spots to try for grouse.

*A brace of woodcock
and a grouse.*

Looking for Sign

Grouse droppings are about an inch long and pencil size in diameter. Tracks can be found in muddy areas along streams, as well as in the snow. The hairlike projections on the toes are a sure giveaway and are easily spotted in snow. The birds do not move around as much on the ground as pheasants, and when you find tracks, birds should be fairly close by.

Hunting Methods

On frosty mornings in particular, grouse are not especially early risers. Wait until mid-morning, when the frost is burning off the cover, to start your hunt. Otherwise, many of the birds will still be roosted in trees, leaving no scent for your dog to work.

The last hour or so before sunset can also be a very productive time.

Although grouse will flush much more readily than the woodcock with whom they often share coverts, they will also sit tight and allow dogless hunters to pass by quite closely. The stop and go technique will flush more birds than walking a steady pace through the woods.

A pair of hunters and a dog make a very effective team for pursuing grouse. One of the two should attempt to remain in the open and ready to shoot if the other is traversing cover which makes it impossible for him to use his gun. When working edges, leaving one gunner on the outside, in the open, is a good idea. And although Iowa law does not require it, ALWAYS wear hunter orange in the woods. Especially in dim light, a hunter wearing any other color becomes very difficult to see.

Remember to look up from time to time. Early in the morning and during cold weather, grouse will spend a lot of time sitting in trees. They favor evergreens in cold weather. If they are roosting in the pines, one hunter will probably have to walk amongst the evergreens to flush the birds—which he almost certainly will not see. Hopefully, his partner will get a good look and perhaps a shot.

Hunting Dogs

Many hunters favor the pointing breeds for grouse. A dog that points its birds will allow the hunters time to prepare for a shot, maneuvering themselves so that they have an open field of fire.

But pointing breeds tend to range farther out, and grouse are often set on a hair trigger, flushing with little provocation. Don't expect your pointing dog, particularly one inexperienced in working grouse, to point most of his birds as he might with quail or woodcock. Eventually, dogs learn how close they can get to grouse without causing a flush, but it takes time and contact with birds.

Always use a bell or beeper on your grouse dog. If you don't, you risk spending most of your time hunting for the dog in the thick cover.

A flushing dog, working well within gun range, may be a better choice than an inexperienced pointing dog with a tendency to cover a lot of ground. Labs and springer spaniels both have many devotees among experienced grouse hunters.

Grouse are not hard to knock down, although some will run if lightly hit. Generally, however, a dog's main retrieving chore will be locating these well-camouflaged birds which typically will be found quite close to where they fall.

Table Preparations

Many bird hunters judge the ruffed grouse their favorite table game. The meat is light and delicate, quite reminiscent of bobwhite. Most hunters I know skin the birds. Although this method is faster, care must be taken to insure that the meat does not dry out during cooking. The birds are best served with a light wine that does not overpower their delicate flavor.

Shot and Choke Suggestions

Early in the season, when I also encounter woodcock and when the foliage is thick, I like ⅞ or an ounce of No. 9 shot. When shots may be somewhat longer, 8s are

Heidi on point in grouse and woodcock cover.

a better choice, and 7½s are even better late in the season. I see no need for any more than an ounce of shot under any circumstances, or for anything larger than 7½.

Cylinder or skeet is best early in the year. Even on a late season hunt, improved cylinder should be tight enough for virtually all situations.

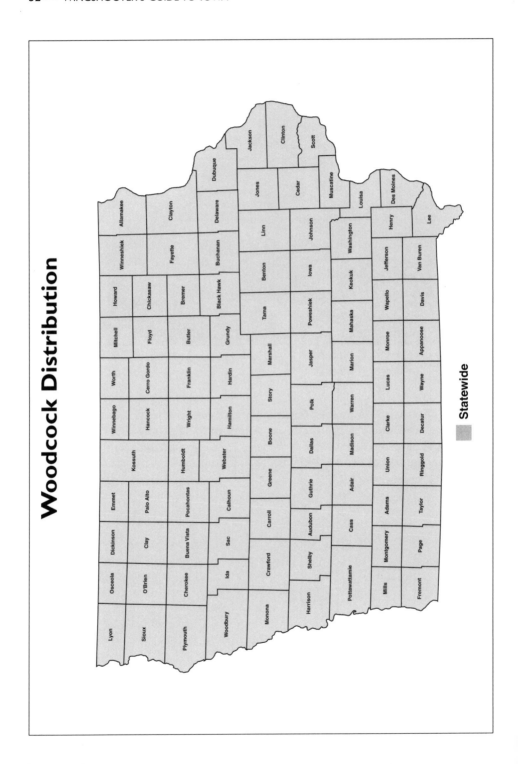

Woodcock Distribution

Statewide

Woodcock

Scolopax minor (formerly *Philohela minor*)

FIELD FACTS

Local Names
Timberdoodle, Bogsucker

Size
Length is 10–12 inches, wingspan is 18–20 inches, weight is 6–8 ounces.

Identification in Flight
Woodcock appear small, chunky, and brownish colored in flight. The long bill is usually visible. Woodcock have an erratic flight path and seldom fly more than 100 yards when flushed by hunters. Flushing woodcock make a twittering sound, which is nonvocal since it comes from the bird's wings. Once a hunter has heard that twitter and related it to woodcock, he is unlikely to have further difficulty identifying them on the wing.

- The woodcock has only been legal game in Iowa since 1972 and is without doubt the state's least hunted upland gamebird.
- Although woodcock are often found near streams, rivers, and damp soil, they avoid standing water.
- Woodcock are migratory and appear to follow highways as well as rivers on their spring and fall journeys.
- Woodcock can be found statewide, but they are most numerous in Iowa during fall migration, which occurs from about mid-October to mid-November.

Color

The woodcock's bill, measuring 2.5 to 3 inches in length, is extremely long for a bird of its size. Woodcock also have very large, black eyes, set far back on the head. The bird's breast is light brown, while the back, wing, and tail are barred with black, dark brown, and gray. Females, which are larger than males, can be distinguished by the length of their bill, which is always longer than a dollar bill is wide. The smaller male's bill is always shorter than the width of a dollar bill. Other than the difference in size and bill length, males and females look virtually identical.

Sound and Flight Patterns

Although male woodcock are very vocal during the spring mating season, neither sex gives voice in the fall. The wing twitter, which many hunters mistakenly believe to be a vocal sound, is the only noise woodcock make during hunting season.

Because they spend much of their time in dense forest, especially during hunting season, a woodcock's flight is not so much fast as it is elusive. The little birds are masters at dodging trees. Woodcock flight in the open might reach 30 mph, but they are so seldom seen there—at least while hunted—that speed is academic where these birds are concerned.

Siimilar Gamebirds

The woodcock bears some resemblance to its long-billed cousin, the common snipe. At times, both birds can be found in similar habitat—either on the fringes of wetlands, or in woods bordered by wet farm fields or pastures. Once seen in flight, however, the distinction is fairly easy to make. The snipe is much slimmer and more streamlined, with a whitish breast. Snipe fly both faster and farther than woodcock when flushed and nearly always emit a shrill cry when taking wing.

Flock or Covey Habits

The woodcock is not a covey bird. Usually, however, when a hunter finds one woodcock, there will be another somewhere nearby.

During migration, hunters speak of "flights" of woodcock, as if they migrate like ducks or geese. In fact, biologists have determined that the woodcock migration is done not so much in flights as in a sort of steady trickle southward.

Although they may migrate separately, woodcock do often drop into coverts already occupied by other migrants. At times, especially in dry years, many woodcock can crowd into a fairly small area. When a hunter chances upon such a spot, he will talk of finding a flight of woodcock.

Reproduction and Life Span

Woodcock mate in the spring, shortly after returning from their winter habitat along the Gulf Coast. Although some woodcock mate and raise their young in Iowa, the major breeding area for the birds in the Midwest is in the states to our north and in Canada.

In the spring, these usually quiet and secretive birds become very vocal and demonstrative. Right around sunset, the male makes a noise described by biologists as a "peent," although to me it sounds more like a buzz made by an insect than a bird's song. After peenting several times on the ground, the males take to the air and fly to an impressive height. Just at the peak of their ascent, they come spiraling back down, making a high-pitched whistling sound until they reach the ground. The purpose of this display is to attract females. The areas where woodcock perform their spring "sky dance" are referred to as singing fields, and research has shown that males will return to the same singing field year after year.

Woodcock lay very few eggs compared to other upland gamebirds—almost always four in a clutch. The chicks are precocious, and as soon as their fluff dries, they leave the nest and start feeding on their own. However, the mother remains quite attentive until the chicks are nearly grown. Brood survival is very high.

Dave Prine and Heidi with woodcock.

Throughout the bird's range, there is a fairly active group of woodcock banders. As a result, quite a bit of data on woodcock travel and life span has been accumulated from returned bands. Two-year-old woodcock are not at all unusual, and some birds older than five have been noted.

Feeding Habits and Patterns

A woodcock's diet consists largely of earthworms. The birds probe in the soft earth with their long bills, listen for worms, and are able to open their bills underground to capture their food. Because a worm's body is mostly water, woodcock have to spend a lot of time feeding in order to satisfy their nutritional requirements. They are nocturnal feeders, and if necessary move from their daytime "resting" cover to areas where they can find worms at night. Peak feeding times are right around dusk and dawn.

Preferred Habitat and Cover

Because woodcock are small birds that spend much of their time walking around on the ground in search of worms, their habitat requirements are quite specific. Woodcock cover must be open at ground level, so the birds can move and feed unimpeded. At the same time, they prefer denser cover above them to protect them from predators. Regenerating forest, especially of species such as aspen that grow closely enough together to shade out ground vegetation, is the best woodcock habitat. In Iowa, where young forest growth is relatively scarce, the birds tend to use saplings or sapling-like species such as sumac and willows. In northeast Iowa, mixed stands of conifers and smaller hardwoods provide good woodcock cover.

I have never found a woodcock in thick, grassy cover. I have, however, shot birds that flushed from standing corn and from horse weeds. But mostly, as its name implies, the woodcock is a bird of the woods.

Locating Hunting Areas

Because a relatively small percentage of Iowa is forested, woodcock cover is quite restricted.

1. Look for woodcock along the timbered banks of streams.
2. Eliminate all open, parklike forest areas with only mature trees.
3. Especially during migration in late October and early November, hunt the "big woods" areas of northeast and southern Iowa.
4. Although woodcock can be found statewide, most hunting takes place in northeast Iowa, with many woodcock taken incidental to ruffed grouse.
5. If you find woodcock sign but no birds, return to the cover again. Woodcock tend to use the same stopover spots during migration, and you may have simply missed the "flight."

Looking for Sign

Woodcock leave two telltale signs, and the presence of either is a sure indicator that birds have been around. They leave probe holes, made by their bills when thrust into the ground searching for worms. You will usually find these in moist, relatively bare ground. The second sign is "whitewash," their characteristic white droppings about the size of a quarter. A lot of probe holes and whitewash is proof that a flight is either in residence or has just departed.

Hunting Methods

Woodcock hunting is a real brush busting sport. These birds are small and secretive, and the only way to find them is to plunge into their habitat. Because most of these spots contain thorns that puncture and rip, branches that whip off caps and glasses, and foliage that hides departing birds, the whole experience can be quite frustrating. One reason so few Iowans hunt woodcock is that bird hunting to them means pheasants—big, gaudy birds that, for the most part, flush out in the open. Somehow it doesn't seem natural to go crashing through thick woods in pursuit of a little bird the size of a quail.

Fortunately, most woodcock coverts in Iowa are relatively small. It doesn't take a lot of time to determine whether woodcock are present, simply because their habitat is quite restricted. Hunt the thick stuff, and if the birds aren't there or if you don't see sign, move on to the next spot.

Phil Bourjaily and woodcock.

Woodcock hunting is just about impossible without a dog. Normally, the birds hold very tight and their camouflage is so good that the only ones you'll flush without a dog are those you nearly step on.

Early in the season, the cover can be so thick that, while plunging through it may produce birds, the flush will seldom offer a shot. About the only alternative under such conditions is to hunt with a partner and swap—one hunter busting brush (preferably accompanied by a dog) and the other staying out on the edge where it's open and where there is some chance of a shot.

Actually, a pair of hunters and a dog or two make just about the perfect team for hunting woodcock. At least one will usually have a shot at a fleeing bird, and because coverts are small, two gunners can usually work them quite effectively.

Late in the season, when migrants start passing through Iowa from the north, woodcock shooting can be very good, indeed. I usually plan a hunt in northeast Iowa the week before pheasant season opens. By then, most of the leaves are down, and the shooting is much more open. Last year, I timed it just right and got into some very fast action. Alternating my mother-daughter team of shorthairs, I worked small pockets of woods along a little waterway that flows into a scenic smallmouth bass river. Woodcock were scattered everywhere—not stacked on top of each other, where things can get so hectic that both a veteran dog and an experienced hunter can come unglued, but just right to provide steady action. Both my girls got to work several birds, and it was a good tuneup for them—and for my shooting—prior to the pheasant opener only a few days later.

Hunting Dogs

Although the pointing breeds tend to be regarded as classic woodcock dogs by most hunters, woodcock can also be hunted very effectively with a close working retriever or spaniel. But my personal preference is dogs that point their game, and in the case of woodcock, this has an additional benefit—not only do you have advance warning of the bird's presence, but you have time to maneuver through the thick stuff so that either you or your partner stands a good chance at an open shot.

Dogs, especially pointing breeds, should never be turned loose in the woods without a bell or beeper collar. While most pointers learn to shut down their range in the thick cover, you can lose track of a silent dog in woodcock country when it's still well within gunshot.

Probably because they eat meat (in the form of worms) rather than vegetable matter as do most other gamebirds, woodcock put out a different scent. On your dog's first woodcock outing, you may have to shoot a bird or two before Old Spot figures out what it is you're hunting. Just about every dog I've owned, even those well experienced on other birds, showed this initial confusion. All, however, have adapted to woodcock quite quickly.

Woodcock are very fragile birds, and it only takes a pellet or two to bring them down. Cripples hardly ever run far, but their coloring blends in perfectly with dead leaves on the forest floor. A dog that will hunt dead on command will seldom lose a woodcock. However, some will show a reluctance to pick them up and retrieve them—again, probably due to the different scent. But in my experience, most will take to fetching them proficiently if properly encouraged.

The best woodcock dogs I've owned are those that work relatively close and cover their ground thoroughly but are not necessarily slow plodders. A bobwhite quail hunter would be well advised to choose his singles specialist over a covey dog when hunting woodcock.

Table Preparations

The meat on a woodcock is the reverse of what it is on most gamebirds: the breast is dark and the legs are white. The breast meat has a strong taste that I compare to chicken liver. While they are one of my favorites on the table, some hunters do not care for the taste at all. A simple method of preparation is to drench the pieces

A trio of woodcock.

in flour seasoned with salt and pepper and then simply sautee them in butter. Woodcock are best served with a hearty red wine.

Although I've made several trips to France and immensely enjoy most of their cuisine, I have yet to try their woodcock specialty: the bird served whole, with intestines, on a piece of toast. It's usually referred to as "toast and trail" in English, and I'm quite content to stick to my own American recipe above.

Shot and Choke Suggestions

If I'm hunting strictly woodcock, 7/8 ounce of 9s works perfectly well—making the bird an excellent target for a 28- or 20-gauge or for light loads from a 16 or 12. If you have a gun with choke tubes, screw in the most open choke you have—skeet, or even true cylinder. A 25–30 yard shot is long on woodcock, and anything tighter than improved cylinder is more choke than you need.

Floaters and Rockets

At age 11, Heidi, my old shorthair, is long past the preliminaries. Releasing her from her kennel before I've slipped into my vest and uncased my shotgun is a definite mistake. Once more I forget that, and once more I hear her bell disappearing up the wooded ridge above us before I've dropped a pair of shells into my double.

A whistle brings her back. Together, we cross the cable that blocks the road to all but the hatchery truck. Rather than put-and-take trout, which provide the attraction for most visitors to this corner of scenic northeast Iowa, the grouse and woodcock that inhabit the timbered hills above the stream are what we seek.

As we wade the stream at the shallow ford, I think back to my first encounter with this classic upland duo. While it doesn't seem that over 20 years have passed, there have been changes. Deke, the little Brittany that pointed my first woodcock, is long dead. Jake and Rebel, father and daughter English pointers, provided many enjoyable days in the woods, both here in Iowa and in the more traditional grouse coverts of Upper Michigan. They, too, are gone, after all too few yet memorable seasons afield.

Heidi is the link in the connecting chain. Rebel's old kennelmate, she is now the veteran, with a decade of experience searching out grouse and woodcock. Her daughter, Blitz, now entering her third season, will continue the tradition.

But for now, it's just me, Heidi, and the birds. The tinkling of her bell reminds me to be about my business and get off the well worn path. Luck might bring me a wild flush out in the open, but the cover is too big for that to be very probable. Chances are I'm going to have to plunge into the thick stuff, sooner or later, to find Heidi on point. And sooner is better, because the birds—especially a nervous grouse—may not be inclined to hold for a point.

Heidi's bell has stopped now, not more than 50 feet ahead. I figure that she must be near the little spring that runs down the hillside. The thorns slow my progress, but then I spot her by the white tip of her raised tail—by far the most visible part of her otherwise almost all liver body. Her head is low and cocked to the left. That tells me the bird is probably very close. The fact that she's standing with her front paws in the mud by the spring seep makes me guess she's pinned one of those damp corner-loving woodcock.

There's no such thing as a clear shot in grouse and woodcock cover. Veteran hunters of these two birds tell you that if the cover knocks your hat off—which it often does—and if your hat makes it to the ground, it's not thick enough. You can't fall down in the stuff, they say. The trees and bushes are too thick.

Here, I'm relatively lucky. There isn't much cover up at eye level, where it will allow the bird to disappear from sight upon flushing. It's mostly low, thorny stuff—made neither for a pleasant stroll in the forest or for doing the Macarena, but not bad for shooting birds as long as your brush pants keep most of the stickers out of your legs.

I proceed toward the dog as best I can. About the time I reach her tail, the woodcock launches from a couple of feet in front of her nose. There's none of the clatter or roar of a pheasant or grouse making a hasty departure—only that odd twitter, which is caused by the bird's wings rather than its vocal cords. Wait a bit on a woodcock, I tell myself; they are not particularly fast fliers. However, delay too long and they're likely to dodge behind something.

I take the shot at about 15 yards, which sounds close until you've shot a few woodcock in heavy cover. The light load of 9s tumbles the bird, trailing feathers above the leaf-carpeted forest floor. "Fetch," I tell Heidi. Excellent marker that she is, she needs neither the command or directions to the bird's fall.

Only one of my dogs has ever exhibited any distaste over retrieving woodcock, and it wasn't Heidi, who, as most versatile dogs, will retrieve just about anything. On a couple of unfortunate occasions, she's tried retrieving porcupines. I'm telling myself how lucky we are not to be "blessed" with quill pigs in our Iowa forests about the time Heidi comes trotting back with the woodcock.

I praise her as I take the dead bird from her. Hefting it in my hand as I examine it, I see it's a female. Unlike most upland birds, female woodcocks are larger than males. Otherwise, the two sexes look exactly alike. The female also has a longer beak, and in questionable cases, bill length will almost always distinguish the two: a female's bill will be longer than a dollar bill is wide, and a male's will be shorter.

We continue along the ridge above the stream. Looking below me, I see a fisherman working a deep hole for hatchery trout. If he's like most Iowans, even in the northeast corner of the state where all the grouse and most of the woodcock hunting takes place, he probably wonders what I'm doing up here. Chasing squirrels with a dog maybe? When hunting pheasants, you're lucky to find a decent 80-acre field unoccupied by a hunting party on opening day, but on the grouse opener you may even have a public hunting area to yourself.

And today is well past the opener. In fact, pheasant season is only a few days away. The fact that Heidi has found me a hen woodcock tells me that there's at least a couple weeks of good shooting to come, since the females migrate first. Males won't get much attention this year, I tell myself, not even from people like me who know about Iowa woodcock and bother to hunt them. Once pheasant season opens in Iowa, everything else takes a back seat.

But this is a day for grouse and woodcock. Heidi's bell changes tempo, alerting me to the fact that she's working scent. I push ahead through the cover, now growing thicker. She stops briefly, then begins to catfoot ahead. "Easy, girl," I caution her, at the same time heading off on a parallel course myself. There's a trail above her, in the direction she's heading. Given the way she's working, I'm guessing grouse, and they aren't as accommodating about waiting around as are woodcock.

Now she's pointing on the far side of the trail. At the moment, however, there's nothing I can do about it. I'm in the middle of a real tangle and would almost swap shotgun for machete just to get me out.

I'm pushing aside the last clinging branches as the grouse blasts off. No twitter or hesitation here: just the sound of furious wingbeats. I throw a desperation shot at the rapidly departing fan tail, but I see the bird emerge unscathed on the far side of a big oak, curving on up the ridge. "Maybe we'll get another chance at him," I tell Heidi. Maybe not, her look tells me.

I decide to give myself a break for awhile and walk the trail. Heidi works first one side, then the other, seeking one of the two scents she knows so well. Near where I last saw the grouse, I direct her into the cover on the uphill side. It's fairly open, and I remain below.

Coming up to a slightly thicker patch, where a maple has shed a big limb thanks to a passing storm, Heidi skids to a halt. No fooling around, just bang stop, head high, eyes seeming to focus on the far side of the log.

She's got the grouse in a place where I might get a shot for a change. I move forward carefully. Heidi is death on woodcock, but her points on grouse are far less frequent, and I want to do my best by her.

Now I'm past Heidi, almost to the log. If she were Jake, I'd know what this was about. The only fur the big pointer ever locked up on were chipmunks, and he pointed them with great style and consistency—always, it seemed, right around a log where you might expect a grouse.

I cast a quick glance back at Heidi, who remains staunch. As I plant my left foot over the log, up it comes. Ready for grouse, I scarcely know it's a woodcock before I cut loose with the right barrel. It dodges behind a wide-trunked oak as I'm about to try with the left. But I'm patient, and when it comes back into view, I touch off the tight barrel and drop it hard, back down near the trail.

We don't find grouse—or any more woodcock, for that matter—anywhere along the ridge. Heidi stops for a long drink as we reford the stream.

The ridge above the parking lot is much smaller than the covert we've just hunted on the far side of the stream—maybe a quarter its size, if that. However, I've seen the days when there were enough woodcock crowded into its thickets to provide limits for two or three gunners—if they could shoot. It is at least as thick as the stuff we've just come out of, which was no picnic.

A narrow strip of cover follows the lane out to the main road. Working above the lane, Heidi seems to make game a time or two but never pins anything down. "Have the woodcock been here and gone?" I ask her. They do have that disconcerting habit: when you most expect them, they're not around.

A nice brace of woodcock.

Having only found a couple on the far side of the stream, it's entirely possible that the ones on this side have also left for warmer parts.

There's a wider spot here at the far end, and as Heidi works up to the high side of it, she swings into a hard point. She's almost on the edge of the woods, weeds and open field above her. I work around and behind, hoping to come at the bird from out in the open, where I can get a clear shot.

She relocates as I move up beside her—back down into the cover. I duck under a limb and nearly step on the bird, which whistles up past my ear. It's across the road and out of sight before I can straighten up to shoot.

"That one's safe, girl," I tell Heidi, turning to find her still on solid point. "Is there another one?" I ask, being fairly certain of the answer. I've never seen Heidi remain on point after a bird flushes. Two more steps and I discover that indeed there is a pair of woodcock. Number two heads downhill, and my first shot scatters leaves and twigs everywhere.

The bird breaks right, giving me a second opportunity as he heads up the ridgeline. The second shot has no visible impact. I watch the bird closely. Woodcock seldom fly very far, even when shot at, and if they don't disappear in the cover, you can usually mark them down.

This one settles in, again choosing the edge of the woods. "Let's go try him again, Heidi," I tell her, as I drop two fresh shells into the double.

Not having had luck with the more logical approach of coming at the bird from the open side, I decide to stay inside the woodline this time. Heidi has probably marked the bird at least as well as I have, and in a couple of minutes she's on point again.

Her head's up and moving ever so slightly, which leads me to believe that the bird is moving. Some people say that woodcock never run, and I say those people haven't hunted woodcock very much. They're certainly not in a class with pheasants, or even grouse, but I've seen them toddling across the forest floor on their skinny little legs, looking a bit like the Energizer Bunny on stilts.

I push past her and it flushes, but "it" is big and wearing a fan tail, and it has kicked in its afterburners. I recover from the surprise of a grouse rather than a woodcock and drop it with a satisfying thump.

The bird's fluttering on the ground, making it even easier for Heidi to find. She brings it gently to hand. It's a big bird with a long tail. The combination of size and the solid black band across the end of the tailfeathers cause me to guess that it's probably a male. Sexing a grouse is less certain than a woodcock, but females almost never have the unbroken tail band. A broken band, however, doesn't always mean female. Some males have them, too.

I slide the bird into my game pouch. Gun broken across my arm, I start down toward the truck. A pair of woodcock and a grouse is a good afternoon's hunt in Iowa. Then I notice Heidi pointing again.

"Come on, old girl," I tell her. "You know we're done and you're just not ready to quit yet. Besides, that's where the grouse was." I walk up to her, knowing she won't come until I've kicked around one more time. As I do so, up flutters the missing woodcock. I bring the gun to shoulder, slide the safety off, and click on an empty chamber. I hear the twitter of wings as the bird floats across the road to safety.

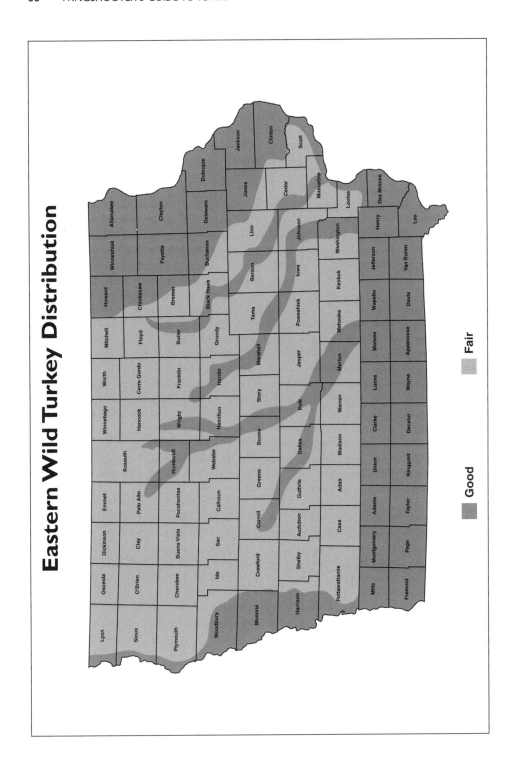

Eastern Wild Turkey Distribution

Good   Fair

Eastern Wild Turkey

Meleagris gallopavo silvestris

FIELD FACTS

Local Names
Gobbler, Wild Turkey, Tom

Size
An adult male (gobbler) in Iowa averages nearly 20 pounds; an immature male (jake) about 14 pounds; and a hen 10–12 pounds..

Identification in Flight
Turkeys spend much more time on the ground than in the air. However, when they do take wing, they are impressive birds, hard to mistake for anything else because of their size and body profile.

- Turkeys were native to Iowa, but were wiped out when white settlers arrived, hunting them without regulation and clearing forest habitat.
- Initial restoration attempts in Iowa in the 1950s and '60s, using Rio Grande and Merriam's turkeys, were failures. It was not until Eastern wild turkeys were released that the birds survived, reproduced, and adapted to the habitat.
- Because of Iowa's relatively limited amount of forest land (about 2.5 million acres), much of which is in small, scattered parcels, initial predictions were for an annual harvest of at most 1,000 birds. But because of the ready availability of food in the form of corn, turkeys in Iowa thrive in much smaller parcels of timber than elsewhere. Iowa hunters take over 10,000 turkeys in a typical year.

Color

Although a male's body feathers are bronzelike in color, the tips are black. This gives the male a shiny, almost jet black appearance when seen on the ground. The head will vary in color between red and white during breeding season, but a gobbler will almost always wear a distinctive white cap on the very top of his head. Especially when seen from the side, a male's beard, composed of long, threadlike feathers, is a distinguishing characteristic. The beard will average about 9 inches in length on an adult, and around 6 inches long on a jake. Occasionally, hens will also have beards, and those that do are legal game in Iowa. The male will also have prominent spurs on his legs, which on an adult may be over an inch long.

Hens are more dark brown in color and have a duller appearance than gobblers. A hen's head will appear blue or brown. Unlike gobblers, hens do not have spurs.

Sound

Turkeys are perhaps the most vocal of all our upland gamebirds and certainly have the widest vocabulary. Hens will yelp, purr, and putt. They also do what callers describe as a kee-kee run, and they will use a reassembly call when a brood is broken up. The male's well-known and impressive gobble is primarily a mating call used in the spring, both to attract hens and to warn off potential rivals from his territory.

The ability to imitate as many of these sounds as possible, and to know when and where to do so, is one of the keys to successful turkey hunting.

Flock or Covey Habits

Other than in the spring, when the males separate to establish breeding territories, turkeys spend most of their time in flocks. After hatching her young, the hen and the poults will stay together throughout the summer. Jakes begin striking out on their own in the fall. In winter, the birds will once again flock, establishing themselves near food and in the best cover available. Large, late winter flocks of two dozen birds or more can often be seen feeding on waste grain in cornfields.

Reproduction and Life Span

Depending on the arrival of true spring weather, mating season can start as early as the beginning of April, and may last throughout most of May. Turkeys are polygamous, and a dominant gobbler will attract numerous hens to his harem, fighting to keep all other male rivals away. The hen makes her nest in the woods—a depression in the ground lined with leaves and well concealed by bushes, branches or logs. The average clutch is about 12 eggs, although a hen may lay up to 20. The incubation period is about four weeks.

The poults are able to fend for themselves almost immediately, although they cannot fly until they are about two weeks old. Like most ground-nesting gamebirds, turkey hatchlings are extremely vulnerable to predators and inclement weather. Long periods of cold and rain are particularly lethal to the poults right after hatching.

Although turkeys can live for up to 10 years or more, a bird that survives half that long in the wild is quite rare.

Feeding Habits and Patterns

Throughout much of its range, the turkey's major source of food is mast—for example, acorns and nuts gathered from the timber where the birds spend most of their time. However, turkeys are extremely adaptable when it comes to food, and in Iowa, they have adapted readily to the grain fields—especially corn—which are almost always located quite close to their wooded habitat. Particularly in winter, waste grain is an important source of food for Iowa turkeys.

Like most upland species, turkeys tend to feed shortly after sunup. They will often spend the middle of the day loafing and dusting. The birds will feed again an hour or two before roosting.

Iowa's turkeys have thrived even without large amounts of forest due to the ready availability of food.

Although winter with its attendant shortage of food somewhat stresses turkeys, they seldom have trouble finding enough to survive. However, the Iowa DNR has found birds dead from starvation following long periods of heavy icing late in the winter.

Preferred Habitat and Cover

Iowa's largest tracts of unbroken timber, in the northeast, southeast, and south central parts of the state, were the areas to which reintroduced turkeys first adapted. Since then, they have been released and have survived along virtually all of the state's major rivers, including the Wapsipinicon, the Cedar, the Iowa, the Des Moines, and the Raccoon. There are also good numbers of birds in the timbered Loess Hills of western Iowa.

Eastern wild turkeys tend to prefer relatively open, mature timber as opposed to newer regrowth.

Locating Hunting Areas

Virtually all significant tracts of timber in Iowa will hold turkeys. Become as familiar with an area as you possibly can, keeping a lookout for the birds themselves and for sign. If you are in good turkey habitat, you are likely to spot birds while still hunting for squirrels or bow hunting for deer.

Looking for Sign

Turkeys move around a lot on the ground, and they leave numerous indications of their passing. These include:

1. Droppings, which are much larger than other birds. A male's droppings will be hooked on the end.
2. Shed feathers.
3. Scratched-up spots in the forest where the birds have been feeding. (Squirrels do the same thing, but turkey scratchings will be much larger and can be found all over an area where the birds feed regularly.)
4. Tracks. These are especially easy to find in late winter snow, just before the spring season; on muddy or dusty trails; in cornfields; and along muddy or sandy streambanks.

Hunting Methods

Iowa offers both a spring and fall season for turkeys. In the spring, the hunter attempts to attract a courting male by imitating a hen turkey. The hunter must camouflage himself well, and be disciplined enough not to move once a bird comes into view.

In the fall, when all turkeys are legal game, the object is to scatter a flock and then sit down, waiting for them to reassemble. Calling is often unnecessary.

Table Preparations

Wild turkey meat is delicious—far superior to the bird's domestic kin. I like to filet the breast into strips and soak them in marinade prior to cooking. On a big, older tom, legs and wings are often quite tough and are best thrown into a crockpot for all-day cooking.

Shot and Choke Suggestions

Although I've taken turkeys with a 16-gauge, they are really 12-gauge game. Iowa regulations limit turkey hunters to nothing larger than 4 shot, and you should never use anything smaller than 6. My own preference is a load of at least 1.5 ounces of copper-plated, buffered 5s in a full or extra-full choke.

Trophy Time

Putting in for a license for the first of Iowa's four spring turkey seasons is a bit of a crapshoot. Because the first season is only four days long and does not include a weekend, odds of getting a license are quite high. Also, you're guaranteed turkeys that have yet to become hunter-savvy.

Then there's the downside. The first season starts in early to mid-April, when Iowa weather is notoriously unreliable. It can be beautiful, true early spring weather, with mild nights and the woods alive with wildflowers. Or it can be like it was in 1996, when I opened the spring season in several inches of snow. I would have been better off wearing a bedsheet with holes cut out rather than my brown and green camo. As much action as I saw and heard from the turkeys, who were probably doing a better job of keeping warm than I was, I should have stayed in bed like a sane person.

But I'm drawn to the early season like my bird dogs to the scent of pheasant because of what happened the first time I tried it.

It was April 1990, and I was teaching an afternoon schedule at Iowa State University, leaving my weekday mornings open. Frustrated by past hunts done later in the spring when the birds seemed all too wary, I decided to gamble on an early hunt.

I also lived conveniently close to a large public hunting area—less than half an hour's drive. On a romp there with the dogs in late winter, after pheasant season closed, I'd seen a lot of turkey sign.

A week before my turkey season opened, I returned alone to the public area to do some scouting. Again, I found turkey sign—numerous fresh tracks in the mud of an old farm road. I followed the road to a ridge overlooking the Des Moines River. There, where a stand of timber met a small corn field, was the spot I chose to set up.

Although I'm not averse to rising early, I don't exactly bound out of bed when the alarm rings at 4 a.m. The morning of April 9, the first day of turkey season, I lingered just a little too long. By the time I reached my destination, there were two other cars in the parking lot.

Both hunters were still in the process of gathering their gear together. The rule I've always played by on public areas is first come, first choice. I find that much more ethical than sneaking off like a thief in the night, hoping the other guys aren't headed your way. Besides, in a sport like turkey hunting, it makes sense from a safety standpoint to know where everyone else is.

The three of us held a brief conference, and I held my breath. The first to arrive selected a deep ravine not far from the parking lot. The second was going the opposite way from me. I exhaled in relief, told them where I was headed, and started down the road on my long walk.

Even with the aid of my small flashlight, progress along the old, rutted road was slower than it had been in daylight. But knowing where I was headed, and having selected the specific tree where I intended to make my initial effort, made things a good bit easier. By the time I was in position and all situated, my watch indicated 6:15—exactly half an hour before sunrise. Had a gobbler appeared at that very moment, it would have been legal to shoot.

I was nearly that lucky. No sooner was I in position than I heard at least two birds gobble. Neither was especially close. I held off on calling, waiting to see what would happen.

Then a hen yelped. She sounded quite close, not much over 100 yards behind me. I'll take no credit for skill in picking my spot, but luck seemed to have put me almost directly between the gobblers and what I hoped would be the object of their affection.

I grabbed my push-button yelper, deciding to give the hen some help. I yelped three or four times over the next ten minutes or so. Meanwhile, the real hen off behind me must have taken me either for an acquaintance or a rival—she yelped whenever I did.

We got some gobbles in response, but they still seemed fairly distant.

Turkeys, until they have been pressured quite a bit, seem to prefer the path of least resistance. One reason I'd set up near the old trail was in hopes of catching an unsuspecting bird as he wandered along the road from his roost in the timber to the small patch of corn just above me. I was fairly well concealed, my back against a big oak on the downhill side of the trail. The terrain sloped up on the opposite side, topping out in a little rise not 30 yards from my location. My second option, if a bird was just a bit too cautious to come waltzing up the road, was that it might approach from behind the rise.

At about 6:30, I heard a loud and very close gobble, which sounded like the bird was right behind the hill on the far side of the trail. I glanced that way. Seeing nothing, I scooted just a bit to my left, adjusting to where I thought the bird should be. Once in position, I gave a series of soft yelps.

At first I got no response, and I began to wonder whether the gobbler had spotted me even though I hadn't seen him. Then he let out with a gobble that nearly lifted my hat right off my head. I moved my old 16 gauge double barrel almost up to my shoulder in anticipation.

I heard the leaves rustle on the far side of the hill and got a fleeting glance of a huge, black form which almost immediately disappeared behind a thick tree trunk. I flipped off the safety and moved my finger back to the second trigger, ready to give him my full choke barrel.

The big bird emerged from behind the tree, in full strut. I had never been this close to a displaying gobbler, and he looked enormous. I rode his head on the top of my front beed sight and squeezed the trigger. At my shot, he disappeared over the rise.

I jumped up, dashed across the trail and up the hill. As it turned out, there was no need to hurry. The turkey had taken the 1-1/4 ounce load of copper 6s in the head, and was thrashing his last just over the hill.

My watch said 6:35—a 20-minute hunt. I gathered up the bird, put him down where he'd been standing when I shot, and paced off the distance to my stand—I made it 25 yards, give or take a couple of yards either way.

On the local grocery scale, the bird weighed in at 25-1/4 pounds. His beard was just shy of 10 inches, and his spurs were just over 1 inch long. He was big enough to get me a Trophy Turkey Award from the Iowa DNR and well worth getting up at 4 o'clock.

I had had an ideal morning to hunt: temperature about 50 degrees, partly cloudy sky, almost no wind. But by mid-morning, as I cleaned the bird in my garage, I heard the sound of rain on the roof. By noon it had turned to sleet. The weather for the rest of that first season was miserable.

With the weather conditions I've had to put up with the last couple of times I've hunted first season, I think I'm paying for that trophy bird on the installment plan. But every time I prepare to fill out my license application, I see that huge tom in full strut. Although I'll probably never be so lucky again, I still have trouble picking any season other than the first one.

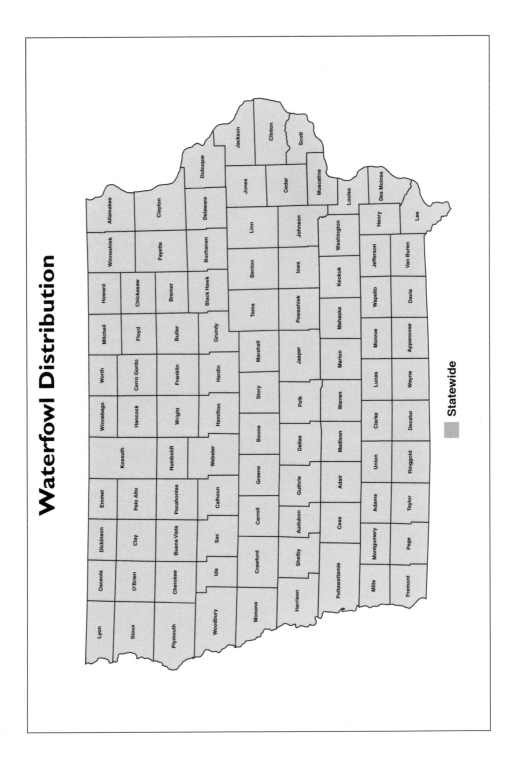

Waterfowl Distribution

Statewide

Waterfowl

A significant portion of Iowa is located within the prairie pothole region, which contained some of the finest natural waterfowl breeding habitat in North America. The southeastern tip of the region, formed by glaciers that left behind large lakes as well as numerous shallow marshes, ends just north of Des Moines.

Iowa's portion of the prairie pothole region was once characterized by the large and mostly shallow natural lakes of the northwest and northcentral parts of the state, and by hundreds of mostly small marshes scattered throughout the remainder of the area. But with the development of modern agricultural equipment and technology, the majority of these smaller wetlands were drained, plowed, and converted to farmland.

In recent years, however, the federal government and various conservation groups have combined their efforts to re-emphasize the importance of wetlands. Iowans, concerned by such issues as soil conservation and the preservation of safe drinking water, are supporting efforts to protect and restore wetlands. Over the past few years, the annual loss of wetland acres—a trend in Iowa since white settlers first arrived in the state—has actually been reversed. Now, more acres per year are being protected or returned to wetland status than are being destroyed or drained. Iowa farmers are eagerly embracing programs such as the Wetlands Reserve. This is an extremely positive trend for Iowa waterfowl and for waterfowl hunters.

Ducks and geese are the major targets for waterfowl hunters in Iowa, although snipe and two species of rail are also legal game and are quite common in the state. Depending on such factors as weather and the progress of the harvest, waterfowl hunting can be quite good almost anywhere in the state. Ducks can be found along all of the state's rivers and larger creeks, as well as on ponds, lakes, and marshes. Geese usually require larger bodies of water but will also feed actively in picked corn, where they can be hunted quite effectively.

DUCKS

Ducks are generally divided into two categories: diving ducks and puddle ducks. Diving ducks prefer big bodies of water and are bottom feeders. From a hunting standpoint, divers play an insignificant role in Iowa.

The surface-feeding, or puddle ducks, are much more common in Iowa and include those species most often found in hunters' bags. Mallards, wood ducks, and teal are especially numerous in Iowa. In fact, mallards and wood ducks together usually account for well over half of all the ducks bagged in Iowa in a given year.

Hunting Methods

Most ducks in Iowa are taken either over decoys or by jumpshooting. Decoys are especially effective on marshes, lakes, and larger rivers. Hunters typically shoot from some sort of blind, either permanent or temporary. With a very few exceptions,

Hunting an Iowa marsh.

permanent blinds are not permitted on public marshes in Iowa. However, unlike many other states, there is neither a check-in procedure nor a quota on waterfowl hunters using most of the state's public marshes.

Jumpshooting is very effective on Iowa's smaller waters. The northern part of the state has numerous private wetlands of just a few acres in size; south of Interstate 80, farm ponds are very common. Both types of habitat can provide very good jump shooting.

Early in the fall, most of Iowa's larger interior rivers hold good numbers of ducks. Floating a section of otherwise inaccessible river in a canoe or a johnboat can produce very good jumpshooting action. Woodies and teal are the species most often taken on a jumpshooting float.

Jump shooting in general is pretty uncrowded hunting compared to the large numbers of hunters that focus on the state's more popular lakes and marshes.

Some hunters also bag ducks as they fly from food to water and back. Most ducks passing through Iowa spend a lot of time feeding in corn, and if they establish regular routes from food to resting place, they can be intercepted and gunned very effectively.

GEESE

Four species of geese are hunted in Iowa: Canada, snow, white-fronted, and brant. In terms of birds bagged, white-fronted geese and brants are insignificant. Of the other two species, about ten times as many Canadas as snows were bagged in 1995.

A hunting partner helps carry the goose home.

This represents a change in a long term trend. As recently as the mid-1980s, Iowa hunters were killing more snows than Canadas. Since then, the number of Canadas bagged has about tripled, reaching a record high of 35,500 in 1995. At the same time, the snow goose harvest fell from 22,000 in 1984 to 4,000 in 1995.

There are several reasons for this change. In recent years, the population of giant Canadas—many of them spending much of the year in Iowa when there is open water—has increased significantly. Although some of these are concentrated in flocks of "urban geese" that spend nearly all their time in areas off limits to hunting, there has also been a population increase in other areas as well. The result is that more Canadas are spending more of the year in Iowa than they did in the past.

The decline in the snow goose harvest is not the result of a falling population. In fact, Iowa plays host to hordes of snows, sometimes numbering into the hundreds of thousands. Nearly all of these birds, however, are concentrated in refuges along the Missouri River. They have become so adept at utilizing refuges as to be nearly unhuntable.

Wildlife managers across North America are working to reduce snow goose numbers, because the population has grown so large that the birds are now endangering their own fragile breeding habitat in the Arctic. As part of this effort, Iowa offered its first-ever spring snow goose season in 1996. Until the snow goose population drops significantly, it is likely that Iowa will continue to offer a spring season.

Hunting opportunities for Canada geese have improved throughout the 1990s.

Most of the snow goose hunting in Iowa is concentrated around the Riverton and Forney areas in Fremont County, in the southwestern corner of the state. These state areas are partial refuges and, on the portions open to hunting, have permanent blinds that are assigned by drawing.

However, the most effective hunting probably takes place in nearby cornfields. Once hunters specializing in snow geese have established the birds' feeding patterns, they will secure permission from the landowner and then put out a "Texas rag set"— up to 1,000 decoys, most of which are nothing more than large white rags. The huge flocks of snows tend to ignore smaller spreads of 100—200 decoys. Hunters using rag sets will simply don white coveralls and, without digging a pit or preparing a blind, lie down in the midst of their decoys. The shooting can be incredible, and if there are many juveniles in the flock, the birds will often land well within gunshot of hunters and pay them absolutely no attention until the shooting starts.

Canadas can be hunted statewide and are found on everything from Iowa's largest rivers and lakes to farm ponds. Large flocks often gather around the state's big reservoirs, such as Red Rock and Rathbun in the southcentral region (both of these areas are partial refuges). There are several areas in Iowa that are closed to Canada goose hunting. These are described in general in the hunting regulations, and detailed maps of the closed areas can be obtained from the DNR.

Canadas can be hunted in fields using methods similar to that described above for snows. However, they are more sensitive to realistic decoys and to motion on the part of hunters. Those who hunt Canadas in grain fields often do so from pit blinds.

Water spreads and traditional blinds are also quite effective for Canadas, particularly on larger lakes and marshes. On smaller bodies of water, such as farm ponds, a stealthy jump shooter can be very effective.

SNIPE AND RAIL

The common snipe, as well as both sora and Virginia rails, are undoubtedly Iowa's least hunted gamebirds. With a season that opens early in September—nearly a month ahead of all other bird seasons—they provide a lot of unexploited potential, especially for waterfowl hunters.

Description

The common snipe (*Capella gallinago*) looks something like a streamlined woodcock, with a long bill, light brown back and wings, and whitish breast. Although a snipe will weigh only about 5 ounces, it appears much larger in the air. Its wingspan may approach 20 inches. Snipe almost always emit a harsh cry when flushed.

The sora rail (*Porzana carolina*) is the most common member of the rail family in Iowa. This bird is mostly dark gray with a slightly lighter breast, and it has a short, thick, yellow beak. I've always thought of sora rail as resembling miniature coots. The sora is about the same size as a snipe, but because it also has a large wingspan relative to body size, it looks larger in the air.

Iowa's other rail, the Virginia (*Rallus limicola*), is mostly brown in color and has a slightly hooked beak that is longer than a sora's but shorter than a snipe's. Sora and Virginia rails are about the same size and are hard to tell apart on the wing. Although biologists say both birds are very vocal, they both flush silently, fly slowly and close to the water, and dangle their feet. These two rails appear to be very clumsy in flight, and once you have seen a rail on the wing, you will never mistake it for anything else.

Hunting Methods

Although they are classified as a shore bird, snipe require very little water. They can be found in wet cornfields and along muddy creek banks, as well as around the edges of larger marshes and on the muddy shores of lakes. They flush readily and can be walked up, with or without the aid of a dog. After an initial exposure to them, some pointing dogs will point snipe. However, the birds prefer open areas—such as mud flats or sparse grass—and cannot be approached too closely before flushing.

Dave Kalkwarf and his Lab with sora rail.

Snipe are fast fliers, twisting and turning almost as soon as they are airborne, and present a very challenging target. When there are a lot of them around—and that is frequently the case on some Iowa marshes in early fall—you will see snipe in the air almost constantly. They can be pass shot, somewhat like doves, but are even harder to hit this way than when walked up.

Unlike snipe, rail require at least some standing water, and marshes are the only places where they can be found in good numbers. They will swim and run through the marsh grass, preferring not to fly unless forced to do so. Flushing retrievers, such as Labs and goldens, will do an excellent job on rail once they determine that these little birds are what you're after.

On the wing, rail are the exact opposite of snipe—they fly slow and straight. They often flush quite close, and the tendency is to wait before taking your shot. Unfortunately, they also have the disconcerting habit of dropping back into cover while still in range.

Because both snipe and rail are migratory, regulations require that they be hunted with steel shot only. (A duck stamp, however, is not required.) The most open choke you have—nothing tighter than improved cylinder—and a steel target load of the smallest shot you can find (probably 8s) works best for these small, fragile birds.

Western Livestock Region

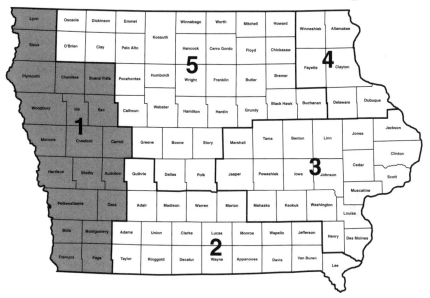

This region runs the length of Iowa's western border. Bounded by the Big Sioux and Missouri Rivers, and the states of South Dakota and Nebraska, much of this region is very good pheasant country. The terrain is relatively flat in the northwest corner of the state but gets more hilly as one heads south. The Loess Hills, a unique geological formation created by windblown soil deposited on the east side of the Missouri River, run like a narrow spine bordering the flat floodplain from Sioux City down to the Missouri border.

The southwestern corner of the state is perhaps the best place to head for a mixed-bag quail and pheasant hunt. After a mild winter or two, quail numbers in this part of the state can actually be quite good well north of Highway 30—much farther north than huntable populations of bobwhites are found anywhere else in the state. The Loess Hills in particular have a solid quail population in an unusual, rugged setting, as well as good numbers of wild turkeys.

Although channelization has destroyed much of the best habitat along the Missouri, waterfowling is still good in old river chutes and oxbows. In the extreme southwest corner of the state, the Forney and Riverton Areas provide what is perhaps the best public waterfowling anywhere in Iowa. Thousands of snow geese migrate along the Missouri, and the Iowa DNR has recently opened a spring season, offering a unique gunning opportunity in this region.

Western Livestock Region Pheasant Distribution

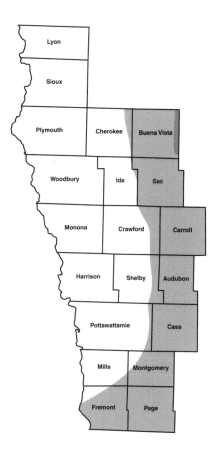

Good   Fair   Poor

Western Livestock Region
Bobwhite Quail Distribution

Fair ▢ Poor

Western Livestock Region
Hungarian Partridge Distribution

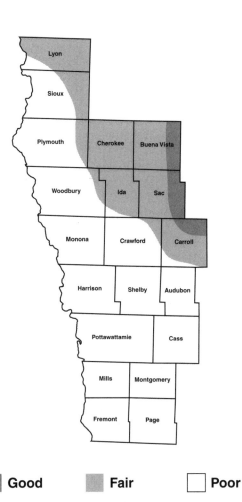

Good   Fair   Poor

Western Livestock Region
Woodcock Distribution

Region 1 Woodcock

Found throughout

Western Livestock Region Wild Turkey Distribution

Good Fair

Shenandoah
Fremont and Page Counties

County Population:
  Fremont–8,226
  Page–16,870
County Area:
  Fremont–517 sq. mi.
  Page–535 sq. mi.
	Shenandoah Population–5,610
	Annual Precipitation–32"
	November temperature–39°
	CRP Acres:
	  Fremont–5,685
	  Page–19,397

This extreme southwestern corner of Iowa is very good pheasant and quail country. However, with the exception of the 700-acre Lake Shawtee area in Fremont County and the upland portions of the Riverton and Forney Lake areas, there is little public land. Best upland opportunities will be on private farms.

Forney and Riverton, with about 4,000 acres between them, are prime waterfowling spots. Choice of blinds is by drawing.

UPLAND BIRDS
Pheasant, Bobwhite Quail, Hungarian Partridge, Woodcock, Wild Turkey

WATERFOWL
Ducks and Geese (special spring Snow Goose season)

ACCOMMODATIONS
59er Motel and Campground, Hwy 59 & 48, Shenandoah 51601 / 712-246-2925 / 18 rooms, smoking and nonsmoking / Dogs permitted in rooms / Bird cleaning room / $

Days Inn, 108 North Fremont Street, Shenandoah 51601 / 712-246-5733 / 33 rooms, smoking and nonsmoking / No dogs / $$

CAMPGROUNDS
59er Motel and Campground, Hwy 59 & 48, Shenandoah 51601 / 712-246-2925 / 17 sites, 5 full hookups, 9 water and electric, 3 electric, 4 pull-thrus / $12–15 per 2 persons / Open all year

RESTAURANTS
The Headquarters, 1001 West Sheridan Avenue, Shenandoah 51601 / 712-246-1608 / Tuesday–Saturday, 10AM–10PM, full service or buffet; Sunday, 11AM–2PM (brunch)

Mondo's Restaurant, 309 South Fremont Street, Shenandoah 51601 / 712-246-1325 / Monday–Saturday, 6:30AM–11:30PM; Sunday, 8AM–11PM / Full menu

Godfather's Pizza, Orchard Corners Mall, Shenandoah 51601 / 712-246-4100 / Sunday–Thursday, 11AM–9:30PM; Friday and Saturday, 11AM–10:30PM

Depot Deli and Lounge, 101 North Railroad Street, Shenandoah 51601 / 712-246-4444 / Monday–Thursday, 6AM–9PM; Friday and Saturday, 6AM–10PM; Sunday, 6AM–8PM / Full menu

VETERINARIANS

Dr. Gary Connell, 1109 West Ferguson, Shenandoah 51601 / 712-246-2563

SPORTING GOODS

Pamida Discount Center, Hwy 59, Shenandoah 51601 / 712-246-2341

Wal-Mart, Shenandoah 51601 / 712-246-4033

AUTO REPAIR

Beecher Chevrolet, Hwy 59 South, Shenandoah 51601 / 712-246-1014

AIRPORT AND AUTO RENTAL

See Council Bluffs

MEDICAL

Shenandoah Memorial Hospital, 300 Pershing Avenue, Shenandoah 51601 / 712-246-1230

FOR MORE INFORMATION

Chamber of Commerce
614 West Sheridan Avenue
Shenandoah, IA 51601
712-246-3260

Council Bluffs
Harrison, Mills, Montgomery, and Pottawattamie Counties

County Population:
  Harrison–14,730
  Mills–13,202
  Montgomery–12,076
  Pottawattamie–82,628
County Area:
  Harrison–701 sq. mi.
  Mills–441 sq. mi.
  Montgomery–424 sq. mi.
  Pottawattamie–959 sq. mi.

Council Bluffs Population–54,315
Annual Precipitation–30"
November temperature–39°
CRP Acres:
  Harrison–10,466
  Mills–2,581
  Montgomery–11,079
  Pottawattamie–6,746

Council Bluffs, located conveniently across the river from Omaha, is the only large city in southwest Iowa and a good location from which to hunt this four-county area. This is good pheasant country east of the Missouri River floodplain, with best opportunities for bobwhite quail in Mills and Montgomery Counties.

Harrison County is the only one of the four with a significant amount of public hunting land. Over 3,500 acres in the Loess Hills State Forest provide good opportunities for quail and wild turkeys, as well as some pheasants.

Harrison County's numerous public areas along the Missouri River (California Bend, Deer Island, Noble's Lake, Soldier Bend, Tyson Bend) are good waterfowling spots. Upland hunters looking for a unique possibility for a "triple" can hunt these same areas in late October and early November for pheasant and quail, with the very good chance of also encountering migrating woodcock. (The Missouri River is the woodcock's westernmost major migration route.)

UPLAND BIRDS
Pheasant, Bobwhite Quail, Hungarian Partridge, Woodcock, Wild Turkey

WATERFOWL
Ducks and Geese (special spring Snow Goose season)

ACCOMMODATIONS
Econo Lodge, 3208 South 7th Street, Council Bluffs 51501 / 712-366-9699 / 60 rooms, smoking and nonsmoking / Dogs permitted with $25 deposit (refundable) / $$

Heartland Inn, 1000 Woodbury Avenue, Council Bluffs 51503 / 712-322-8400 / 89 rooms, smoking and nonsmoking / Dogs in smoking rooms only, $7 extra / $$

Motel 6, 3032 South Expressway Street, Council Bluffs 51501 / 712-366-2405 / 84 rooms, smoking and nonsmoking / Dogs allowed / $

CAMPGROUNDS

Bluffs Run RV Park, 800-238-2946 / From Jct I-29/I-80 (exit 1B) and South 24th Street: go ½ mile north on 24th, then ½ mi west on 23rd Avenue, entrance on left / 123 sites with water and electric, 17 pull thrus / $17–20 per vehicle / Open all year

Lake Manawa State Park, 712-366-0220 / From two, go 1 mile south on Hwy 192 / 68 sites, 35 electric, dump station / Open all year

RESTAURANTS

The Bleu Ox West, 3549 West Broadway, Council Bluffs 51501 / 712-323-6848 / Open 6AM–10PM daily / Daily specials for lunch and dinner

Happy Chef, I-80 & 24th Street, Council Bluffs 51501 / 712-328-0898 / Open 24 hours a day, 7 days a week / Complete menu

Perkins Restaurant, 3250 South Expressway Street, Council Bluffs 51501 / 712-366-0585 / Open 24 hours a day, 7 days a week / Complete menu

Village Inn Restaurant, 2935 West Broadway, Council Bluffs 51501 / 712-328-7377 / Sunday–Thursday, 6AM–12AM; Friday and Saturday, 6AM–3AM / Family restaurant

VETERINARIANS

Midlands Animal Clinic, 2410 West Broadway, Council Bluffs 51501 / 712-323-0939

Animal Hospital of Council Bluffs, 1735 McPherson Avenue, Council Bluffs 51503 / 712-323-0598

SPORTING GOODS

K-Mart, 2803 East Kanesville Boulevard, Council Bluffs 51503 / 712-325-0930

AUTO REPAIR

McMullen Ford, 3401 South Expressway Street, Council Bluffs 51501 / 712-366-0531

Tim O'Neill Chevrolet, 1010 34th Avenue, Council Bluffs 51501 / 712-366-2541

AUTO RENTAL

Epply Airfield, Omaha, NE: Alamo, 800-327-9633 / Avis, 800-831-2847 / Budget, 800-527-0700 / Hertz, 800-654-3131 / National, 800-227-7368

AIRPORT

Eppley Airfield, 4501 Abbott Drive, Omaha, NE 68110 / 402-422-6817 / Airlines: America West, American, Continental, Frontier, Delta, Midwest Express, Northwest, Southwest, TWA, United, Comair, Mesaba, US Air Express

MEDICAL

Health Center West, 3434 West Broadway, Council Bluffs 51501 / 712-325-0022

FOR MORE INFORMATION

Chamber of Commerce
119 South Main Street
Council Bluffs, IA 51503
712-325-1000

Atlantic
Audubon, Cass, and Shelby Counties

County Population:
  Audubon–7,334
  Cass–15,128
  Shelby–13,230
County Area:
  Audubon–445 sq. mi.
  Cass–564 sq. mi.
  Shelby–591 sq. mi.
	Atlantic Population–7,432
	Annual Precipitation–31"
	November temperature–36°
	CRP Acres:
	  Audubon–10,708
	  Cass–13,817
	  Shelby–5,445

Atlantic, the Cass County seat located near I-80, makes a good base from which to hunt these three counties. Although this is good pheasant country, there is almost no public land. In addition to pheasants, there are also opportunities for quail, mostly in southern Cass County. Waterfowling is largely limited to farm ponds and jumpshooting along rivers and creeks.

UPLAND BIRDS
Pheasant, Bobwhite Quail, Hungarian Partridge, Woodcock, Wild Turkey

WATERFOWL
Ducks and Geese (special spring Snow Goose season)

ACCOMMODATIONS
Super 8, 1902 East 7th Street, Atlantic 50022 / 712-243-4723 / 44 rooms, smoking and nonsmoking / No dogs in rooms but may stay in heated garage if kenneled / Bird cleaning room / Free continental breakfast / $$
Econo-Lodge, Jct I-80 & 71 North, Atlantic 50022 / 712-243-4067 / 52 rooms, smoking and nonsmoking / No dogs / $$
Hawkeye Motel, 1104 East 7th Street, Atlantic 50022 / 712-243-1603 / 16 rooms, smoking and nonsmoking / Dogs allowed (extra charge) / $

RESTAURANTS
Country Kitchen, I-80 & Hwy 71, Atlantic 50022 / 712-243-1284 / Open 24 hours a day, 7 days a week / Complete menu
Bob's Downtowner, 14 East 4th Street, Atlantic 50022 / 712-243-2183 / Open 5AM–4PM; closed Sunday / Breakfast and lunch specials daily
Martin Steak House, 5th & Poplar Street, Atlantic 50022 / 712-243-5589 / Tuesday–Saturday, 11AM–11PM / Beef tenderloins and fresh seafood / Also a bed and breakfast

*Sora rail (left) and snipe (right)—two very common
and underhunted Iowa game birds.*

VETERINARIANS
Atlantic Animal Health Center, 1008 West 6th Street, Atlantic 50022 / 712-243-2121

SPORTING GOODS
K-Mart, 1200 East 7th Street, Atlantic 50022 / 712-243-6616.

AUTO RENTAL
See Council Bluffs

AIRPORT
See Council Bluffs

MEDICAL
Cass County Memorial Hospital, 1501 East 10th Street, Atlantic 50022 /
712-243-3250

FOR MORE INFORMATION
Chamber of Commerce
614 Chestnut Street
Atlantic, IA 50022
712-243-3017

Carroll
Carroll and Crawford Counties

County Population:	Carroll Population–9,579
Carroll–21,423	Annual Precipitation–33"
Crawford–16,775	November Temperature–35°
County Area:	CRP Acres:
Carroll–570 sq. mi.	Carroll–2,696
Crawford, 714 sq. mi.	Crawford–11,040

Like the counties immediately to the south, this region also has very little public land. However, pheasant hunting is typically very good on private ground. Also, the more hilly areas of western Crawford County can hold good numbers of quail following a mild winter or two. That same part of the region also has more timber than much of Iowa and has fair numbers of wild turkeys. Waterfowling will take place mainly around ponds and streams, with some field shooting for geese.

UPLAND BIRDS
Pheasant, Bobwhite Quail, Hungarian Partridge, Woodcock, Wild Turkey

WATERFOWL
Ducks and Geese (special spring Snow Goose season)

ACCOMMODATIONS
Burke Inn, Hwy 30 East, Carroll 51401 / 712-792-5156 / 41 rooms, smoking and nonsmoking / No dogs / $$
Motel 71-30, US Hwys 71 & 30, Carroll 51401 / 712-792-1100 / 27 rooms, smoking and nonsmoking / Dogs allowed / $
Super 8 Motel, Hwy 71 North, Carroll 51401 / 712-792-4753 / 30 rooms, smoking and nonsmoking / No dogs / $$
Best Western Holiday Motel, Hwy 30 West, Carroll 51401 / 712-792-9214 / 38 rooms, smoking and nonsmoking / Dogs allowed / $

RESTAURANTS
Denny's, 227 North Carroll Street, Carroll 51401 / 712-792-9151 / Open 6AM–11PM; closed Sunday / Complete menu
Family Table Restaurant, Hwy 30 West, Carroll 51401 / 712-792-3260 / Open 6AM–11PM, 7 days a week / Complete menu

MC's Cafe, Hwy 30 East, Carroll 51401 / 712-792-6331 / Monday–Friday, 6AM–4PM; Saturday, 6AM–2PM; Sunday, 8AM–12PM / Daily breakfast and lunch specials

Tony's Restaurant, Hwys 30 & 71, Carroll 51401 / 712-792-3792 / Open 8AM–10PM, 7 days a week / Family restaurant

VETERINARIANS
Carroll Small Animal Clinic, 416 North Grant Road, Carroll 51401 / 712-792-3708

SPORTING GOODS
K-Mart, 715 Hwy 30 West, Carroll 51401 / 712-792-5938
Wal-Mart, 425 Hwy 30 West, Carroll 51401 / 712-792-2280

AUTO REPAIR
Wittrock Chrysler Plymouth, 218 West 6th Street, Carroll 51401 / 712-792-9234
Griffith Ford-Mercury, Hwy 30 & 71, Carroll 51401 / 712-792-1505

AUTO RENTAL
See Fort Dodge

AIRPORT
See Fort Dodge

MEDICAL
St. Anthony Regional Hospital, 311 South Clark Street, Carroll 51401 / 712-792-3581

FOR MORE INFORMATION
Chamber of Commerce
223 West 5th Street
Carroll, IA 51401
712-792-4383

Sioux City
Monona, Plymouth, and Woodbury Counties

County Population:
  Monona–10,034
  Plymouth–23,388
  Woodbury–98,276
County Area:
  Monona–699 sq. mi.
  Plymouth–864 sq. mi.
  Woodbury–877 sq. mi.
	Sioux City Population–80,505
	Annual Precipitation–28"
	November temperature–36°
	CRP Acres:
	  Monona–9,879
	  Plymouth–12,613
	  Woodbury–25,719

The best pheasant hunting is generally in the eastern halves of these three border counties. There are good public opportunities for pheasants on Plymouth County's 1000-acre Deer Creek. The Missouri River accesses in Monona and Woodbury Counties are excellent for waterfowl and also offer that unique upland "triple"—pheasant, quail, and woodcock—also found along the river in Harrison County.

Some 6,000 acres of Monona County in the Loess Hills provides hunters with very good chances at wild turkey and quail.

UPLAND BIRDS
Pheasant, Bobwhite Quail, Hungarian Partridge, Woodcock, Wild Turkey

WATERFOWL
Ducks and Geese (special spring Snow Goose season)

ACCOMMODATIONS
Comfort Inn, 4202 South Lakeport Street, Sioux City 51106 / 712-274-1300 / 70 rooms, smoking and nonsmoking / No dogs / $$$
Holiday Express, 4230 South Lakeport Street, Sioux City 51106 / 712-274-1400 / 58 rooms, smoking and nonsmoking / No dogs / $$$
Super 8 Motel, 4307 Stone Avenue, Sioux City 51106 / 712-274-1520 / 60 rooms, smoking and nonsmoking / Dogs allowed / $$

CAMPGROUNDS
KOA Campgrounds of Sioux City, 601 Streeter Drive, North Sioux City, SD 57049-4071 / 605-232-4519 / Go 6 miles north on I-29 to Exit 4 (McCook Road), then 100 yards west on McCook, then ¾ mile south on west service road /
Stone State Park, northwest of Sioux City / 712-255-4698 / 32 campsites, 12 with electric, flush toilets and showers / Open all year

RESTAURANTS

Copper Kettle, 525 Pearl Street, Sioux City 51101 / 712-252-1260 / Open 6AM–2PM; closed Sunday / Complete breakfast and lunch menu

El Fredo Pizza, 523 West 19th Street, Sioux City 51103 / 712-258-0691 / Sunday–Thursday, 4PM–9PM; Friday, 4PM–11PM; Saturday, 11AM–11PM / Pasta, ribs, sandwiches, and salads as well as pizza

Truck Haven Cafe, 2815 Outer Drive, Sioux City 51111 / 712-258-0777 / Open 24 hours a day, 7 days a week / Truck stop with large dining room

San Francisco Restaurant, 3105 North US Hwy 7, Sioux City 51103 / 712-258-7616 / Open daily 11AM–2:30PM for lunch, 4–8:30PM for dinner

VETERINARIANS

Companion Animal Hospital, 801 Hamilton Boulevard, Sioux City 51103 / 712-252-5342

Elk Creek Animal Hospital, 6003 Morningside Avenue, Sioux City 51106 / 712-276-5368

SPORTING GOODS

Scheels Sport Shop, 2829 Hamilton Boulevard, Sioux City 51104 / 712-252-1551

K-Mart, 5700 East Gordon Dr., Sioux City 51106 / 712-276-0290

Wal-Mart, 5901 East Gordon Dr., Sioux City 51106 / 712-276-4451

AUTO REPAIR

Knoepfler Chevrolet-Geo, 100 Jackson Street, Sioux City 51101 / 712-279-7100

Crown Lincoln-Mercury-Toyota, 2201 6th Street, Sioux City 51101 / 712-277-4271

AUTO RENTAL

Sioux Gateway Airport: Avis, 800-831-2847; Hertz, 800-654-3131; National, 800-227-7368

AIRPORT

Sioux Gateway Airport, 2403 Ogden Avenue, Sioux City 51110 / 712-279-6165 / Airlines: Northwest, TW Express

MEDICAL

Saint Lukes Regional Medical Center, 2720 Stone Park Boulevard, Sioux City 51104 / 712-279-3500

FOR MORE INFORMATION

Sioux City Chamber of Commerce
101 Pierce Street
Sioux City, IA 51101
712-255-7903

Storm Lake
Buena Vista, Cherokee, Ida, and Sac Counties

County Population:	Storm Lake Population–8,769
Buena Vista–19,965	Annual Precipitation: 29"
Cherokee–14,098	November temperature: 34°
Ida–8,365	CRP Acres:
Sac–12,324	Buena Vista–2,098
County Area:	Cherokee–2,639
Buena Vista–580 sq. mi.	Ida–6,170
Cherokee–577	Sac–1,839
Ida–432	
Sac–578	

Storm Lake, the county seat of Buena Vista County, is located well as a base from which to hunt this area. Pheasant hunting is typically fair to good, with decent numbers of Hungarian partridge, especially in Cherokee and Buena Vista Counties.

Other than the perimeter of Storm Lake, the majority of public land in this area is in Sac County. There, several marshes and a shallow lake (Black Hawk) provide good waterfowling and some pheasant hunting as well.

UPLAND BIRDS
Pheasant, Bobwhite Quail, Hungarian Partridge, Woodcock, Wilt Turkey

WATERFOWL
Ducks and Geese (special spring Snow Goose season)

ACCOMMODATIONS
Super 8 Motel, 101 West Milwaukee Avenue, Storm Lake 50588 / 712-732-3063 / 59 rooms, smoking and nonsmoking / No dogs / $$

Vista Economy Inn, 1316 North Lake Avenue, Storm Lake 50588 / 712-732-2342 / 37 rooms, smoking and nonsmoking / No dogs / $

Crossroads Motel, Hwys 3 & 71, Storm Lake 50588 / 712-732-1456 / 21 rooms, smoking and nonsmoking / Dogs allowed in some rooms, preferably in kennels / $

Budget Inn Motel, Hwy 71 North, Storm Lake 50588 / 712-732-2505 / 50 rooms, smoking and nonsmoking / Dogs allowed / $

RESTAURANTS

Villager Restaurant, 421 Flindt Drive, Storm Lake 50588 / 712-732-2372 / Sunday–Thursday, 1PM–9PM; Friday and Saturday, 10AM–10PM / Lunch and dinner specials

Lakeshore Cafe, 1520 North Lake Avenue, Storm Lake 50588 / 712-732-9800 / Open 6AM–10PM daily / Complete menu

Mrs. Mom's Family Restaurant, 401 Flindt Drive, Storm Lake 50588 / 712-732-7853 / Open 5AM–7PM Closed Sundays and holidays / Features home cooking

VETERINARIANS

Lake Animal Hospital, 1710 North Lake Avenue, Storm Lake 50588 / 712-732-2033

SPORTING GOODS

Wal-Mart, 1280 North Lake Avenue, Storm Lake 50588 / 712-732-7940

AUTO REPAIR

Schuelke Auto Co., 211 West 5th Street, Storm Lake 50588 / 712-732-3619

Rasmussen Ford-Mercury, Hwy 71 North, Storm Lake 50588 / 712-732-1310

AUTO RENTAL

See Spencer

AIRPORT

See Spencer

MEDICAL

Family Health Center, 2015 West 5th Street, Storm Lake 50588 / 712-732-6650

FOR MORE INFORMATION

Chamber of Commerce
119 West 6th Street
Storm Lake, IA 50588
712-732-3780

Sioux Center
Sioux and Lyon Counties

County Population:	Sioux Center Population–5,074
Sioux–29,903	Annual Precipitation–27"
Lyon–11,952	November Temperature–35°
County Area:	CRP Acres:
Sioux–769 sq. mi.	Sioux–1,982
Lyon–588	Lyon–2,686

This extreme northwestern corner of the state has decent pheasant hunting and some Hungarian partridge as well. However, there is little public land in either county. Waterfowling and wild turkey hunting is fair to good along the Big Sioux and other streams in the area.

UPLAND BIRDS
Pheasant, Bobwhite Quail, Hungarian Partridge, Woodcock, Wild Turkey

WATERFOWL
Ducks and Geese (special spring Snow Goose season)

ACCOMMODATIONS
Colonial Motel, 1367 South Main Avenue, Sioux Center 51250 / 712-722-2614 / 17 rooms, smoking and nonsmoking / Dogs occasionally allowed / $
Country Home Motel, 3741 US 75 Avenue, Sioux Center 51250 / 712-722-2309 / 7 large units with up to 4 beds, all have kitchenettes / Smoking and nonsmoking / Dogs allowed, preferably in kennels / $
Econo Lodge, 86 9th Street, Sioux Center 51250 / 712-722-4000 / 56 rooms, smoking and nonsmoking / Dogs allowed in some rooms / $$

CAMPGROUND
Country Home Campground / 800-919-2309 / 15 sites, 12 full hookups, 3 water and electric, 4 pull-thrus / $12 per 2 persons / Open all year

RESTAURANTS
Doc's Cafe, 130 3rd Street NW, Sioux Center 51250 / 712-722-2531 / Monday–Saturday, 5AM–2PM; closed Sunday / Full breakfast and lunch menu

VETERINARIANS
Avenue Veterinary Clinic, 349 North Main Avenue, Sioux Center 51250 / 712-722-2522

SPORTING GOODS
Wal-Mart, 1921 South Main Avenue, Sioux Center 51250 / 712-722-1990

Canada goose numbers have improved throughout the 1990s.

AUTO REPAIR
Ver Hoef Chevrolet, 517 North Main Avenue, Sioux Center 51250 / 712-722-0143

AUTO RENTAL
See Sioux City

AIRPORT
See Sioux City

MEDICAL
Sioux Center Medical Clinic, 159 South Main Avenue, Sioux Center 51250 / 712-722-2609

FOR MORE INFORMATION
Chamber of Commerce
303 North Main Avenue
Sioux Center, IA 51250
712-722-3457

Western Iowa Smorgasbord

"Look at that!" called my friend, Jim Cole. Heidi was on a solid point, head cocked left and down toward the fencerow that marked the boundary of the set-aside field.

"Looks like she's got another single," I replied, moving in behind her.

"But she's pointing with the first bird in her mouth!" exclaimed Jim. He was coming in from a different angle and was able to see what I couldn't. I hadn't noticed that she'd picked up the single I just dumped before almost immediately locking on point again.

"Does she do that often?" asked Arnold, our landowner host.

"Sometimes with quail, and I've seen her do it once with a woodcock," I answered. "Arnold, why don't you go ahead and take this bird? Jim, back him up."

Arnold moved cautiously past my immobile shorthair. A single bobwhite buzzed out of the thigh-high brome grass, and Arnold's shot sent him tumbling. I took the first bird from Heidi before sending her on for the second.

"That's four birds from that covey," said Arnold, as Heidi retrieved his bird. "Expect we ought to let the rest of them go."

"You're right," I replied. "We just don't see that many quail in Iowa, and we don't want to overshoot a covey. Besides, I'll bet there are more pheasants around that we haven't found yet."

We were midway through the morning of a mixed bag bird hunt in western Iowa's Crawford County. My companions, Jim Cole and Doug Carpenter, were old high school classmates from three decades earlier. We'd gotten reacquainted on the skeet range, and when they said they knew of some good pheasant and quail hunting in western Iowa—a part of the state with which I wasn't very familiar—I volunteered the services of my dogs to help corral the birds.

Jim had family in the area and access to a number of farms. Arnold's place was the first stop. Not only did he have ground set aside in the CRP, but he'd also put in food plots for the birds. The mix was obviously to their liking. We'd already put two pheasants in the bag. Then, just on the edge of a little sorghum patch, we got the icing on the cake—a big covey of quail. We'd managed two on the covey rise and two more from the scattered singles.

After we finished with the quail, we looped back to the vehicles where I swapped dogs. Rebel, my little pointer bitch, sliced up the remaining cover thoroughly without turning up any more birds. Another brief, birdless stop and we decided it was time for lunch.

Over big, juicy burgers and Cokes at the local cafe in town, we mapped out our strategy for the afternoon. We'd picked up teenager Greg Thomsen, mostly a deer and coyote hunter who wanted to see what all this fuss was about hunting birds with dogs.

"You should have seen Heidi this morning," Jim told Greg. "There she was, pointing a quail with a dead bird in her mouth!" Doug verified the story.

"You guys want quail?" offered Greg. "I can take you a couple of places where we've found them before. But I can't ever hit the darned little things."

"It works better with a dog," I assured him.

He was as good as his word. Our first stop was an L-shaped CRP field with a creek slicing up the middle. Reb locked on point about five minutes into the hunt, and Greg and Doug fired a departing salute at a big rooster.

"How can you miss when the dog tells you where they are?" Doug critiqued himself.

"Larry and I were wondering the same thing," chided Jim.

Jim and Greg had the next try, with better results. "There's how you do it!" Jim told Doug.

"Don't count that rooster yet!" I yelled. "He hit and took off on the run. Go get him, Reb!" I encouraged the dog, hot on the bird's trail. Just shy of a fence, where the bird might have given her the slip, Reb made a diving grab. She proudly returned to us with the still very-much-alive rooster. I dispatched the bird and stuffed it in Jim's vest.

"You guys are making it tough on the dogs," I told them.

The cover angled, and we changed directions with it. Reb headed to the creek. Assuming she needed a drink, I didn't pay much attention when her bell went silent.

"Hey!" yelled Greg. "Reb's got another bird over here by the creek!" We all hustled over to find her locked up, nose almost into a clump of multiflora rose.

"Are there quail on this place?" I asked Greg.

"Yeah—I usually find them along the creek somewhere," he said.

"Well, watch out!" I warned them, kicking into the thorny brush.

A dozen bobwhites burst out, and a volley of shots accompanied them.

"I got one!" called Jim. "So did I," said Doug. "I still can't hit the darned things," complained Greg.

"Mark your birds down—I dropped one, too," I told them.

We recovered the trio. Jim's had dropped dead, and he had it marked well. Reb found mine and Doug's fairly quickly.

We worked back to the trucks without any more action.

"What's left?" I asked Greg.

"Buzzy's, across the road," he said. "It's loaded with birds—both pheasants and quail."

We followed the gravel road for half a mile, then through an open gate into a cut cornfield. Greg directed me to park near a wide creek.

It was Heidi's turn again. We waded the shallow stream and, once up the far bank, found ourselves in a triangular grass field with fence on one side and creek on the other. There was more cut corn on the far side of the fencerow.

"What's the plan?" asked Jim.

"Greg, you're the guide," I told him.

"I think we should go straight north on the fence," he suggested. "We can hunt all the way to the dirt road. With two of us on each side and Heidi in the middle, we should do OK."

Jim and Greg took the far side, Doug and I in the grass. "I think the kid's figuring out this game," I told Doug. Just as I said that, Heidi swung away from the tree and brush-choked fencerow and slid into a point in front of me. The rooster gave me a perfect straightaway shot, and I sent him tumbling, but only wing-busted.

"We'll have to count on Heidi on this one," I called to the guys on the far side. "I'm not dropping my birds clean, either." But it only took the reliable shorthair about five minutes to return with the bird.

There was a lull in the action for the next 15 minutes or so. I could see a fence blocking our path and, not knowing the property boundaries, called over to ask Greg if we could cross it.

"Yeah, go ahead," he replied.

I looked for Heidi but could neither see her nor hear her bell.

"Look for the dog!" I called. "She must be on point somewhere!"

"I see her!" replied Jim. "She's down in the brush over this way. I can go in on her if you want."

I agreed. Jim instructed Greg to remain out in the open, then moved into the heavy stuff.

"Quail!" he called, as the covey broke. Several roared out our side, and I was aware of shots from both sides of the cover. I was on with my right barrel but missed my second chance. From the corner of my eye, I saw Doug drop one as well.

Heidi brought in our two birds. "Anything down over there?" I called.

"Naw—I still can't hit those darned things!" said Greg.

"I was so tangled up in the brush that I was lucky to get off a shot," said Jim, excusing his miss.

We followed Greg's plan, working the fenceline to the road some quarter mile distant. Not only did we pick up a couple more singles but another large covey as well. The shooting was fast and furious. I was doing well with my first shot but never did manage one of those all-too-infrequent bobwhite doubles. Jim and Doug each pocketed an additional brace apiece, and Greg finally connected—nearly obliterating a bird as it zipped across the road.

"What's that gun choked?" I asked him.

Author and pheasants.

"Full," he replied.

"That'll either miss 'em, or else do what you just did to that bird," I advised him.

We followed the creek back, picking up one more pheasant along the way. We arrived back at the trucks at 4:15, just a quarter of an hour to closing time.

"Pretty fair hunt," said Jim. Doug nodded in agreement. Heidi wolfed down her post-hunt snack, and from the other side of the double kennel, Reb indicated she was ready for more.

"Those dogs sure make a difference," said Greg.

"Put your deer slug barrel on next time we hunt quail," I told him. "Then you'll find out that those little birds aren't quite so hard to hit."

Southern Pasture Region

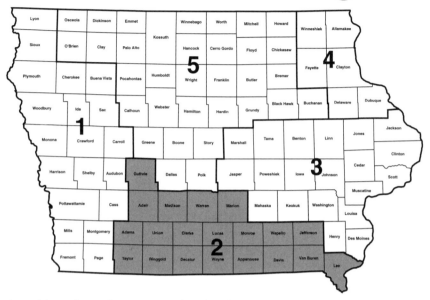

Stretching along the Missouri border from the southeast corner of the state nearly to Nebraska, this part of Iowa is dominated by cattle raising rather than row crop farming. The terrain varies from rolling to hilly, and there are tracts of forest larger than in any other part of the state except the northeast. This region also has more land enrolled in the CRP than any other part of Iowa.

This is turkey and quail country, but there is good pheasant hunting wherever one finds a fair amount of corn. Waterfowling is good on the Mississippi, on the region's two large reservoirs (Red Rock and Rathbun), and on the numerous farm ponds and smaller rivers. Woodcock hunting can be good in wooded areas during migration, usually in early November. Some counties in this region have thousands of acres of public hunting ground, and others have almost none.

Southern Pasture Region
Pheasant Distribution

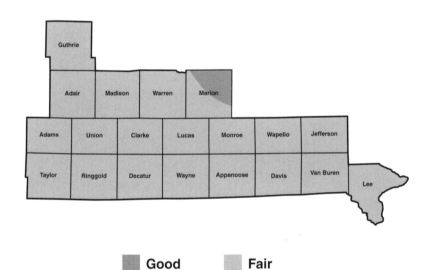

Good   Fair

Southern Pasture Region
Bobwhite Quail Distribution

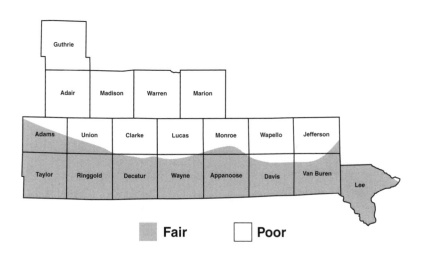

Guthrie

Adair · Madison · Warren · Marion

Adams · Union · Clarke · Lucas · Monroe · Wapello · Jefferson

Taylor · Ringgold · Decatur · Wayne · Appanoose · Davis · Van Buren · Lee

■ Fair   □ Poor

Southern Pasture Region
Woodcock Distribution

Region 2 Woodcock

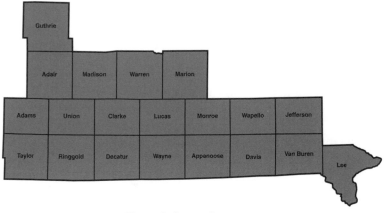

Found throughout

Southern Pasture Region
Wild Turkey Distribution

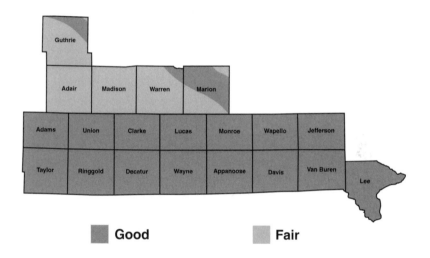

Fort Madison
Lee and Van Buren Counties

County Population:	Fort Madison Population–11,618
Lee–38,687	Annual Precipitation–38"
Van Buren–7,676	November Temperature–40°
County Area:	CRP Acres:
Lee–540 sq. mi.	Lee–16,238
Van Buren–489 sq. mi.	Van Buren–24,379

Two river towns of almost identical size—Fort Madison and Keokuk—are the population centers of this area. However, Keokuk's location in the extreme southeast corner of the state gives Fort Madison the edge in ease of access to the rest of the area.

Lee and Van Buren Counties share the 7,000 acres of Shimek State Forest, one of Iowa's best public hunting areas for turkeys. Quail hunting is also good in the clearings and around old fields. There is another good, large public area around Lake Sugema in Van Buren County, with possibilities for both pheasant and quail. Bobwhite numbers are strong in both counties. The best bet for pheasants is Van Buren County north of Highway 16. Waterfowling along the Mississippi in Lee County can be very good.

UPLAND BIRDS
Pheasants, Bobwhite Quail, Woodcock, Wild Turkey

WATERFOWL
Ducks and Geese

ACCOMMODATIONS
Best Western Iowan Motor Lodge, Hwy 61 South, Fort Madison 52627 / 319-372-7510 / 140 rooms, smoking and nonsmoking / Dogs allowed / $$
The Madison Inn Motel, 3440 Avenue L, Fort Madison 52627, 319-372-7740 / 20 rooms, smoking and nonsmoking / No dogs / $
Mericana Motel, Hwy 61 West, Fort Madison 52627 / 319-372-5123 / 28 rooms, smoking and nonsmoking / Dogs allowed / $
Super 8 Motel, Hwy 61 West, Fort Madison 52627 / 319-372-8500 / 42 rooms, smoking and nonsmoking / No dogs / $$

CAMPGROUNDS AND RV PARKS
Lake Wilderness Camping Inc., 5 miles West of Denmark on Highway, Fort Madison 52627 / 319-372-1511
Wally World Camp Ground, 2698 241st Street, Fort Madison 52627 / 319-372-3600

RESTAURANTS
Alpha's on the Riverfront, 709 Avenue H, Fort Madison 52627 / 319-372-1411 /
Open Monday–Saturday, 11AM–11PM; Sunday, 8AM–11AM (breakfast buffet)
Country Kitchen, 5102 Avenue 0, Fort Madison 52627 / 319-372-1932 / Open 24
hours daily / Complete menu
The Cottage Cafe, Hwy 61 West, Fort Madison 52627 / 319-372-5043 / Open
Monday–Friday, 5:30AM–2PM; Saturday, 5:30AM–2PM; closed Sunday

VETERINARIANS
Fort Madison Veterinary Clinic, 1215 36th Street and Hwy 61 West, Fort Madison
52627 / 319-372-9000

SPORTING GOODS
Jacks Discount Inc., 4810 Avenue 0, Fort Madison 52627 / 319-372-4217

AUTO REPAIR
Jim Baier Inc. Ford–Lincoln–Mercury, Hwy 61 West, Fort Madison 52627 / 319-
372-1012

AUTO RENTAL
See Burlington

AIRPORT
See Burlington

MEDICAL
Fort Madison Community Hospital, Hwy 61 West, Fort Madison 52627 /
319-372-6530

FOR MORE INFORMATION
Fort Madison Chamber of Commerce
922 Avenue H
Fort Madison, IA 52627-4540
319-372-5471

Fairfield and Jefferson County

County Population–16,310	Fairfield Population–9,768
County Area–440 sq. mi.	Annual Precipitation–35"
CRP Acres–27,467	November Temperature–41°

Fairfield is a county seat town, relatively large by southern Iowa standards, and home to Maharishi International University. There are no large public hunting areas in the county. The terrain is mostly rolling farm ground and is good mixed bag, pheasant and quail country, with pheasant numbers better north of Highway 34, and bobwhites more numerous to the south. Wild turkey numbers are very good in wooded areas.

UPLAND BIRDS
Pheasants, Bobwhite Quail, Woodcock, Wild Turkey

WATERFOWL
Ducks and Geese

ACCOMMODATIONS
Economy Inn, 2701 West Burlington Avenue, Fairfield 52556 / 515-472-4161 / 42 rooms, smoking and nonsmoking / Dogs occasionally allowed / $
Super 8 Motel, 3001 West Burlington Avenue, Fairfield 52556 / 515-469-2000 / 45 rooms, smoking and nonsmoking / Dogs not normally allowed / When permitted, there is an additional $5 charge per day, plus a $50 deposit (refundable) / $$

RESTAURANTS
Country Kitchen, 2803 West Burlington Avenue, Fairfield 52556 / 515-472-3106 / Open 24 hours daily / Complete menu
Torino Pizza and Steak House, 115 West Broadway Avenue, Fairfield 52556 / 515-472-9071 / Open Sunday–Thursday, 5PM–Midnight; Friday and Saturday, until 2:30AM

VETERINARIANS
Fairfield Animal Hospital, 1115 East Madison Avenue, Fairfield 52556 / 515-472-6983

SPORTING GOODS
Wal-Mart, 1800 West Burlington Avenue, Fairfield 52556 / 515-472-6858

AUTO REPAIR
Fesler Inc. Chevy–Olds–Geo–Ford, 3200 West Burlington Avenue, Fairfield 52556 / 515-472-2161

Author with bobwhite quail.

AUTO RENTAL
See Ottumwa

AIRPORT
See Ottumwa

MEDICAL
Jefferson County Hospital, 400 Highland Street, Fairfield 52556 / 515-472-4111

FOR MORE INFORMATION
Chamber of Commerce
204 West Broadway Avenue
Fairfield, IA 52556
515-472-2111

Ottumwa
Wapello and Davis Counties

County Population:
  Wapello–35,687
  Davis–8,312
County Area:
  Wapello–436 sq. mi.
  Davis–505 sq. mi.
	Ottumwa Population–24,488
	Annual Precipitation–34"
	November Temperature–40°
	CRP Acres:
	  Wapello–16,999
	  Davis–35,740

Ottumwa is the largest city in the Southern Pasture Region and an agribusiness center. The largest public hunting areas are Fox Hills in Wapello County and Eldon in Davis County. Both offer good hunting for turkey and quail. A 2,000-acre unit of the Stephens State Forest, located in Davis County, also has good turkey hunting.

In both counties, where there is a good mix of cropland, CRP, and pasture, hunters will also find good pheasant hunting.

UPLAND BIRDS
Pheasants, Bobwhite Quail, Woodcock, Wild Turkey

WATERFOWL
Ducks and Geese

ACCOMMODATIONS
Colonial Motor Inn, 1534 Albia Road, Ottumwa 52501 / 515-683-1661 / 26 rooms, smoking and nonsmoking / Dogs permitted ($10 fee) / $

Heartland Inn, 125 West Joseph Avenue, Ottumwa 52501 / 515-682-8526 / 88 rooms, smoking and nonsmoking / Dogs permitted ($10 fee) / $$

Super 8 Motel, 2823 North Court Street, Ottumwa 52501 / 515-684-5055 / 62 rooms, smoking and nonsmoking / No dogs / $$

RESTAURANTS
Briana's Mexican Food, Hwy 34 East, Ottumwa 52501 / 515-682-9447 / Open Sunday–Thursday, 11AM–9PM; Friday and Saturday, until 10PM / American dishes also

Country Kitchen, 1107 North Quincy Avenue, Ottumwa 52501 / 515-682-0776 / Open 24 hours daily / Complete menu

Ellis Famous Tenderloins, Vine & Sheridan, Ottumwa 52501 / 515-683-1105 / Open Monday–Thursday, 11AM–7PM; Friday and Saturday, until 8PM; closed Sunday

Nester's Cafe, 536 East Main Street, Ottumwa 52501 / 515-683-1808 / Open Monday–Saturday, 11AM–8PM; closed Sunday / Complete menu

VETERINARIANS
Animal Clinic Southside, 301 Richmond Avenue, Ottumwa 52501 / 515-682-8701
Ottumwa Veterinary Clinic, 2305 North Court Street, Ottumwa 52501 /
515-682-2291

SPORTING GOODS
K-Mart, 1131 North Quincy Avenue, Ottumwa 52501 / 515-673-4636
Wal-Mart, 1110 North Quincy Avenue, Ottumwa 52501 / 515-682-1715

AUTO REPAIR
Ottumwa Ford Lincoln Mercury Inc., 613 Richmond Avenue, Ottumwa 52501 /
515-682-3009

AUTO RENTAL
Enterprise / 515-682-2020

AIRPORT
Ottumwa Airport, 14802 Terminal Street, Ottumwa 52501 / 515-682-5141 /
Airline: United Express

MEDICAL
Ottumwa Regional Health Center, 1001 Pennsylvania Avenue, Ottumwa 52501 /
515-682-7511

FOR MORE INFORMATION
Ottumwa Area Chamber of Commerce
108 East 3rd Street
Ottumwa, IA 52501
515-682-3465

Chariton and Centerville
Lucas, Monroe, Appanoose, and Wayne Counties

County Population:	Chariton Population–4,616
Lucas–9,070	Centerville Population–5,936
Monroe–8,114	Annual Precipitation–37"
Appanoose–13,743	November Temperature–38°
Wayne–7,067	CRP Acres:
County Area:	Lucas–38,481
Lucas–435 sq. mi.	Monroe–20,881
Monroe–434 sq. mi.	Appanoose–21,088
Appanoose–515 sq. mi.	Wayne–53,160
Wayne–527 sq. mi.	

This is an area of small towns, with one of the state's largest public hunting areas—Rathbun Reservoir—sitting right in the middle of a rectangle formed by the four county seat towns. The two largest of these, Chariton and Centerville, provide the best access and accommodations.

Rathbun's 16,000 acres have very good turkey and waterfowl hunting (it is a partial refuge) and fair numbers of pheasants and quail. Stephens State Forest (3,000 acres), which is divided into several small tracts mostly in Lucas County, also provides good turkey hunting. Pheasant numbers will generally improve the farther north you go, with best quail numbers along the Missouri border.

UPLAND BIRDS
Pheasants, Bobwhite Quail, Woodcock, Wild Turkey

WATERFOWL
Ducks and Geese

ACCOMMODATIONS

Perrin Motel, 1519 Court Avenue, Chariton 50049 / 515-774-7533 / 20 rooms, smoking and nonsmoking / Dogs permitted with $25 deposit (refundable) / $

Royal Rest Motel, Bypass 34 East, Chariton 50049 / 515-774-5961 / 27 rooms, smoking and nonsmoking / Dogs permitted in some rooms / $

Super 8 Motel, Bypass 34 East, Chariton 50049 / 515-774-8888 / 35 rooms, smoking and nonsmoking / No dogs / $$

Don Elen Motel, Hwy 2 East, Centerville 52544 / 515-437-4780 / 25 rooms, smoking and nonsmoking / Dogs allowed ($2 per dog per day additional charge) / Game cleaning room, free breakfast / $

Motel 60 & Villa, Hwy 5 North, Centerville 52544 / 515-437-7272 / 52 rooms, smoking and nonsmoking / Dogs allowed / $

Super 8 Motel, 1021 North 18th Street, Centerville 52544 / 515-856-8888 / 41 rooms, smoking and nonsmoking / No dogs / $$

CAMPGROUNDS

Island View (Rathbun Lake), northwest of Centerville / 515-647-2464 / 251 sites, 113 electric / Open all year

Rolling Cove (Rathbun Lake), northwest of Centerville / 515-647-2464 / 80 sites / Open all year

Red Haw State Park, southwest of Chariton / 515-774-5632 / 80 sites, 60 electric / Open all year

RESTAURANTS

Blue Grass Inn, Bypass 34 E, Chariton 50049 / 515-774-2213 / Open Tuesday–Sunday, 5PM–9:30PM; closed Monday / Daily specials / Buffet Thursday–Sunday

Country Chef Restaurant, Bypass 34 East, Chariton 50049 / 515-774-8117 / Open Monday–Thursday, 6:30AM–9PM; Friday and Saturday until 10PM; Sunday, 7–2

Mary's Pizza and Steak House, 126 North Grand Street, Chariton 50049 / 515-774-8111 / Open Monday–Saturday, 11AM–9PM / Sandwiches and spaghetti as well as steaks and pizza

Green Circle Inn, Hwy 5 S, Centerville 52544 / 515-437-4472 / Open Monday–Friday, 11AM–2PM for lunch, 4:30–9PM for dinner; Saturday, 9AM–2PM and 4:30–10PM; Sunday, 10:30AM–2PM for brunch and 4:30–8PM for dinner

Pucci's Family Restaurant, 717 North 18th Street, Centerville 52544 / 515-437-4128 / Open Sunday–Thursday, 11AM–9PM; Friday and Saturday, until 10PM / Noon buffet daily

VETERINARIANS

Eastridge Animal Center, 730 South 4th Street, Chariton 50049 / 515-774-8486

SPORTING GOODS

Wal-Mart, 1101 North 18th Street, Centerville 52544 / 515-437-7181

AUTO REPAIR

Chariton Ford–Mercury, 124 South Main Street, Chariton 50049 / 515-774-2586

AUTO RENTAL

Chariton–See Des Moines

Centerville–See Ottumwa

AIRPORT

Chariton–See Des Moines

Centerville–See Ottumwa

MEDICAL

Lucas County Health Center, 1200 North 7th Street, Chariton 50049 / 515-774-3000

FOR MORE INFORMATION

Chariton Chamber & Development Corp.
104 North Grand Street
Chariton, IA 50049
515-774-4059

Chamber of Commerce
128 North 12th Street
Centerville, IA 52544
515-437-4102

Knoxville and Marion County

County Population–30,001	Knoxville Population–8,232
County Area–575 sq. mi.	Annual Precipitation–35"
CRP Acres–25,045	November Temperature–39°

Although Pella—a town with a distinctly Dutch flavor—is slightly larger, Knoxville is the county seat and is more centrally located. It is just south of Red Rock Reservoir, which at 25,000 acres is the state's largest public hunting area. Red Rock has good waterfowling (part of it is a refuge) and decent pheasant hunting, as well as turkey hunting in wooded areas. One major drawback is its proximity to Des Moines, the state's largest city.

Pheasant hunting on private ground can also be quite good, although the competition from resident hunters out of Des Moines can make access more difficult than in other parts of the state.

UPLAND BIRDS
Pheasants, Bobwhite Quail, Woodcock, Wild Turkey

WATERFOWL
Ducks and Geese

ACCOMMODATIONS
Red Carpet Motel, Hwy 14 N, Knoxville 50138 / 515-842-3191 / 40 rooms, smoking and nonsmoking / No dogs / $

Super 8 Motel, Hwy 14 N, Knoxville 50138 / 515-828-8808 / 40 rooms, smoking and nonsmoking / No dogs / $$

CAMPGROUNDS
Elk Rock State Park, 7 miles north on Hwy 14 / 515-842-6008 / 92 sites, 32 electric, dump station / Open all year

RESTAURANTS
Kin Folks Inc., 1711 High Street, Knoxville 50138 / 515-943-2362 / Open 10:30AM–9PM daily / Texas-style barbeque

Mr. C's Steakhouse, Hwy 14 N, Knoxville 50138 / 515-828-8909 / Open Monday–Saturday, 6AM–9PM; Sunday, 6AM–3PM

Udders, 1265 Hayes Drive, Knoxville 50138 / 515-828-7821 / Open Sunday–Thursday, 5PM–9PM; Friday and Saturday until 10PM / Bar and grill; grill your own steak

SPORTING GOODS
Avery's Hardware, 322 East Main Street, Knoxville 50138 / 515-842-2121

An unusual, mostly-white pheasant shot by the author in 1996.

AUTO REPAIR
Plymouth & Dodge Inc., 1705 North Lincoln Street, Knoxville 50138 / 515-842-3200

AUTO RENTAL
See Des Moines

AIRPORT
See Des Moines

MEDICAL
Knoxville Area Community Hospital, 1002 South Lincoln Street, Knoxville 50138 / 515-842-2151

FOR MORE INFORMATION
Knoxville Chamber of Commerce
305 South 3rd Street
Knoxville, IA 50138
515-828-7555

Indianola
Warren and Madison Counties

County Population:	Indianola Population–11,340
Warren–36,033	Annual Precipitation–35"
Madison–12,483	November Temperature–38°
County Area:	CRP Acres:
Warren–573 sq. mi.	Warren–25,046
Madison–563 sq. mi.	Madison–17,871

These two counties both adjoin the Des Moines metro area, and their county seats—Indianola and Winterset—are rapidly becoming bedroom communities for the capital city. Although Madison County has Hollywood connections—Winterset was John Wayne's birthplace and the county's covered bridges the subject of a Clint Eastwood movie—Indianola has better accommodations and access.

The only public hunting area of any size is Badger Creek in Madison County, which has a good pheasant population; it also draws numerous hunters from Des Moines. This is mainly pheasant country, and hunting on private ground can be good. As you get farther away from Des Moines, hunting competition will decrease.

UPLAND BIRDS
Pheasants, Bobwhite Quail, Woodcock, Wild Turkey

WATERFOWL
Ducks and Geese

ACCOMMODATIONS
Apple Tree Inn, 1215 North Jefferson Street, Indianola 50125 / 515-961-0551 / 60 rooms, smoking and nonsmoking / No dogs / $$
Frontier Motel, 901 West 2nd Avenue, Indianola 50125 / 515-961-6283 / 10 rooms, smoking and nonsmoking / Dogs allowed ($3 extra per day) / $$

CAMPGROUNDS
Woods Motel and RV Park, 906 South Jefferson Street, Indianola 50125 / 515-961-5311 / 13 rooms, smoking and nonsmoking / Dogs allowed ($5 extra per day) / $ / **RV Park:** 17 spaces with electricity, water, sewer / $8 per day
Lake Ahquabi State Park, southwest of Indianola / 515-961-7101 / from jct Hwy 92 and US65-69, go 5½ miles south on US65-69, then 2 miles west on Hwy 349 / 161 sites, 35 ft. maximum RV length, 85 electric, dump station / Open all year

RESTAURANTS

Country Kitchen of Indianola, 1303 North Jefferson Street, Indianola 50125 / 515-961-4919 / Open 24 hours daily / Complete menu

Crouse Cafe, 115 East Salem Avenue, Indianola 50125 / 515-961-3362 / Open Monday–Thursday, 6AM–8PM; Friday and Saturday until 9PM; Sunday, 8AM–2PM

VETERINARIANS

All Creatures Small Animal Hospital, 2300 West 2nd Avenue, Indianola 50125 / 515-961-7882

Indianola Veterinary Clinic, 972 Hwy 65-69 North, Indianola 50125 / 515-961-6201

SPORTING GOODS

Wal-Mart, 1500 North Jefferson Street, Indianola 50125 / 515-961-8955

AUTO REPAIR

Noble Ford–Lincoln–Mercury, Hwy 65-69 North, Indianola 50125 / 515-961-8151

AUTO RENTAL

See Des Moines

AIRPORT

See Des Moines

FOR MORE INFORMATION

Indianola Chamber of Commerce
515 North Jefferson Street
Indianola, IA 50125-1750
515-961-6269

Osceola
Clarke and Decatur Counties

County Population:	Osceola Population–4,164
Clarke–8,287	Annual Precipitation–35"
Decatur–8,338	November Temperature–38°
County Area:	CRP Acres:
Clarke–431 sq. mi.	Clarke–35,381
Decatur–535 sq. mi.	Decatur–38,675

Formerly one of the state's prime pheasant and quail areas, Clarke and Decatur Counties have seen bird numbers tumble—but both species are on the rebound. Decatur County has three public hunting areas—Dekalb, Little River, and Sand Creek—all of about 2,000 acres and all with decent numbers of pheasants, quail, and turkeys. Little River also can have good duck shooting.

There is a lot of CRP ground in this part of the state. The trick to finding the best quail and pheasant hunting is to locate cornfields in close proximity. Turkey numbers are good wherever there are large tracts of woods.

UPLAND BIRDS
Pheasants, Bobwhite Quail, Woodcock, Wild Turkey

WATERFOWL
Ducks and Geese

ACCOMMODATIONS
Blue Heaven Motel, 325 South Main Street, Osceola 50213 / 515-342-2115 / 24 rooms, smoking and nonsmoking / Dogs allowed / $
Super 8 Motel, I-35 and US 34, Osceola 50213 / 515-342-6594 / 54 rooms, smoking and nonsmoking / No dogs / $$

RESTAURANTS
Family Table Restaurant, Jeffreys Street, Osceola 50213 / 515-342-4153 / Open 6AM–10PM daily / Lunch buffet
Redman's Pizza and Steak House, 123 South Main Street, Osceola 50213 / 515-342-6116 / Open Monday–Saturday, 11AM–10PM; closed Sunday

SPORTING GOODS
The Outdoor Store (factory outlet for Boyt and Bob Allen hunting and shooting products), 220 South Main, Osceola 50213 / 515-342-6461

Matt Brown swings on a flushing bobwhite.

AUTO REPAIR
Oliver Motors Chrysler Plymouth, 1120 Jeffreys Drive, Osceola 50213 /
515-342-2537

AUTO RENTAL
See Des Moines

AIRPORT
See Des Moines

MEDICAL
Clarke County Hospital, 800 South Fillmore Street, Osceola 50213 / 515-342-2184

FOR FURTHER INFORMATION
Osceola Chamber of Commerce
100 South Fillmore Street
Osceola, IA 50213
515-342-4200

Guthrie Center and Greenfield
Guthrie and Adair Counties

County Population:	Guthrie Center Population–1,614
Guthrie–10,935	Greenfield Population–2,074
Adair–8,409	Annual Precipitation–33"
County Area:	November Temperature–36°
Guthrie–594 sq. mi.	CRP Acres:
Adair–570 sq. mi.	Guthrie–22,601
	Adair–17,074

Interstate 80 nearly follows the line dividing these two counties, making access to them and their small county seats quite easy. There is more row crop farming in these counties than in most of this region, and pheasant hunting—mostly on private land—can be quite good. Best quail numbers are in southern Adair County. These two counties are also less heavily wooded than those along the Missouri border. The best turkey hunting will be along stream courses. Streams and farm ponds provide decent duck shooting.

Adair County has little public land. In Guthrie County, there are two medium-sized public hunting areas: heavily timbered Elk Grove, mainly for turkey hunters; and Bays Branch, which does have some quail and waterfowl as well as pheasants.

UPLAND BIRDS
Pheasants, Bobwhite Quail, Woodcock, Wild Turkey

WATERFOWL
Ducks and Geese

ACCOMMODATIONS
Midway Motel, Hwy 44 East, Guthrie Center 50115 / 515-747-2261 / 13 rooms, smoking and nonsmoking / No dogs / Bird cleaning room / $
Ember Motel, 301 SE Kent Street, Greenfield 50849 / 515-743-2171 / 13 rooms, smoking and nonsmoking / Dogs allowed in rooms if in kennel / $

CAMPGROUND
Springbrook State Park, northeast of Guthrie Center / 515-747-3591 / from jct Hwy 4 and Hwy 25, go 7 miles north on Hwy 25, then 1 mi southeast on Hwy 384 / 200 sites, 32 ft. maximum RV length, 55 electric, dump station / Open all year

RESTAURANTS
Breadeaux Pisa, 409 State Street, Guthrie Center 50115 / 515-747-8323 / Open Sunday–Thursday, 11AM–10PM; Friday and Saturday until 10:30PM / Pasta, salads, sandwiches / Lunch buffet 11AM–1:30PM Monday–Friday

VETERINARIANS

Wells Veterinary Clinic, 702 North 1st Street, Guthrie Center 50115 / 515-747-8345
Adair County Veterinary Clinic PC, 407 SE Noble Street, Greenfield 50849 /
515-743-2138

AUTO RENTAL

See Des Moines

AIRPORT

See Des Moines

MEDICAL

Adair County Memorial Hospital, 609 SE Kent Street, Greenfield 50849 /
515-743-2123

FOR MORE INFORMATION

Chamber of Commerce
PO Box 61
Greenfield, IA 50849
515-743-8444

Creston
Union and Ringgold Counties

County Population:
  Union–12,750
  Ringgold–5,402
County Area:
  Union–427 sq. mi.
  Ringgold–536 sq. mi.
	Creston Population–7,911
	Annual Precipitation–35"
	November Temperature–39°
	CRP Acres:
	  Union–25,075
	  Ringgold–59,618

Lots of CRP acres characterize the countryside in what was once one of the strongholds of Iowa quail and pheasant hunting. Numbers of both have declined, but they have been improving recently.

Creston, the largest town in a several county area, has good accommodations and convenient access to both counties. Best public land opportunities are in Ringgold County, where the Mount Ayr and Ringgold areas—each over 1,000 acres—have decent numbers of pheasants and quail, as well as turkeys. The area around Twelve Mile Lake in Union County, also open to public hunting, has waterfowl as well as pheasants.

UPLAND BIRDS
Pheasants, Bobwhite Quail, Woodcock, Wild Turkey

WATERFOWL
Ducks and Geese

ACCOMMODATIONS
Holiday Motel, 800 South Walnut Street, Creston 50801 / 515-782-2524 / 14 rooms, smoking and nonsmoking / No dogs / $$
Moonlite Motel, 704 New York Avenue, Creston 50801 / 515-782-4422 / 10 rooms, smoking and nonsmoking / No dogs / $
Super 8 Motel, 804 West Taylor Street, Creston 50801 / 515-782-6541 / 84 rooms, smoking and nonsmoking / No dogs / $$

CAMPGROUND
Green Valley State Park, north of Creston / 515-782-5131 / From jct US34 and Hwy 25, go 3 miles north on Hwy 25, then 1 mile east on CRH24 / 139 sites, 81 electric, dump station / Open all year

RESTAURANTS
A & G Pizza and Steak House, 211 West Adams Street, Creston 50801 / 515-782-7871 / Open Monday–Saturday, 11AM–9PM; closed Sunday
Berning Cafe, 301 West Adams Street, Creston 50801 / 515-782-7001 / Open Monday–Saturday, 5:30AM–10:30PM; Sunday, 7AM–2PM
Happy Chef, 802 West Taylor Street, Creston 50801 / 515-782-4238 / Open 24 hours daily / Complete menu

Don't leave home without one!

VETERINARIANS
Creston Veterinary Clinic PC, 509 West Townline Street, Creston 50801 /
515-782-2224

SPORTING GOODS
Wal-Mart, 612 New York Avenue, Creston 50801 / 515-782-6954

AUTO REPAIR
Creston Motor Co., 410 West Adams Street, Creston 50801 / 515-782-2179

AUTO RENTAL
See Des Moines

AIRPORT
See Des Moines

MEDICAL
Hospice Greater Community Hospital, 1700 West Townline Street, Creston 50801 /
515-782-7091

FOR MORE INFORMATION
Creston Chamber of Commerce
116 West Adams Street
Creston, IA 50801-3103
515-782-7021

Corning
Adams and Taylor Counties

County Population:	Corning Population–1,806
Adams–4,866	Annual Precipitation–35"
Taylor–7,114	November Temperature–38°
County Area:	CRP Acres:
Adams–426 sq. mi.	Adams–23,336
Taylor–537 sq. mi.	Taylor–53,571

Corning, a small county seat town, has the best location and accommodations from which to hunt these two counties. Almost all hunting opportunities will be on private ground, although the area around Lake Icaria is open to public hunting and has both waterfowl and pheasants. Typically, this is a good area for both pheasants and quail, with turkeys most abundant along creeks and rivers.

UPLAND BIRDS
Pheasants, Bobwhite Quail, Woodcock, Wild Turkey

WATERFOWL
Ducks and Geese

ACCOMMODATIONS

La Conn E Motel, South Hwy 148, Corning 50841 / 515-322-4003 / 17 rooms, smoking and nonsmoking / No dogs / $

Sunset Motel, Old Hwy 34 East, Corning 50841 / 515-322-3191 / 10 rooms, all smoking / Dogs occasionally allowed / $

RESTAURANTS

Kay's Kafe, 608 Davis Avenue, Corning 50841 / 515-322-4297 / Open Monday–Saturday, 6AM–9PM; closed Sunday / Daily specials

Ken's, Hwy 148 at 9th Street, Corning 50841 / 515-322-4919 / Open Tuesday–Sunday, 10AM–9PM; closed Monday

AUTO REPAIR

Miller Chevrolet, 601 Benton Avenue, Corning 50841 / 515-322-4112

AUTO RENTAL

Omaha, NE (see Council Bluffs)

AIRPORT

Omaha, NE (see Council Bluffs)

MEDICAL

Mercy Hospital, Rosary Drive, Corning 50841 / 515-322-3121

FOR MORE INFORMATION

Chamber of Commerce
710 Davis Avenue
Corning, IA 50841
515-322-3243

Eastern Livestock Region

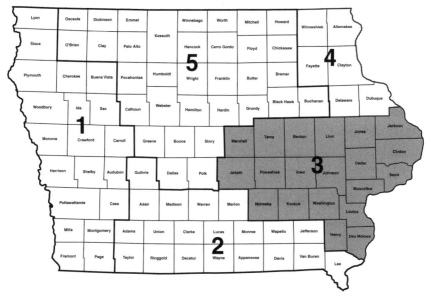

Extending from the Mississippi River west to the center of the state, this region of eastern and eastcentral Iowa is comprised mostly of rolling terrain: not as flat as much of the Cash Grain Region, but not as hilly as either the Southern Pasture or Northeast Dairy Regions.

The Eastern Livestock Region is pheasant country, with several of its counties ranking among the best spots in the state for ringnecks. Turkey hunting is good in the southern counties and along major river valleys. There are good waterfowling opportunities on the Mississippi, as well as on other streams, lakes, and reservoirs. Quail are relatively common in the southern part of the region and Hungarian partridge in the north.

Although some parts of this region have fairly large public hunting areas, in general there is not a lot of public land. In particular, the best pheasant hunting will be found on private ground.

Eastern Livestock Region
Pheasant Distribution

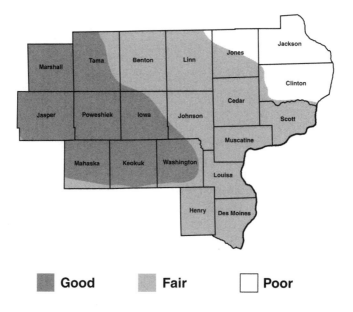

Eastern Livestock Region
Bobwhite Quail Distribution

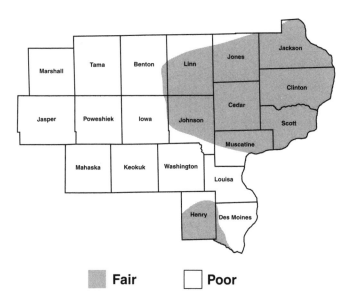

Fair   Poor

Eastern Livestock Region
Hungarian Partridge Distribution

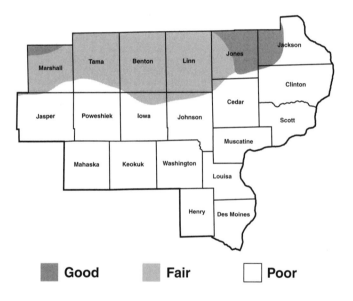

Good   Fair   Poor

Eastern Livestock Region
Woodcock Distribution

Found throughout

Eastern Livestock Region
Wild Turkey Distribution

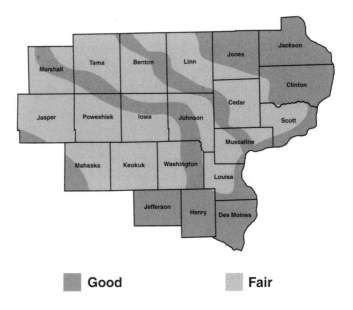

Good   Fair

Eastern Livestock Region
Ruffed Grouse Distribution

Clinton
Clinton and Jackson Counties

County Population:	Clinton Population–29,201
Clinton–51,040	Annual Precipitation–35"
Jackson–19,950	November Temperature–40°
County Area:	CRP Acres:
Clinton–710 sq. mi.	Clinton–18,019
Jackson–650 sq. mi.	Jackson–35,038

Clinton, a medium-sized city on the Mississippi River, is a good town from which to hunt these two eastern Iowa counties. Along the river itself, there is very good hunting for waterfowl and wild turkeys. The best pheasant hunting is in the western half of both counties.

The Barber Creek and Syracuse Areas in Clinton County and Big Mill in Jackson County, all in the 600- to 800-acre range, are good for turkeys. The best public pheasant hunting will be found on the nearly 1,000-acre Goose Lake Area in Clinton County. Goose Lake and the big Green Island Area (nearly 4,000 acres) in Jackson County are good waterfowl bets.

UPLAND BIRDS
Pheasants, Bobwhite Quail, Hungarian Partridge, Ruffed Grouse, Woodcock, Wild Turkey

WATERFOWL
Ducks and Geese

ACCOMMODATIONS
Best Western Frontier Inn, 2300 Lincolnway Street, Clinton 52732 / 319-242-7112 / 116 rooms, smoking and nonsmoking / Dogs allowed ($3 fee) / $$$
Super 8, 1711 Lincolnway Street, Clinton 52732 / 319-242-8870 / 63 rooms, smoking and nonsmoking / No dogs / $$
Clinton Travelodge, 302 6th Avenue South, Clinton 52732 / 319-243-4730 / 51 rooms, smoking and nonsmoking / Dogs allowed / $$
Ramada Inn, 1522 Lincolnway Street, Clinton 52732 / 319-243-8841 / 103 rooms, smoking and nonsmoking / Dogs allowed / $$$

CAMPGROUND
Riverview RV Park (City Park) / 319-243-1260 / 24 sites, all electric, all pull-thrus / Open all year

RESTAURANTS
Country Kitchen, 1516 Camanche Avenue, Clinton 52732 / 319-242-2312 / Open 24 hours daily / Complete menu

J & D Steak House, 320 South 2nd Street, Clinton 52732, 319-242-9831 / Open Monday–Saturday, 11AM–8PM; Sunday, 11AM-2PM / Catfish, chicken, pork chops as well as steaks

Village Inn, 1710 Lincolnway Street, Clinton 52732 / 319-242-7121 / Open Sunday-Thursday; Friday and Saturday until 3AM / Complete menu

Mississippi Cafe, 212 South 2nd Street, Clinton 52732 / 319-243-1009 / Open Monday–Saturday, 5:30AM–2PM; Sunday, 6AM–2PM

VETERINARIANS
Clinton Veterinary Clinic, 1574 Main Avenue, Clinton 52732 / 319-242-8761

SPORTING GOODS
K-Mart, 1800 Lincolnway Street, Clinton 52732 / 319-242-6612

AUTO REPAIR
Rose Ford, 2716 South 19th Street, Clinton 52732 / 319-242-7011
Southgate Motors, 2715 South 19th Street, Clinton 52732 / 319-242-0441

AUTO RENTAL
See Davenport

AIRPORT
See Davenport

MEDICAL
Medical Associates, 915 13th Avenue North, Clinton 52732 / 319-243-3325

FOR MORE INFORMATION
Chamber of Commerce
333 4th Avenue South
Clinton, IA 52732
319-242-5702

Anamosa
Jones and Cedar Counties

County Population: Jones–19,444 Cedar–17,381 County Area: Jones–576 sq. mi. Cedar–582 sq. mi.	Anamosa Population–5,100 Annual Precipitation–35" November temperature–38° CRP Acres: Jones–12,513 Cedar–9,035

Although this is primarily pheasant country, three of the state's larger rivers—Cedar, Wapsipinicon, and Maquoketa—flow through the two counties, providing good possibilities for wild turkey and waterfowl.

There is little public land in Cedar County. In Jones County, Indian Bluffs (410 acres) and Pictured Rocks (over 1,000 acres) both have good turkey hunting. Muskrat Slough has both pheasants and waterfowl.

Anamosa is a typical Iowa county seat town with some facilities. Visitors looking for a wider variety of accommodations, restaurants, and services should look to Cedar Rapids or Iowa City.

UPLAND BIRDS
Pheasants, Bobwhite Quail, Hungarian Partridge, Ruffed Grouse, Woodcock, Wild Turkey

WATERFOWL
Ducks and Geese

ACCOMMODATIONS
Super 8 Motel, 100 Grant Wood Drive, Anamosa 52205 / 319-462-3888 / 33 rooms, smoking and nonsmoking / No dogs / $$

CAMPGROUND
Wapsipinicon State Park, in town off US151 / 319-462-2761 / 30 sites, 15 electric / Open all year

RESTAURANTS
McOtto's Family Restaurant, Hwy 151 & 64, Anamosa 52205 / 319-462-4200 / Open Sunday–Thursday, 8AM–10PM; Friday and Saturday until midnight

Opera House Family Restaurant, 221 West Main Street, Anamosa 52205 / 319-462-2302 / Open 6:30AM–9PM daily / Featuring home cooking and homemade soups

A beautiful bobwhite quail, brought to hand. (Photo by Dave Meisner)

SPORTING GOODS
Wal-Mart, Chamber Drive, Anamosa 52205 / 319-462-4314

AUTO REPAIR
Schoon's Auto and Truck Center, Hwys 151 & 1, Anamosa 52205 / 319-462-3567

AUTO RENTAL
See Cedar Rapids

AIRPORT
See Cedar Rapids

MEDICAL
Anamosa Community Hospital, 104 Broadway Place, Anamosa 52205 /
319-462-6131

FOR MORE INFORMATION
Anamosa Chamber of Commerce
209 West Main Street
Anamosa, IA 52205
319-462-4879

Davenport and Scott County

County Population–150,979	Davenport Population–95,333
County Area–469 sq. mi.	Annual Precipitation–36"
CRP Acres–2,884	November Temperature–40°

Scott County is one of Iowa's smallest and most densely populated areas. Davenport is its county seat, and together with the adjacent Illinois cities of Moline, East Moline, and Rock Island, it forms the "Quad Cities" metropolitan area.

Because of Scott County's urban nature, hunting land—either private or public—is at a premium. However, there is some decent pheasant hunting in the more rural, northern part of the county. There are also two large (1,000-acre plus) public areas: Lost Grove Lake, primarily for pheasants, and Princeton, mostly for waterfowl. Both do receive significant hunting pressure from the nearby city.

Although Scott County itself does not rank as a top hunting hotspot, Davenport is not a bad choice as a base from which to hunt extreme eastcentral Iowa.

UPLAND BIRDS
Pheasants, Bobwhite Quail, Hungarian Partridge, Woodcock, Wild Turkey

WATERFOWL
Ducks and Geese

ACCOMMODATIONS
Days Inn, 101 West 65th Street, Davenport 52806 / 319-388-9999 / 64 rooms, smoking and nonsmoking / Dogs allowed ($10 fee) / $$

Exel Inn, 6310 North Brady Street, Davenport 52806 / 319-386-6350 / 103 rooms, smoking and nonsmoking / No dogs / $

Motel 6, 6111 North Brady Street, Davenport 52806 / 319-391-8997 / 98 rooms, smoking and nonsmoking / No dogs / $

Heartland Inn, 6605 North Brady Street, Davenport 52806 / 319-386-8336 / 85 rooms, smoking and nonsmoking / Dogs allowed / $$

CAMPGROUNDS
Interstate RV Park & Campground, From jct I-80 (exit 292) and Hwy 130, go 1 mil west on Hwy 130, then ¼ miles south on Fairmount Road, entrance on right / 319-386-7292 / 88 sites, 54 full hookups, 28 water and electric, 42 pull-thrus / Open all year

Lakeside Manor Park / 319-381-3413 / 110 sites, 50 full hookups, 50 water and electric, 40 pull-thrus / Open all year

*Darwin Linn
of Pheasants Galore
and a brace
of ringnecks.*

Scott County Park, From jct I-80 (exit 295) and US 61, go 7 miles north on US 61 (exit 129), then ¾ mile east on 267th Street, then ¼ mile north on Scott Park Road, then 1¼ mile east on 270th Street, entrance on left / 319-285-9656 / 398 sites, 48 water and electric, 37 electric / Open all year

West Lake Park, From juc I-280 (exit 6) and US 61, go ½ mile west on US 61, then ¾ mile north on CR Y48, entrance on right / 319-381-3589 / 140 sites, 75 full hookups, 48 water and electric, 3 electric, 48 pull-thrus / Open 3/1 thru 11/30

RESTAURANTS

Country Kitchen, 5324 North Brady Street, Davenport 52806 / 319-386-2203 / Open 24 hours daily / Complete menu

Fat Boy's Pizza, 1627 Washington Street, Davenport 52804 / 319-322-5446 / Open Sunday–Thursday, 11AM–midnight; Friday and Saturday until 1AM / Deli with sandwiches as well as pizza / Bar

Machine Shed Restaurant, 7250 Northwest Boulevard, Davenport 52806 / 319-391-2427 / Open Monday–Saturday, 6AM–10PM; Sunday, 7AM–9PM / Featuring stuffed roast pork, homemade pies, apple dumplings

Village Inn Restaurant, 1919 North Harrison Street, Davenport 52803 / 319-323-9933 / Open Monday–Thursday, 6AM–3AM; Friday and Saturday until 4AM; Sunday closes at 1AM

Riefe's Restaurant, 1417 West Locust Street, Davenport 52804 / 319-324-4732 / Open 7AM-11PM daily / Family dining

VETERINARIANS
Bell Animal Hospital, 1316 West Locust Street, Davenport 52804 / 319-322-4901

SPORTING GOODS
Wal-Mart, 3785 Elmore Avenue, Davenport 52806 / 319-355-6923
K-Mart, 3616 West Kimberly Road, Davenport 52806 / 319-386-6560

AUTO REPAIR
River City Ford, 3921 West River Drive, Davenport 52802 / 319-326-4011.
Ron Buysse Dodge, 4100 North Brady Street, Davenport 52806 / 319-391-4100

AUTO RENTAL
At Airport: **Avis** / 800-831-2847; **Budget** / 800-527-0700; **Hertz** / 800-654-3131; **National** / 800-227-7368

AIRPORT
Quad City Airport, 2200 59th Avenue, Moline, IL 61265 / 309-757-1530 / Airlines: Air Trans, American Eagle, Northwest, TWA, United

MEDICAL
Davenport Medical Center, 1111 West Kimberly Road, Davenport 52806 / 319-328-7575

FOR MORE INFORMATION
Davenport Chamber of Commerce
102 South Harrison Street
Davenport, IA 52801
319-322-1706

Muscatine
Muscatine and Louisa Counties

County Population:	Muscatine Population–22,881
Muscatine–39,907	Annual Precipitation–36"
Louisa–11,592	November temperature–40°
County Area:	CRP Acres:
Muscatine–449 sq. mi.	Muscatine–8,475
Louisa–417 sq. mi.	Louisa–11,386

These two Mississippi River counties have very good waterfowling on the big river itself and decent pheasant hunting farther west, away from the river. You are also likely to encounter the occasional covey of quail while pheasant hunting. There is also fair turkey hunting along the Mississippi as well as in the timber along the Cedar River in Muscatine County and the Iowa River in Louisa County.

Public areas are mostly wetlands maintained with waterfowl in mind. The best are Wiese Slough (1,700 acres) in Muscatine County and Lake Odessa (almost 4,000 acres) in Louisa County.

Muscatine is a medium-sized river town with good facilities from which to hunt both counties.

UPLAND BIRDS
Pheasants, Bobwhite Quail, Hungarian Partridge, Woodcock, Wild Turkey

WATERFOWL
Ducks and Geese

ACCOMMODATIONS
Super 8 Motel, Jct 61 & 38, Muscatine 52761 / 319-263-9100 / 63 rooms, smoking and nonsmoking / No dogs / $$
Lamplight Inn, 2107 Grandview Avenue, Muscatine 52761 / 319-263-7191 / 39 rooms, all smoking / Dogs allowed / $
Muskie Motel, 1620 Park Avenue, Muscatine 52761 / 319-263-2601 / 36 rooms, smoking and nonsmoking / No dogs / $

CAMPGROUNDS
Fairport State Recreation Area, From jct US61 and Hwy 22, go 5 miles east on Hwy 22 / 319-263-3197 / 43 sites, all electric, dump station / Open all year
Wildcat Den State Park, From jct US61 and Hwy 22, go 11 miles northeast on Hwy 22 / 319-263-4337 / 28 sites, 30 ft. maximum RV length, non-flush toilets / Open all year

RESTAURANTS

Country Kitchen, 2406 Park Avenue, Muscatine 52761 / 319-263-8832 / Open 24 hours daily / Complete menu

Downtown Cafe, 220 Walnut Street, Muscatine 52761 / 319-263-9813 / Open Monday–Friday, 6AM–4PM; from midnight Friday–noon Saturday; and from midnight Saturday–noon Sunday

Mazzio's Pizza, 2515 Park Avenue, Muscatine 52761 / 319-263-4415 / Open Sunday–Thursday, 11AM–10PM; Friday and Saturday until midnight / Pasta and sandwiches as well as pizza

Bootlegger's, 215 East 3rd Street, Muscatine 52761 / 319-264-2686 / Open Monday–Friday, 11AM–2PM, and 5–9PM; Saturday, 11AM–8PM; closed Sunday

VETERINARIANS

Muscatine Veterinary Hospital, 2200 Park Avenue, Muscatine 52761 / 319-263-2831

SPORTING GOODS

Wal-Mart, 1903 Mark Avenue, Muscatine 52761 / 319-263-8312

AUTO REPAIR

M & M Ford, 100 Ford Avenue, Muscatine 52761 / 319-263-5324

AUTO RENTAL

See Davenport

AIRPORT

See Davenport

MEDICAL

Muscatine General Hospital, 1518 Mulberry Avenue, Muscatine 52761 / 319-264-9100

FOR MORE INFORMATION

Muscatine Chamber of Commerce
319 East 2nd Street, Suite 102
Muscatine, IA 52761
319-263-8895

Burlington and Des Moines County

County Population–42,614	Burlington Population–27,208
County Area–429 sq. mi.	Annual Precipitation–36"
CRP Acres–5,379	November Temperature–41°

Burlington, Iowa's first capital (before it became a state), is an historic river town. Des Moines County, which has little public land, has decent pheasant hunting (primarily in the northern half of the county), as well as fair quail hunting. You will find turkeys wherever there are sizable blocks of timber, and there is good waterfowling along the Mississippi.

UPLAND BIRDS
Pheasants, Bobwhite Quail, Hungarian Partridge, Woodcock, Wild Turkey

WATERFOWL
Ducks and Geese

ACCOMMODATIONS
Ramada Inn, 2759 Mt. Pleasant Street, Burlington 52601 / 319-754-5781 / 100 rooms, smoking and nonsmoking / Dogs allowed ($25 refundable deposit) / $$

Super 8 Motel, Jct US 34 & 61, Burlington 52601 / 319-752-9806 / 63 rooms, smoking and nonsmoking / No dogs / $$

RESTAURANTS
Jefferson Street Cafe, 3003 Johannsen Drive, Burlington 52601 / 319-754-1036 / Open Sunday–Thursday, 11AM–9PM; Friday and Saturday until 10PM

Mazzio's Pizza, 616 South Roosevelt Avenue, Burlington 52601 / 319-753-0161 / Open Sunday–Thursday, 11AM–10PM; Friday and Saturday until midnight / Pasta, sandwiches, and salads in addition to pizza

Perkins Family Restaurant, Hwy 61 & Agency Street, Burlington 52601 / 319-753-6581 / Open 24 hours daily / Complete menu

VETERINARIANS
Allgood Animal Hospital, 3106 Johannsen Drive, Burlington 52601 / 319-752-5983

SPORTING GOODS
K-Mart, 3200 Agency Street, Burlington 52601 / 319-752-5466
Wal-Mart, 3320 Agency Street, Burlington 52601 / 319-753-6526

AUTO REPAIR
Delzell Motor Co., 1309 North Roosevelt Avenue, Burlington 52601 / 319-754-8484

Chuck Gates and a rooster.

AUTO RENTAL
At Airport: **Avis** / 800-831-2847; **National** / 800-227-7368

AIRPORT
Burlington Airport, 2501 Summer Street, Burlington 52601 / 319-754-1414 /
Airlines: TW Express, United Express

MEDICAL
Burlington Medical Center, 602 North 3rd Street, Burlington 52601 / 319-753-3011

FOR MORE INFORMATION
Port of Burlington
400 North Front Street
Burlington, IA 52601
319-752-8731

Washington and Mount Pleasant
Washington and Henry Counties

County Population:
  Washington–19,612
  Henry–19,226
County Area:
  Washington–571 sq. mi.
  Henry–436 sq. mi.
	Washington Population–7,074
	Mount Pleasant Population–8,027
	Annual Precipitation–34"
	November Temperature–41°
	CRP Acres:
	  Washington–27,275
	  Henry–20,974

These two counties, with county seats of similar sizes and facilities, are both good bets for upland birds. Washington County is the better of the two for pheasants, while there are decent quail numbers south of Mount Pleasant in Henry County. Wild turkey numbers will generally increase the farther south you go. Waterfowling is mostly jumpshooting along streams and off farm ponds. There is almost no public land in either county.

UPLAND BIRDS
Pheasants, Bobwhite Quail, Hungarian Partridge, Woodcock, Wild Turkey

WATERFOWL
Ducks and Geese

ACCOMMODATIONS
Hawkeye Motel, 1320 West Madison, Washington 52353 / 319-653-7510 / 21 rooms, smoking and nonsmoking / Dogs allowed / $
Super 8 Motel, 119 Westview Drive, Washington 52353 / 319-653-6621 / 56 rooms, smoking and nonsmoking / Dogs allowed ($25 refundable deposit) / $$
Heartland Inn, Hwy 218 North, Mt. Pleasant 52641 / 319-385-2102 / 58 rooms, smoking and nonsmoking / Dogs allowed ($8 fee) / $$
Super 8 Motel, Hwy 218 North, Mt. Pleasant 52641 / 319-385-8888 / 55 rooms, smoking and nonsmoking / Dogs allowed / $$

RESTAURANTS
Dinos Pizza & Steak House, 109 East Washington Street, Washington 52353 / 319-653-5014 / Open 11AM–9PM daily
Winga's Restaurant, 106 West Main Street, Washington 52353 / 319-653-2093 / Open Tuesday–Sunday, 6AM–7:30PM; closed Monday / Homemade pie / Family dining since 1928

The Feed Bin, Hwy 34 West, Mt. Pleasant 52641 / 319-385-4714 / Open
10:30AM–9:30PM daily / Features build your own sandwich and potato bar

Hawkeye Pizza & Steak House, 115 South Jefferson Street, Mt. Pleasant 52641 /
319-385-4664 / Open Monday–Saturday, 10AM–2PM, and 4–10PM; closed
Sunday / Varied menu in addition to pizza and steaks

VETERINARIANS

Northeast Animal Hospital, 1909 220th Street, Mt. Pleasant 52641 / 319-385-9533

SPORTING GOODS

Wal-Mart, 530 Hwy 1 South, Washington 52353 / 319-653-7213

AUTO REPAIR

Buckwalter Motors, 1738 East Washington Street, Washington 52353 /
319-653-7266

Shottenkirk Automotive, Hwy 34 East, Mt. Pleasant 52641 / 319-385-2261

NEAREST AIRPORT AND AUTO RENTAL

Washington—See Cedar Rapids

Mt. Pleasant—See Burlington

MEDICAL

Washington County Hospital, 400 East Polk Street, Washington 52353 /
319-653-5481

Henry County Health Center, Saunders Park, Mt. Pleasant 52641 / 319-385-3141

FOR MORE INFORMATION

Chamber of Commerce
212 North Iowa Avenue
Washington, IA 52353
319-653-3272

Chamber of Commerce
124 South Main Street
Mt. Pleasant, IA 52641
319-385-3101

Cedar Rapids
Linn and Benton Counties

County Population:
Linn–168,767
Benton–22,429
County Area:
Linn–724 sq. mi.
Benton–718 sq. mi.

Cedar Rapids Population–108,751
Annual Precipitation–36"
November Temperature–39°
CRP Acres:
Linn–10,749
Benton–12,324

These two neighboring counties present an interesting contrast: Linn, with Cedar Rapids, the state's second largest city; and Benton, which is mostly rural. What they have in common, however, is very good pheasant hunting wherever you can find the right habitat. Simply because of Linn County's more urban nature, possibilities are better in Benton County. However, northern Linn County is also quite good. Turkey hunting is fair, but timber tends to be in small, scattered tracts (except along streams). You may encounter an occasional covey of Huns, especially in the northern part of either county. Waterfowling is mostly along rivers, although Dudgeon Lake near Vinton is a good public area. Pleasant Creek, on the border between the two counties, is a public area with some pheasants.

Although Cedar Rapids has excellent facilities, Vinton—the county seat of Benton County—shouldn't be written off, especially if you prefer a smaller town atmosphere.

UPLAND BIRDS
Pheasants, Bobwhite Quail, Hungarian Partridge, Woodcock, Wild Turkey

WATERFOWL
Ducks and Geese

ACCOMMODATIONS
Days Inn, 3245 Southgate Place SW, Cedar Rapids 52404 / 319-365-4339 / 40 rooms, smoking and nonsmoking / Dogs allowed in smoking rooms only / $$
Econo Lodge, 622 33rd Avenue SW, Cedar Rapids 52404 / 319-363-8888 / 50 rooms, smoking and nonsmoking / Dogs allowed / $$
Heartland Inn, 3315 Southgate Court SW, Cedar Rapids 52404 / 319-362-9012 / 115 rooms, smoking and nonsmoking / Dogs sometimes allowed / $$
Super 8 Motel, 720 33rd Avenue SW, Cedar Rapids 52404 / 319-362-6002 / 61 rooms, smoking and nonsmoking / No dogs / $$

RESTAURANTS

Country Kitchen, 555 33rd Avenue SW, Cedar Rapids 52404 / 319-363-7305 / Open 24 hours daily / Complete menu

Flamingo Pizza Palace, 1211 Ellis Boulevard NW, Cedar Rapids 52405 / 319-364-9926 / Open 11:30AM–10PM daily / Ribs, chicken and lunch specials

Lone Star Steakhouse, 4545 1st Avenue SE, Cedar Rapids 52402 / 319-393-9648 / Open Sunday–Thursday, 11AM–10PM; Friday and Saturday until 11PM / Mesquite-grilled steaks

Outback Steak House, 3939 1st Avenue SE, Cedar Rapids 52402 / 319-366-6683 / Open Sunday–Thursday, 4PM–10PM; Friday until 11PM; Saturday, 3–11PM / Shrimp and chicken "on the barbie" as well as steaks

Perkins Family Restaurant, 315 Collins Road NE, Cedar Rapids 52402 / 319-393-0202 / Open 24 hours daily / Complete menu

VETERINARIANS

All Pets Veterinary Clinic, 400 Edgewood Road NW, Cedar Rapids 52405 / 319-396-7759

Family Pet Hospital, 1101 J Avenue NE, Cedar Rapids 52402 / 319-365-7111

SPORTING GOODS

Fin & Feather, 712 3rd Avenue SE, Cedar Rapids 52401 / 319-364-4396

K-Mart, 2727 16th Avenue SW, Cedar Rapids 52404 / 319-366-2339

Wal-Mart, 2645 Blairs Ferry Road NE, Cedar Rapids 52402 / 319-393-0444

AUTO REPAIR

Pat McGrath Chevyland, 1600 51st Street NE, Cedar Rapids 52402 / 319-393-6300

Jim Miller Lincoln-Mercury, 1510 Collins Road NE, Cedar Rapids 52402 / 319-393-6500

AUTO RENTAL

At Airport: **Avis** / 800-831-2847; **Budget** / 800-527-0700; **Hertz** / 800-654-3131; **National** / 800-227-7368

AIRPORT

Cedar Rapids Airport, 2515 Wright Bros. Boulevard SW, Cedar Rapids 52404 / 319-362-8336 / Airlines: Northwest, United, TWA, American Eagle, Delta, US Airways

MEDICAL

St. Luke's Hospital, 1026 A Avenue NE, Cedar Rapids 52402 / 319-369-7211

FOR MORE INFORMATION

Cedar Rapids Area Chamber of Commerce
424 1st Avenue NE
Cedar Rapids, IA 52401
319-398-5317

Iowa City
Iowa and Johnson Counties

County Population:	Iowa City Population–59,738
Johnson–96,119	Annual Precipitation–36"
Iowa–14,630	November Temperature–40°
County Area:	CRP Acres:
Johnson–623 sq. mi.	Johnson–18,133
Iowa–588 sq. mi.	Iowa–36,048

This is another urban/rural contrast, with Johnson County home to Iowa City and the University of Iowa, and Iowa County, which is sparsely populated. Although Iowa City has excellent facilities, visitors should be aware that they may have to seek lodging elsewhere on those Saturdays when the University of Iowa has a home football game.

Both counties are typically among the best in the state for pheasants. Over 13,000 acres of public hunting land, the Hawkeye Wildlife Area, surround the Coralville Reservoir in northern Johnson County. This area is good for pheasants, waterfowl, and turkey, but it does receive relatively heavy hunting pressure from the Cedar Rapids-Iowa City area. The Iowa River Corridor in Iowa County is less heavily hunted and is also good for pheasants, waterfowl, and turkeys.

UPLAND BIRDS
Pheasants, Bobwhite Quail, Hungarian Partridge, Woodcock, Wild Turkey

WATERFOWL
Ducks and Geese

ACCOMMODATIONS
Hampton Inn, I-80 at Exit 242, Coralville 52241 / 319-351-6600 / 115 rooms, smoking and nonsmoking / No dogs / $$$

Motel 6, 810 1st Avenue, Coralville 52241 / 319-354-0030 / 103 rooms, smoking and nonsmoking / No dogs / $

Super 8 Motel, 611 1st Avenue, Coralville 52241 / 319-337-8388 / 87 rooms, smoking and nonsmoking / No dogs / $$

Heartland Inn, 87 2nd Street, Coralville 52241 / 319-351-8132 / 170 rooms, smoking and nonsmoking / Dogs sometimes allowed / Ask in advance / $$

CAMPGROUNDS
At Coralville Lake north of Iowa City:
Tailwater West / 25 sites / 319-338-3543

Lake MacBride State Park, north of Iowa City, west of Solon / 319-644-2200 / North Unit: modern with 40 sites, 20 electrical, showers, dump station; South Unit: nonmodern with 60 campsites, nonflush restroom

RESTAURANTS

Country Kitchen, 2208 North Dodge Street, Iowa City 52245 / 319-354-0270 / Open 24 hours daily / Complete menu

Highlander Supper Club, Hwy 1 and I-80 Exit 246, Iowa City 52241 / 319-351-3150 / Open Monday–Friday, 8AM–9PM; Saturday until 10PM; Sunday, 8AM–2PM for brunch

Sam's Pizza, 321 South Gilbert Street, Iowa City 52240 / 319-337-8200 / Open Monday–Saturday, 11AM–midnight; Sunday until 10PM / Pasta and subs as well as pizza

VETERINARIANS

Animal Clinic Inc., 408 Highland Avenue, Iowa City 52240 / 319-337-2123

SPORTING GOODS

Fin & Feather, 943 South Riverside Drive, Iowa City 52246 / 319-354-2200

K-Mart, 901 Hollywood Boulevard, Iowa City 52240 / 319-354-1201

Wal-Mart, 1001 Hwy 1 West, Iowa City 52246 / 319-337-3116

AUTO REPAIR

Winebrenner Ford, 217 Stevens Drive, Iowa City 52240 / 319-338-7811

AUTO RENTAL

See Cedar Rapids

AIRPORT

See Cedar Rapids

MEDICAL

Mercy Hospital, 500 East Market Street, Iowa City 52245 / 319-339-0300

FOR MORE INFORMATION

Iowa City Area Chamber of Commerce
325 East Washington Street, Suite 100
Iowa City, IA 52240
319-337-9637

Oskaloosa
Mahaska and Keokuk Counties

County Population:	Oskaloosa Population–10,632
Mahaska–21,522	Annual Precipitation–34"
Keokuk–11,624	November Temperature–39°
County Area:	CRP Acres:
Mahaska–572 sq. mi.	Mahaska–27,829
Keokuk–580 sq. mi.	Keokuk–48,216

More rural and farther removed from the population centers of eastern Iowa, these two counties are both excellent for pheasants. Hunters will also encounter quail, especially in the southern part of either county. Waterfowling will be mainly jumpshooting off small ponds and streams. There are turkeys wherever you can find more than a few acres of timber.

Several public areas in Keokuk County along the Skunk River (Rubio, Skunk, South Skunk) have decent turkey hunting, while the Hawthorn Lake and Hull areas in Mahaska County can be good for pheasants.

UPLAND BIRDS
Pheasants, Bobwhite Quail, Hungarian Partridge, Woodcock, Wild Turkey

WATERFOWL
Ducks and Geese

ACCOMMODATIONS
Super 8 Motel, 306 South 17th Street, Oskaloosa 52577 / 515-673-8481 / 51 rooms, smoking and nonsmoking / No dogs / $$

Traveler Budget Inn, 1210 A Avenue, Oskaloosa 52577 / 515-673-8333 / 27 rooms, smoking and nonsmoking / No dogs / Bird cleaning room / $

Oskaloosa Motel, Hwy 92 West, Oskaloosa 52577 / 515-673-8367 / 14 rooms, smoking and nonsmoking / Dogs allowed / $

Roadway Inn, 1315 A Avenue, Oskaloosa 52577 / 515-673-8351 / 40 rooms, smoking and nonsmoking / No dogs / $

CAMPGROUND
Lake Keomah State Park, From jct US63 and Hwy 92, go 6 miles southeast on Hwy 92 & Hwy 371 / 515-673-6975 / 88 sites, 52 electric, dump station / Open all year

RESTAURANTS

Country Kitchen, 200 High Avenue West, Oskaloosa 52577 / 515-673-9527 / Open 24 hours daily / Complete menu

Dr. Salami's, 702 A Avenue, Oskaloosa 52577 / 515-673-4532 / Open Monday–Saturday, 11AM–10PM; closed Sunday / Features excellent sandwiches

Stout's, 112 1st Avenue, Oskaloosa 52577 / 515-673-7336 / Open Monday–Saturday, 5AM–8:30PM; closed Sunday

The Pepper Tree, 1244 C Avenue East, Oskaloosa 52577 / 515-673-9191 / Open Monday–Saturday, 5PM–10PM; Sunday, 11AM–2PM (brunch buffet) / Specials every evening

VETERINARIANS

Mahaska Veterinary Clinic, 2348 Hwy 92, Oskaloosa 52577 / 515-673-0431

SPORTING GOODS

K-Mart, 200 1st Avenue West, Oskaloosa 52577 / 515-673-4636

Wal-Mart, 1714 3rd Avenue East, Oskaloosa 52577 / 515-673-3839

AUTO REPAIR

Carriker Ford, 1201 South 17th Street, Oskaloosa 52577 / 515-673-8373

AUTO RENTAL

See Ottumwa

AIRPORT

See Ottumwa

MEDICAL

Mahaska County Hospital, 1229 C Avenue East, Oskaloosa 52577 / 515-673-3431

FOR MORE INFORMATION

Oskaloosa Chamber of Commerce
124 North Market Street
Oskaloosa, IA 52577
515-672-2591

Grinnell and Poweshiek County

County Population–19,033	Grinnell Population–8,902
County Area–586 sq. mi.	Annual Precipitation–36"
CRP Acres–23,573	November Temperature–37°

Grinnell is a prosperous college town (Grinnell College) that becomes bird-hunting headquarters for numerous nonresidents who come to sample Iowa's pheasant hunting. Poweshiek is nearly always one of the top pheasant counties in the state. However, it has almost no public land, and opportunities for species other than ringnecks—outside of jumpshooting ducks or fieldshooting geese—are fairly limited.

UPLAND BIRDS
Pheasants, Bobwhite Quail, Hungarian Partridge, Woodcock, Wild Turkey

WATERFOWL
Ducks and Geese

ACCOMMODATIONS
Best Western, Hwy 146 South, Grinnell 50112 / 515-236-6116 / 38 rooms, smoking and nonsmoking / Dogs allowed (smoking rooms only) / $$
Days Inn, I-80 & Hwy 146, Grinnell 50112 / 515-236-6710 / 41 rooms, smoking and nonsmoking / Dogs allowed ($5 fee per animal) / $$
Super 8 Motel, I-80 & Hwy 146, Grinnell 50112 / 515-236-7888 / 53 rooms, smoking and nonsmoking / Dogs allowed (smoking rooms only), $10 fee / $$

RESTAURANTS
City Limits Restaurant, I-80 & Hwy 146, Grinnell 50112 / 515-236-3533 / Open 7AM–9PM daily
J D's Restaurant, 922½ Main Street, Grinnell 50112 / 515-236-4900 / Open Monday–Friday, 11AM–2PM for lunch; Tuesday–Saturday, 5–9PM for dinner; closed Sunday
Pagliai's Pizza, 816 5th Avenue, Grinnell 50112 / 515-236-5331 / Open 5–11PM daily / Italian dishes in addition to pizza

SPORTING GOODS
Wal-Mart, 86 West Street, Grinnell 50112 / 515-236-4999

AUTO REPAIR
Tiger Ford, Grinnell 50112 / 515-236-7918

AUTO RENTAL
See Des Moines

Labs are great at fetching pheasants.

AIRPORT
See Des Moines

MEDICAL
Grinnell Regional Medical Center, 210 4th Avenue, Grinnell 50112 / 515-236-7511

FOR MORE INFORMATION
Chamber of Commerce
719 4th Avenue
Grinnell, IA 50112
515-236-6555

Newton and Jasper County

County Population–34,795	Newton Population–14,789
County Area–732	Annual Precipitation–34"
CRP Acres–15,518	November Temperature–38°

Jasper County, slightly more urban than neighboring Poweshiek and attracting more resident hunters from nearby Des Moines, is excellent pheasant country. While some public opportunities for waterfowl and pheasants occur on Rock Creek Marsh and the Colfax area, most hunting in the county will be on private land. Newton, the county seat, is home to the headquarters of the Maytag Corporation.

UPLAND BIRDS
Pheasants, Bobwhite Quail, Hungarian Partridge, Woodcock, Wild Turkey

WATERFOWL
Ducks and Geese

ACCOMMODATIONS
Days Inn, Hwy 14 & I-80, Newton 50208 / 515-792-2330 / 58 rooms, smoking and nonsmoking / Dogs allowed ($5 fee) / $$

Super 8 Motel, 1635 South 12th Avenue West, Newton 50208 / 515-792-8868 / 43 rooms, smoking and nonsmoking / No dogs / $$

Newton Inn Best Western, Hwy 14 & I-80, Newton 50208 / 515-792-4200 / 118 rooms, smoking and nonsmoking / Dogs allowed / $$

Ramada Inn, Hwy 14 & I-80, Newton 50208 / 515-792-8100 / 79 rooms, smoking and nonsmoking / Dogs allowed / $

RESTAURANTS
Country Kitchen, Hwy 14 & I-80, Newton 50208 / 515-792-4582 / Open 24 hours daily / Complete menu

Mason's Cafe, 110 East 3rd Street North, Newton 50208 / 515-792-6063 / Open Monday–Saturday, 5:30AM–2PM and 4:30–8PM; closed Sunday / Lunch and dinner specials

Perkins Family Restaurant, Hwy 14 & I-80, Newton 50208 / 515-792-1042 / Open 24 hours daily / Complete menu

VETERINARIANS
Newton Animal Clinic, 2009 1st Avenue West, Newton 50208 / 515-792-4860

SPORTING GOODS
Wal-Mart, 3021 1st Avenue East, Newton 50208 / 515-792-0203

AUTO REPAIR
Axtell Chrysler Plymouth, 2900 1st Avenue East, Newton 50208 / 515-792-2341

AUTO RENTAL
See Des Moines

AIRPORT
See Des Moines

MEDICAL
Medical Specialties, 321 East 3rd Street North, Newton 50208 / 515-792-2062

FOR MORE INFORMATION
Chamber of Commerce
113 1st Avenue West
Newton, IA 50208
515-792-5545

Marshalltown
Marshall and Tama Counties

County Population:	Marshalltown Population–25,178
Marshall–38,276	Annual Precipitation–34"
Tama–17,419	November Temperature–37°
County Area:	CRP Acres:
Marshall–573 sq. mi.	Marshall–7,263
Tama–722 sq. mi.	Tama–20,509

These are two very good pheasant counties in the region, with best bird numbers usually found in the southern halves of both counties. Marshall County's Hendrickson Marsh (800 acres) and Tama County's Otter Creek Marsh (3,400 acres) are good public areas for both pheasants and waterfowl.

Although Marshalltown has very good facilities, some visitors may be attracted to the much smaller twin towns of Tama and Toledo: the state's largest Indian casino is located just to the west of them on Highway 30.

UPLAND BIRDS
Pheasants, Bobwhite Quail, Hungarian Partridge, Woodcock, Wild Turkey

WATERFOWL
Ducks and Geese

ACCOMMODATIONS

Comfort Inn, 2613 South Center Street, Marshalltown 50158 / 515-752-6000 / 62 rooms, smoking and nonsmoking / Dogs allowed ($10 fee) / $$

Days Inn, 403 East Church Street, Marshalltown 50158 / 515-753-7777 / 28 rooms, smoking and nonsmoking / Dogs allowed / $$

Economy Inn, Jct Hwys 30 & 14, Marshalltown 50158 / 515-752-5485 / 22 rooms, smoking and nonsmoking / Dogs allowed / $

Super 8 Motel, Hwy 14 South, Marshalltown 50158 / 515-753-8181 / 61 rooms, smoking and nonsmoking / No dogs / $$

RESTAURANTS

Country Kitchen, 2003 South Center Street, Marshalltown 50158 / 515-752-7363 / Open 24 hours daily / Complete menu

Stone's Restaurant, 507 South 3rd Avenue, Marshalltown 50158 / 515-753-3626 / Open Monday–Saturday, 11AM–9PM; Sunday, 11AM–3PM (brunch buffet) / Lunch and dinner specials

Perkins Restaurant, 3012 South Center Street, Marshalltown 50158 / 515-753-4038 / Open 24 hours daily / Complete menu

VETERINARIANS
Marshalltown Vet Clinic, 113 Nicholas Drive, Marshalltown 50158 / 515-752-1036

SPORTING GOODS
K-Mart, 1720 South Center Street, Marshalltown 50158 / 515-753-0957

AUTO REPAIR
Braga Motor Co., 908 North 3rd Avenue, Marshalltown 50158 / 515-752-3636

AUTO RENTAL
See Des Moines

AIRPORT
See Des Moines

MEDICAL
Marshalltown Medical & Surgical Center, 3 South 4th Avenue, Marshalltown 50158 / 515-754-5151

FOR MORE INFORMATION
Chamber of Commerce
709 South Center Street
Marshalltown, IA 50158
515-753-6645

Northeast Dairy Region

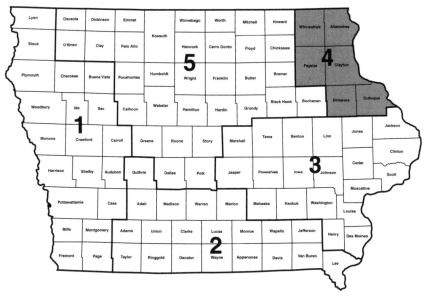

Located in the northeast corner of the state, this region does not fit the non-resident's idea of what Iowa is supposed to look like. Compared to the rest of the state, this region is very hilly and heavily forested. Dubuque is the only major population center.

Extreme northeast Iowa is not a particularly good area for pheasants, although the ringneck population does increase the farther west one goes. It is the state's premier area for wild turkeys, and it also encompasses most of Iowa's ruffed grouse range. Waterfowl hunting can be very good along the Mississippi. There is a higher percentage of public land than in most other regions, and hunting on these public areas for turkey, grouse, and waterfowl can be very good.

Northeast Dairy Region
Pheasant Distribution

Good   Fair   Poor

Northeast Dairy Region
Ruffed Grouse Distribution

Good   Poor

Northeast Dairy Region
Woodcock Distribution

Region 4 Woodcock

Found throughout

Northeast Dairy Region
Wild Turkey Distribution

Good

Waukon and Allamakee County

County Population–13,855	Waukon Population–4,019
County Area–660 sq. mi.	Annual Precipitation–34"
CRP Acres–30,541	November Temperature–35°

Waukon is a small, picturesque county seat town located in the extreme northeast corner of the state. Allamakee County contains one of Iowa's three state forests (Yellow River), as well as large public hunting areas at Lansing and on French Creek. All three areas have very good populations of ruffed grouse, woodcock, and wild turkey. There are several smaller public areas, as well as numerous public accesses to the Mississippi River, where duck hunting is also very good.

UPLAND BIRDS
Pheasant, Ruffed Grouse, Woodcock, Wild Turkey

WATERFOWL
Ducks and Geese

ACCOMMODATIONS

Stony Creek Inn, 407 Rossville Road, Waukon 52172 / 319-568-2220 / 40 rooms / No dogs / $$

RESTAURANTS

S & D Cafe, 13 West Main Street, Waukon 52172 / 319-568-9944 / Monday–Friday, 5:30AM–4:30PM; Saturday, 7AM–3PM; Sunday, 7AM–1:30PM / Daily specials, homemade pies

Gus and Tony's Pizza and Steak House, 508 West Main Street, Waukon 52172 / 319-568-6015 / Sunday–Thursday, 11AM–9:30PM; Friday and Saturday, 11AM–11PM

VETERINARIANS

Waukon Veterinary Service, 508 Rossville Road, Waukon 52172 / 319-568-2487

SPORTING GOODS

Pamida Discount Center, 612 Rossville Road, Waukon 52172 / 319-568-4507

AUTO RENTAL

Nearest is La Crosse, WI

AIRPORT

Nearest is La Crosse, WI / Airlines: Northwest, Northwest Airlink, American Eagle, Skyways

Iowa isn't all rolling prairie and grassland. (Photo by Dave Meisner)

AUTO RENTAL

Nearest at La Crosse, WI airport: Avis / 800-831-2847; Hertz / 800-654-3131
For additional information, call the La Crosse Visitors Bureau / 800-658-9424

MEDICAL

Veterans Memorial Hospital, 22 1st Avenue SE, Waukon 52172 / 319-568-3411

FOR MORE INFORMATION

Waukon Chamber of Commerce
101 Allamakee Street
Waukon, IA 52172
319-568-4110

Decorah and Winneshiek County

County Population–20,847	Decorah Population–8,063
County Area–690 sq. mi.	Annual Precipitation–33"
CRP Acres–24,776	November Temperature–36°

Decorah is a college town (Luther College) located on the Upper Iowa River. There are several public hunting areas in the county, especially east of Decorah along the Upper Iowa and in the northern part of the county around Highlandville. These areas are very good for turkeys, grouse, and woodcock. West of Decorah, the terrain in general is more gently rolling and less wooded, and pheasant hunting (mostly on private ground) improves considerably.

UPLAND BIRDS
Pheasant, Ruffed Grouse, Woodcock, Wild Turkey

WATERFOWL
Ducks and Geese

ACCOMMODATIONS
Super 8 Motel, Highway 9 East, Decorah 52101 / 319-382-8771 / 60 rooms, smoking and nonsmoking / Dogs allowed (refundable deposit) / $
Heartland Inn, 705 Commerce Drive, Decorah 52101 / 319-382-2269 / 58 rooms, smoking and nonsmoking / No dogs / $$

CAMPGROUND
Decorah City Campground, Pulpit Rock Road, Decorah 52101 / 319-382-9941

RESTAURANTS
Clarksville Diner, 504 Heivly Street, Decorah 52101 / 319-382-4330 / Monday–Friday, 6AM–7:30PM; Saturday, 6AM–2PM; closed Sunday / Specials Monday–Thursday
Country Kitchen, 915 Short Street, Decorah 52101 / 319-382-4817 / Sunday–Thursday, 6AM–10PM; Friday and Saturday, 6AM– 12AM / Complete menu
The Hay Market, 201 Washington Street, Decorah 52101 / 319-382-8005 / Open 6:30AM-10PM daily with noon specials Monday–Friday / Tuesday night–Mexican / Friday night–fish and ribs
The Pizza Ranch, 212 College Drive, Decorah 52101 / 319-382-8744 / Sunday–Thursday, 11AM–11PM; Friday and Saturday 11AM–11PM / Also serves chicken and pasta

VETERINARIANS
Decorah Veterinary Clinic, 604 Montgomery Street, Decorah 52101 / 319-382-3806

SPORTING GOODS
Wal-Mart, 915 Short Street, Decorah 52101 / 319-382-8737

AUTO REPAIR
Nelson Repair, 402 1/2 Water Street, Decorah 52101 / 319-382-3735

AUTO RENTAL
Nearest at Rochester, MN Airport: **Avis** / 800-831-2847; **Hertz** / 800-654-3131; **National** / 800-227-7368

AIRPORT
Nearest at Rochester, MN / 507-282-2328 / Airlines: Northwest, American

MEDICAL
Gundersen Clinic, Decorah, 921 Montgomery Street, Decorah 52101 / 319-382-3140

FOR MORE INFORMATION
Decorah Area Chamber of Commerce
111 Winnebago Street
Decorah, IA 52101
319-382-3990

Elkader and Clayton County

County Population–19,054	Elkader Population–1,510
County Area–795 sq. mi.	Annual Precipitation–34"
CRP Acres–42,141	November Temperature–36°

Located on the Turkey River, Elkader is the county seat of Clayton County. Excellent turkey, grouse, and woodcock hunting can be had in the woods and hills. The large Sny Magill/North Cedar Public Hunting Area is good for all three species. Duck hunting is very good along the islands and wooded shoreline of the Mississippi River. Clayton County does not have a very high pheasant population. For those seeking evening entertainment, the twin river towns of Marquette and McGregor offer riverboat gambling.

UPLAND BIRDS
Pheasant, Ruffed Grouse, Woodcock, Wild Turkey

WATERFOWL
Ducks and Geese

ACCOMMODATIONS
Elkader Inn Motel, Highway 13 North, Elkader 52043 / 319-245-2020 / 14 rooms, smoking and nonsmoking / No dogs / $$

RESTAURANTS
Johnson's Restaurant and Supper Club, 916 High Street NE, Elkader 52043 / 319-245-2371 / Open 6AM–10PM daily / Friday night buffet, noon and nightly specials
Keystone, 107 South Main, Elkader 52043 / 319-245-1992 / Monday–Saturday, 11AM-9PM; Sundah, 11AM–3PM for brunch / Daily specials
The Pizza Well, 127 North Main Street, Elkader 52043 / 319-245-2414 / Monday–Friday, 11:30AM–1PM for lunch; open daily at 4 for dinner / Also serves sandwiches and pasta

VETERINARIANS
Elkader Veterinary Clinic, Highway 13, Elkader 52043 / 319-245-1633

AUTO RENTAL
See Dubuque

AIRPORT
See Dubuque

Cover like this makes one appreciate a good hunting dog. (Photo by Dave Meisner)

FOR MORE INFORMATION
Elkader Area Chamber of Commerce
916 High Street NE
Elkader, IA 52043
319-245-2858

West Union and Fayette County

County Population–21,843	West Union Population–2,490
County Area–731 sq. mi.	Annual Precipitation–34"
CRP Acres–10,574	November Temperature–35°

Located at the junction of Highways 18 and 150, West Union sits on a natural dividing line between the wooded hill country to the east, where hunters will find turkeys, woodcock, and grouse, and rolling farm country to the west, where there is a decent pheasant population. The 5,400-acre Volga Recreation Area, located just south of town to the east of Highway 150, has very good populations of turkeys, grouse, and woodcock. Vehicle access is limited on the Volga Area, and those willing to do some walking have good opportunities at uncrowded hunting. The Volga Area does have some pheasants, but better ringneck hunting can be found on private land west of Highway 150. Primitive camping is allowed on the Volga Area.

UPLAND BIRDS
Pheasant, Ruffed Grouse, Woodcock, Wild Turkey

WATERFOWL
Ducks and Geese

ACCOMMODATIONS
Elms Motel, 705 Highway 150 South, West Union 52175 / 319-422-3841 /
   15 rooms, smoking and nonsmoking / Limited rooms for dogs / $
Lilac Motel, junction Highways 18 and 150, West Union 52175 / 319-422-3861 /
   27 rooms, smoking and nonsmoking / No dogs / $

RESTAURANTS
The Long Branch, 106 South Vine Street, West Union 52175 / 319-422-5818 /
   Monday–Saturday, 6AM–2AM; Sunday, 11AM–2AM / Noon and nightly specials
Red Heart Deli and Pizza, 118 South Vine Street, West Union 52175 / 319-422-
   6033 / Monday–Thursday, 4:30–10PM; Friday and Saturday until 11PM;
   Sunday until 9PM / Also serving chicken and salads

VETERINARIANS
West Union Veterinary Clinic, 504 West Bradford Street, West Union 52175 /
   319-422-3519

AUTO RENTAL
See Waterloo

AIRPORT
See Waterloo

Author with Jake.

MEDICAL

Palmer Lutheran Health Center, 112 Jefferson Street, West Union 52175 /
   319-422-3811

FOR MORE INFORMATION

West Union Chamber of Commerce
101 North Vine Street
West Union, IA 52175
319-422-3070

Manchester and Delaware County

County Population–18,035	Manchester Population–5,137
County Area–579 sq. mi.	Annual Precipitation–35"
CRP Acres–10,179	November temperature–35°

Manchester is located on Highway 20, the main east–west corridor across northern Iowa. There is little public land in Delaware County. Basically, the eastern half of the county is better for turkeys, with grouse and woodcock also fairly common in the northeast corner. Pheasant hunting is better in the western half.

UPLAND BIRDS
Pheasant, Ruffed Grouse, Woodcock, Wild Turkey

WATERFOWL
Ducks and Geese

ACCOMMODATIONS
Super 8 Motel, 1020 West Main Street, Manchester 52057 / 319-927-2533 / 42 rooms, smoking and nonsmoking / Dogs allowed in smoking rooms ($5 extra) / $$

East Inn, 948 East Main Street, Manchester 52057 / 319-927-4850 / 16 rooms, smoking and nonsmoking / $$

RESTAURANTS
Argonaut Supper Club, 107 West Main Street, Manchester 52057 / 319-927-3092 / Open 11AM–10PM daily / Full menu for lunch and dinner

Hazel's Cafe, 211 North Franklin Street, Manchester 52057 / 319-927-2058 / Monday–Friday, 5AM–4PM; Saturday, 5AM–2PM; Sunday, 7AM–12:15PM / Lunch specials during week

SPORTING GOODS
Wal-Mart, 1220 West Main Street, Manchester 52057 / 319-927-3377

AUTO REPAIR
Motors Unlimited, 1049 North 3rd Street, Manchester 52057 / 319-927-3221

AUTO RENTAL
See Dubuque

AIRPORT
See Dubuque

FOR MORE INFORMATION
Chamber of Commerce
200 East Main Street
Manchester, IA 52057
319-927-4141

Dubuque and Dubuque County

County Population–86,403	Dubuque Population–57,538
County Area–616 sq. mi.	Annual Precipitation–33"
CRP Acres–16,255	November Temperature–37°

Dubuque, the population center of this region, is a scenic, old river town located on the Mississippi. There is good waterfowling along the river, decent turkey and grouse hunting in the northern part of the county, and some pheasant hunting in the southern part. The only large public area is White Pine Hollow State Preserve in the northwest corner, where there are grouse, woodcock, and turkeys. For after-hours entertainment, riverboat gambling is available in Dubuque and just across the Mississippi in East Dubuque, Illinois.

UPLAND BIRDS
Pheasant, Ruffed Grouse, Woodcock, Wild Turkey

WATERFOWL
Ducks and Geese

ACCOMMODATIONS
Super 8 Motel, 2730 Dodge Street, Dubuque 52003 / 319-582-8898 / 61 rooms, smoking and nonsmoking / Dogs allowed with permission / $$
Motel 6, 2670 Dodge Street, Dubuque 52003 / 319-556-0880 / 98 rooms, smoking and nonsmoking / Dogs in smoking rooms only / $
Heartland Inn West, 4025 Dodge Street, Dubuque 52003 / 319-582-3752 / 88 rooms, smoking and nonsmoking / Dogs in smoking rooms only ($10 extra) / $$$
Days Inn, 1111 Dodge Street, Dubuque 52003 / 319-583-3297 / 154 rooms, smoking and nonsmoking / Dogs with advance permission / $$$

CAMPGROUND
Dubuque Yacht Basin and RV Park / 319-556-7708 / 56 sites, 8 full hookups, 48 water and electric, 48 pull-thrus / Open all year

RESTAURANTS
Bierstube, 1301 Rhomberg Avenue, Dubuque 52001 / 319-588-0361 / Monday–Saturday, 11:30AM–2PM for lunch; Wednesday–Saturday, 5–9PM / Bar open 11AM–11PM
Bishop Buffet, 555 John F. Kennedy Road, Dubuque 52002 / 319-588-2031 / Monday–Thursday, Saturday, 11AM–8PM; Friday until 8:30PM; Sunday, 10:30AM–7:30PM
Country Kitchen, 3187 University Avenue, Dubuque 52001 / 319-556-8405 / Open 24 hours daily / Complete menu

Luigi's Pizza House, 501 Rhomberg Avenue, Dubuque 52001 / 319-588-4275 / Open 6AM–12AM daily / Full menu, featuring chicken and catfish

Perkins, 3500 Dodge Street, Dubuque 52003 / 319-557-9262 / Open 24 hours daily / Complete menu

VETERINARIANS

Animal Clinic, 2611 Rockdale Road, Dubuque 52003 / 319-588-1875

Central Animal Hospital, 1865 Central Avenue, Dubuque 52001 / 319-557-1515

SPORTING GOODS

K-Mart, 2600 Dodge Street, Dubuque 52003 / 319-588-2361

Wal-Mart, 4200 Dodge Street, Dubuque 52003 / 319-582-1003

AUTO REPAIR

Don's Auto Repair, 955 Jackson Street, Dubuque 52003 / 319-588-9647

Bird Chevrolet, 3255 University Avenue, Dubuque 52001 / 319-583-9121

AUTO RENTAL

At Airport: **Avis** / 800-831-2847; **National** / 800-227-7368

AIRPORT

Dubuque Regional Airport, 11000 Airport Road, Dubuque 52003 / 319-589-4127 / Airlines: American Eagle, Northwest Air Link, United Express

MEDICAL

The Finley Hospital, 350 North Grandview Avenue, Dubuque 52001 / 319-582-1881

FOR MORE INFORMATION

Chamber of Commerce
770 Town Clock Plaza
Dubuque, IA 52001
319-557-9200

Cash Grain Region

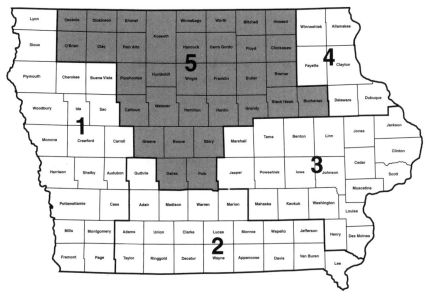

Covering 33 of Iowa's 99 counties, this is the largest of the five regions used in this book. Its name describes it quite aptly: the Cash Grain Region includes most of Iowa's best agricultural land, and much of it is intensively farmed for corn and soybeans.

This is Iowa as typically portrayed in the movies or as seen in the minds of people who have never visited the state: relatively flat and featureless, with continuous fields of corn and soybeans.

Until the 1960s and the era of fencerow to fencerow farming, this was the state's top pheasant region. Since then, most of the best bird habitat has disappeared. Although the CRP was a temporary respite, much of that set-aside ground has now been plowed up as well. However, where there is sufficient cover, hunters will still find good numbers of birds. And it remains Iowa's best region for Hungarian partridge, with bird populations generally increasing the farther north and west one travels.

This region also includes a large slice of Iowa that falls within the Prairie Pothole Region. Waterfowl hunting is very good and improving as wetlands are protected or restored. Although the region does not include many large tracts of timber, there are good numbers of wild turkeys, especially along the courses of major rivers such as the Des Moines, the Raccoon, the Boone, and the Cedar.

The northwest part of the region, around Iowa's large natural lakes, contains thousands of acres of public hunting ground. There are other large public areas scattered throughout the region, mostly around reservoirs, lakes, or wetlands. In general, however, with some counties having almost no state land, this region does not have a lot of public hunting opportunities.

Cash Grain Region
Pheasant Distribution

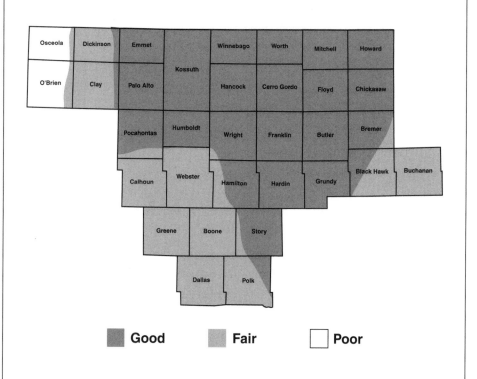

Good   Fair   Poor

Cash Grain Region
Hungarian Partridge Distribution

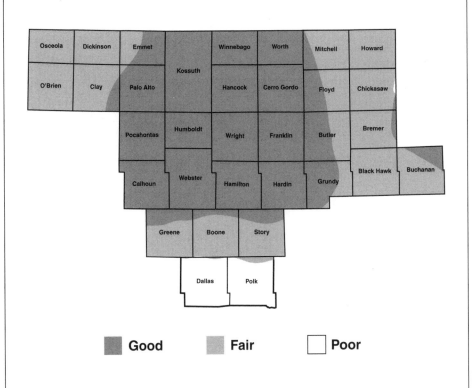

Good   Fair   Poor

Cash Grain Region
Woodcock Distribution

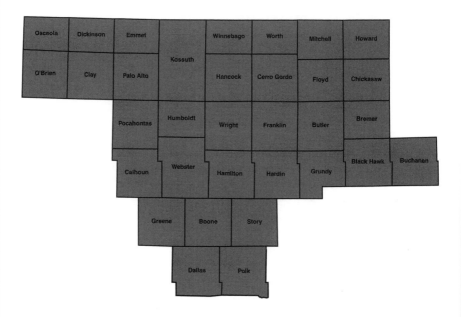

Found throughout

Cash Grain Region
Wild Turkey Distribution

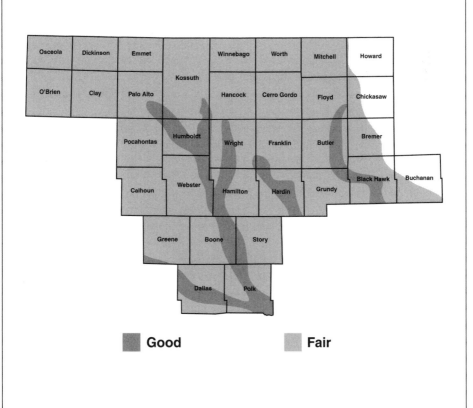

Good   Fair

Charles City
Howard, Mitchell, Floyd, and Chickasaw Counties

County Population:	Charles City Population–7,878
Howard–9,809	Annual Precipitation–33"
Mitchell–10,928	November Temperature–35°
Floyd–17,058	CRP Acres:
Chickasaw–13,295	Howard–12,002
County Area:	Mitchell–4,391
Howard–473 sq. mi.	Floyd–8,595
Mitchell–470 sq. mi.	Chickasaw–5,677
Floyd–501 sq. mi.	
Chickasaw–505 sq. mi.	

In general, the eastern part of this region is the best for pheasants, and Charles City is at the center of a four-county area that can be quite good where there is the right mix of cover and crop ground. Between them, the four counties have only about 1,500 acres of public hunting land, most in fairly small tracts of 100–200 acres. In any case, the best pheasant hunting will be on private ground. With no major population centers in close proximity, permission to hunt private land should not be difficult to secure after about the first two weeks of the season.

The best waterfowl and wild turkey hunting will be found along this area's numerous streams.

UPLAND BIRDS
Pheasants, Hungarian Partridge, Woodcock, Wild Turkeys

WATERFOWL
Ducks and Geese

ACCOMMODATIONS
Hartwood Inn, 1312 Gilbert Street, Charles City 50616 / 515-228-4352 / 35 rooms, smoking and nonsmoking / No dogs / $

Lamplighter Motel, 1416 Gilbert Street, Charles City 50616 / 515-228-6711 / 47 rooms, smoking and nonsmoking / Dogs allowed in rooms (in kennels) / $

Parkview Motel, 1001 South Grand Avenue, Charles City 50616 / 515-228-5163 / 23 rooms, smoking and nonsmoking / Dogs allowed / $

RESTAURANTS
Country Kitchen, 510 Hildreth Street, Charles City 50616 / 515-228-4598 / Open 24 hours daily / Complete menu

Uptown Cafe, 223 North Main Street, Charles City 50616 / 515-228-2801 / Open 6AM–10PM; closed Sunday

Granny's Kitchen, Hwy 218 South, Charles City 50616 / 515-228-7383 / Open Monday–Friday, 6AM–8PM; Saturday, 6AM–1:30PM; Sunday, 7AM–1:30PM

VETERINARIANS
Cedar River Animal Hospital, 900 South Grand Avenue, Charles City 50616 / 515-228-2211.

SPORTING GOODS
K-Mart, 90 South Main Street, Charles City 50616 / 515-228-7040.

AUTO REPAIR
Bob Elthon Ford Mercury, 1207 South Grand Avenue, Charles City 50616 / 515-228-1500.

AUTO RENTAL
See Mason City

AIRPORT
See Mason City

MEDICAL
Floyd County Memorial Hospital, 800 11th Street, Charles City 50616 / 515-228-6830.

FOR MORE INFORMATION
Chamber of Commerce
610 South Grand Avenue
Charles City, IA 50616
515-228-4234

Mason City
Worth, Winnebago, Hancock, and Cerro Gordo Counties

County Population:
  Worth–7,991
  Winnebago–12,122
  Hancock–12,638
  Cerro Gordo–46,733
County Area:
  Worth–402 sq. mi.
  Winnebago–402 sq. mi.
  Hancock–573 sq. mi.
  Cerro Gordo–575 sq. mi.
	Mason City Population–29,040
	Annual Precipitation–32"
	November Temperature–33°
	CRP Acres:
	  Worth–2,853
	  Winnebago–7,172
	  Hancock–3,405
	  Cerro Gordo–5,976

This is another sparsely populated farming region, including only one city with a population over 5,000—Mason City, northcentral Iowa's "metropolis." In general, this area is not as good a bet for pheasants as the counties immediately to the east. However, it does include some fairly large public waterfowl areas, such as Elk Creek Marsh (2,500 acres) and Silver Lake Marsh in Worth County; Rice Lake (1,800 acres), and several smaller wetlands in Winnebago County; Eagle Lake (900 acres) and smaller areas in Hancock County; and Clear Lake, with adjacent Ventura Marsh, totaling over 4,000 acres, in Cerro Gordo County. Many of these marshes and wetlands offer opportunities for pheasant hunters who aren't afraid to get their feet wet. Hungarian partridge, though quite hard to approach, will also be fairly numerous, mostly on harvested crop ground.

UPLAND BIRDS
Pheasants, Hungarian Partridge, Woodcock, Wild Turkeys

WATERFOWL
Ducks and Geese

ACCOMMODATIONS
Comfort Inn, 410 5th Street SW, Mason City 50401 / 515-423-4444 / 60 rooms, smoking and nonsmoking / No dogs / $$$
Days Inn, Hwy 18 W, Mason City 50401 / 515-424-0210 / 50 rooms, smoking and nonsmoking / Dogs allowed / $$
Willow Inn Motel, Hwy 18 West, Mason City 50401 / 515-423-8221 / 14 rooms, all smoking / Dogs allowed / $

RESTAURANTS

Country Kitchen, Willowbrook Plaza, Mason City 50401 / 515-423-4000 / Open 24 hours daily / Complete menu

Prime N' Wine, Hwy 18 West, Mason City 50401 / 515-424-8153 / Open Monday–Friday, 10:30AM–2PM for lunch and 4:30–11PM for dinner; Saturday, 4–11AM; Sunday, 10:30AM–3PM (buffet), 4:30–10PM for dinner

Valentino's, 1631 4th Street SW, Mason City 50401 / 515-424-1458 / Open Monday–Friday, 11AM–2PM for lunch, 5–8:30PM for dinner; Saturday and Sunday, 11AM–8:30PM, noon and evening buffets / Pasta dishes and pizza

VETERINARIANS

Pioneer Animal Hospital, 508 6th Street SW, Mason City 50401 / 515-424-0810

SPORTING GOODS

K-Mart, 2006 4th Street SW, Mason City 50401 / 515-424-1620

Wal-Mart, 2560 4th Street SW, Mason City 50401 / 515-423-6767

AUTO REPAIR

Schukei Chevrolet, 721 South Monroe Avenue, Mason City 50401 / 515-423-5402

Price Motors, 808 South Monroe Avenue, Mason City 50401 / 515-423-8273

AUTO RENTAL

Hertz (at airport) / 800-654-3131

AIRPORT

Mason City Airport, Mason City 50401 / 515-421-3680 / Airlines: United Express, Northwest Airlink

MEDICAL

North Iowa Mercy Health Center, 84 Beaumont Drive, Mason City 50401 / 515-424-7211

FOR MORE INFORMATION

Chamber of Commerce
15 West State Street
Mason City, IA 50401
515-423-5724

Algona
Kossuth, Emmet, and Palo Alto Counties

County Population:	Algona Population–6,015
Kossuth–18,591	Annual Precipitation–28"
Emmet–11,569	November Remperature–34°
Palo Alto–10,669	CRP Acres:
County Area:	Kossuth–3,918
Kossuth–976 sq. mi.	Emmet–4,937
Emmet–402 sq. mi.	Palo Alto–5,075
Palo Alto–568 sq. mi.	

This three-county, mostly rural area of northcentral Iowa has hunting opportunities very similar to those in the Mason City region: average to above pheasant hunting on private ground where there is good cover, and also on public marshes There are very good possibilities for waterfowl around shallow lakes and wetlands. Although Kossuth is larger than Emmet and Palo Alto Counties combined, the latter two have far better public hunting opportunities. Emmet County has over 7,000 acres of state hunting ground, nearly all around marshes or shallow lakes. Palo Alto has over 9,000 acres, with nearly 6,000 in the Dewey Pasture Wetland Complex.

Algona, a county seat town with good facilities situated near major travel routes, makes a good base from which to hunt this area.

UPLAND BIRDS
Pheasants, Hungarian Partridge, Woodcock, Wild Turkeys

WATERFOWL
Ducks and Geese

ACCOMMODATIONS

Acreage Motel, 1914 Hwy 18 E, Algona 50511 / 515-295-2428 / 18 rooms, smoking and nonsmoking / Dogs allowed / $

Burr Oak Motel, Hwy 169 South, Algona 50511 / 515-295-7213 / 42 rooms, smoking and nonsmoking / Dogs allowed / $$.

Super 8 Motel, Hwy 169 N & Norwood Drive, Algona 50511 / 30 rooms, smoking and nonsmoking / No dogs / $

CAMPGROUND

Ambrose A. Call State Park, From jct US18 and US169, go 2 miles southon US169, then 2 miles west on Hwy 274 / 515-581-4835 /^32 sites, 30 ft. maximum RV length, 13 electric, non-flush toilets / Open all year

RESTAURANTS

Happy Chef, 224 East Norwood Drive, Algona 50511 / 515-295-9301 / Open 24 hours daily / Complete menu

Cornfield hunts can be productive, but it takes a well-trained dog.

Sister Sarah's, Hwy 18 East, Algona 50511. 515-295-7757 / Open Monday, 11AM–2PM (lunch); Tuesday–Friday, 11AM–2PM (lunch) and 5–10PM (dinner); Saturday, 5–10:30PM (dinner); closed Sunday

VETERINARIANS
Animal Medical Center, 2222 Hwy 169 North, Algona 50511 / 515-295-5192

SPORTING GOODS
K-Mart, 1501 Hwy 169 N, Algona 50511 / 515-295-7775

AUTO REPAIR
Ken's Auto Service, 1107 North Main Street, Algona 50511 / 515-295-2497

AUTO RENTAL
See Fort Dodge

AIRPORT
See Fort Dodge

MEDICAL
Kossuth County Hospital, 1515 South Phillips Street, Algona 50511 / 515-295-2451

FOR MORE INFORMATION
Chamber of Commerce
117 East Call Street
Algona, IA 50511
515-295-7201

Spencer
Dickinson, Osceola, O'Brien, and Clay Counties

County Population:
  Dickinson–14,909
  Osceola–7,267
  O'Brien–15,444
  Clay–17,585
County Area:
  Dickinson–404 sq. mi.
  Osceola–399 sq. mi.
  O'Brien–574 sq. mi.
  Clay–573 sq. mi,
	Spencer Population–11,066
	Annual Precipitation–28"
	November Temperature–34°
	CRP Acres:
	  Dickinson–6,165
	  Osceola–2,842
	  O'Brien–1,952
	  Clay–5,300

This four-county region encompasses what is known as the "Iowa Great Lakes Region." While most of northern Iowa is dotted with fairly large but mostly shallow lakes, this part of the state has East and West Okoboji and Spirit Lakes. Those three lakes, all relatively deep and boasting very good fisheries, combine to form one of the top vacation spots for Iowa boaters and anglers.

Of the four counties, Clay and Dickinson have far more public hunting land. Most is in or around marshes and lakes and is obviously designed with waterfowl in mind. However, these areas—and adjacent private land—can also be very productive for pheasants. This is also a very good area for Hungarian partridge, but almost all coveys will be found on private ground.

Spencer, the largest town in the region, has excellent facilities and is situated well for hunters visiting this part of the state.

UPLAND BIRDS
Pheasants, Hungarian Partridge, Woodcock, Wild Turkeys

WATERFOWL
Ducks and Geese

ACCOMMODATIONS
Budget Inn, 1004 South Grand Avenue, Spencer 51301 / 712-262-4620 / 42 rooms, smoking and nonsmoking / Dogs allowed (smoking rooms only) / $$
Iron Horse Motel, 14 11th Street SE, Spencer 51301 / 712-262-9123 / 84 rooms, smoking and nonsmoking / Dogs allowed (in 2 rooms only) / $$
Spencer Motel, 1725 Hwy Boulevard, Spencer 51301 / 712-262-2610 / 12 rooms, all smoking / No dogs / $

RESTAURANTS

Country Kitchen, 16 11th Street SW, Spencer 51301 / 712-262-7540 / Open 24 hours daily / Complete menu

The Prime Rib, 1205 South Grand Avenue, Spencer 51301 / 712-262-4625 / Open Monday–Thursday, 5–10PM; Friday and Saturday until 11PM; closed Sunday

Mainstreet Family Cafe, 312 Grand Avenue, Spencer 51301 / 712-262-6803 / Open Monday-Friday, 5AM–4PM; Saturday until 1PM; Sunday, 7–11:30AM (breakfast only)

The Grand Diner, 208 North Grand Avenue, Spencer 51301 / 712-262-4404 / Open Tuesday-Saturday, 6AM–3PM; closed Sunday and Monday

VETERINARIANS

Homestead Small Animal Practice, 205 11th Street SW, Spencer 51301 / 712-262-8990

SPORTING GOODS

K-Mart, 900 11th Street SW, Spencer 51301 / 712-262-2080

AUTO REPAIR

H & N Chevrolet, 713 Grand Avenue, Spencer 51301 / 712-262-3230

AUTO RENTAL

National (at airport) / 800-227-7368

AIRPORT

Spencer Municipal Airport, 1965 330th Street, Spencer 51301 / 712-262-7734 / Airline: United Express

MEDICAL

Spencer Municipal Hospital, 1200 1st Avenue East, Spencer 51301 / 712-264-6198

FOR MORE INFORMATION

Spencer Chamber of Commerce
122 West 5th Street
Spencer, IA 51301-3820
712-262-5680

Fort Dodge
Humboldt, Pocahontas, Calhoun,
and Webster Counties

County Population:	Fort Dodge Population–25,894
Humboldt–10,756	Annual Precipitation–31"
Pocahontas–9–525	November Temperature–36°
Calhoun–11,508	CRP Acres:
Webster–40,342	Humboldt–1,099
County Area:	Pocahontas–1,671
Humboldt–436 sq. mi.	Calhoun–2,223
Pocahontas–578 sq. mi.	Webster–2,658
Calhoun–573 sq. mi.	
Webster–718 sq. mi.	

Fort Dodge, the only sizable city in this part of the state, is a good base from which to hunt these four counties. There are fewer shallow lakes and wetlands than in the counties to the north and west, although Calhoun County does have North and South Twin Lakes (1,200 acres total) with good waterfowl opportunities, and Pocahontas County has several shallow lakes and marshes of under 400 acres. In Webster County, there are nearly 10,000 acres of public hunting ground in the Brushy Creek and Boone Forks areas. Both are fairly heavily timbered and are quite good for wild turkey. Field openings in both areas also have decent numbers of pheasants, although the best pheasant hunting—and good numbers of Hungarian partridge— will be found on private ground.

UPLAND BIRDS
Pheasants, Hungarian Partridge, Woodcock, Wild Turkeys

WATERFOWL
Ducks and Geese

ACCOMMODATIONS

Budget Host Inn, Jct Hwys 20 & 169, Fort Dodge 50501 / 515-955-8501 / 111 rooms, smoking and nonsmoking / Dogs allowed / $

Comfort Inn, 2938 5th Avenue South, Fort Dodge 50501 / 515-573-3731 / 48 rooms, smoking and nonsmoking / Dogs allowed / $$

Super 8 Motel, 3040 5th Avenue South, Fort Dodge 50501 / 515-576-8000 / 81 rooms, smoking and nonsmoking / Hunting dogs allowed / $$

Starlite Village Motel, Jct Hwys 7 and 169, Fort Dodge 50501 / 515-573-7177 / 115 rooms, smoking and nonsmoking / Dogs allowed if in kennels / $$

RESTAURANTS

Happy Chef, 3040 5th Avenue South, Fort Dodge 50501 / 515-576-2021 / Open 24 hours daily / Complete menu

Sports Page Bar & Grill, 2707 North 15th Street, Fort Dodge 50501 / 515-955-1890 / Open Sunday–Thursday, 11AM–Midnight; Friday and Saturday until 2AM

Village Inn, 2002 North 15th Street, Fort Dodge 50501 / 515-955-2002 / Open Sunday–Thursday, 6AM–11PM; Friday and Saturday until 3AM

VETERINARIANS

Stockman's Pet Clinic, 1508 A Street, Fort Dodge 50501 / 515-955-3631

SPORTING GOODS

K-Mart, 3126 5th Avenue South, Fort Dodge 50501 / 515-576-7611

Wal-Mart, 301 South 29th Street, Fort Dodge 50501 / 515-576-7400

AUTO REPAIR

Shimkat Motor Co., 1225 2nd Avenue South, Fort Dodge 50501 / 515-573-7164

AUTO RENTAL

Hertz (at airport) / 800-654-3131

AIRPORT

Fort Dodge Regional Airport, RR2, Fort Dodge 50501 / 515-573-3881 / Airlines: Northwest Airlink

MEDICAL

Trinity Regional Hospital, Fort Dodge 50501 / 515-574-6448

FOR MORE INFORMATION

Greater Fort Dodge Chamber of Commerce
1406 Central Avenue
Fort Dodge, IA 50501-4252
515-955-5500

Webster City
Hamilton, Hardin, Franklin,
and Wright Counties

County Population:	Webster City Population–7,894
Hamilton–16,071	Annual Precipitation–32"
Hardin–19,095	November temperature–36°
Franklin–11,364	CRP Acres:
Wright–14,269	Hamilton–2,816
County Area:	Hardin–3,297
Hamilton–577 sq. mi.	Franklin–4,310
Hardin–569 sq. mi.	Wright–4,508
Franklin–583 sq. mi.	
Wright–582 sq. mi.	

This is mainly pheasant country, with decent numbers of Hungarian partridge (better the farther west you go), and turkeys along timbered streams. In general, this four-county area has very little public land. In Wright County, three public wetlands total slightly over 1500 acres; Franklin County has the 400-acre Whitetail Flats area along the Iowa River, with good potential for both waterfowl and pheasants; and Hamilton County shares the 3,000-acre Boone Forks Area, on the Boone River, with neighboring Webster County.

Although Hardin County has almost no state land, much of the ground adjacent to the Iowa River has been acquired by the county conservation board. This Iowa River Greenbelt offers very good hunting for wild turkeys and decent jumpshooting for waterfowl.

Webster City, the county seat of Hamilton County, is located conveniently near I-35 and makes a good base from which to hunt the region.

UPLAND BIRDS
Pheasants, Hungarian Partridge, Woodcock, Wild Turkeys

WATERFOWL
Ducks and Geese

ACCOMMODATIONS
Super 8 Motel, 305 Closz Drive, Webster City 50595 / 515-832-2000 / 44 rooms, smoking and nonsmoking / No dogs / $$

The Executive Inn, 1700 Superior Street, Webster City 50595 / 515-832-3631 / 39 rooms, smoking and nonsmoking / No dogs / $$

Jim Boone of Indiana with a rooster.

RESTAURANTS

Leon's Pizza, 716 Laura Lane, Webster City 50595 / 515-832-2215 / Open
11AM–11PM daily / Other dishes as well as pizza

Second Street Emporium, 615 2nd Street, Webster City 50595 / 515-832-3463 /
Open Monday–Saturday, 11AM–9:30PM; closed Sunday

SPORTING GOODS

K-Mart, 2307 Superior Street, Webster City 50595 / 515-832-5523

AUTO REPAIR

Moffitt Ford, 2nd & Broadway, Webster City 50595 / 515-832-3333

AUTO RENTAL

See Fort Dodge

AIRPORT

See Fort Dodge

MEDICAL

Webster City Medical Clinic, 1610 Collins, Webster City 50595 / 515-832-6123

FOR MORE INFORMATION

Webster City ABI
628 2nd Street
Webster City, IA 50595
515-832-2564

Waterloo
Black Hawk, Bremer, Buchanan, Butler, and Grundy Counties

County Population:
  Black Hawk–123,798
  Bremer–22,813
  Buchanan–20,844
  Butler–15,731
  Grundy–12,029
County Area:
  Black Hawk–573 sq. mi.
  Bremer–439 sq. mi.
  Buchanan–573 sq. mi.
  Butler–582 sq. mi.
  Grundy–501 sq. mi.
	Waterloo Population–66,467
	Annual Precipitation–33"
	November Temperature–36°
	CRP Acres:
	  Black Hawk–2,145
	  Bremer–3,773
	  Buchanan–2,772
	  Butler–8,004
	  Grundy–874

This five-county area, centered around the city of Waterloo, is good pheasant country. There are also good numbers of wild turkeys where there is sufficient timber, and waterfowl can be found around a couple of large public marshes and along streams.

Best opportunities for pheasants will come on private ground in Butler, Bremer, and Buchanan Counties. Two large marshes—Big Marsh in Butler County and Sweet Marsh in Bremer County, each over 2,000 acres—are good bets for waterfowl and also have good pheasant populations. Other than those areas, public hunting opportunities in this part of the state are quite limited.

UPLAND BIRDS
Pheasants, Hungarian Partridge, Woodcock, Wild Turkeys

WATERFOWL
Ducks and Geese

ACCOMMODATIONS
Comfort Inn, 1945 Laporte Road, Waterloo 50702 / 319-234-7411 / 56 rooms, smoking and nonsmoking / Dogs allowed / $$
Days Inn, 2141 Laporte Road, Waterloo 50702 / 319-233-9191 / 51 rooms, smoking and nonsmoking / Dogs allowed / $$
Heartland Inn, 1809 Laporte Road, Waterloo 50702 / 319-235-4461 / 118 rooms, smoking and nonsmoking / Dogs allowed in smoking rooms only ($10 fee) / $$

Super 8, 1825 Laporte Road, Waterloo 50702 / 319-233-1800 / 62 rooms, smoking and nonsmoking / No dogs / $$

RESTAURANTS

Mama Nick's Circle Pizzaria, 1934 Washington Street, Waterloo 50702 / 319-233-3323 / Open Sunday–Thursday, 11AM–Midnight; Friday and Saturday until 2AM / Features Italian dishes and sandwiches as well as pizza

Country Kitchen, 2855 Crossroads Boulevard, Waterloo 50702 / 319-232-3521 / Open 24 hours daily / Complete menu

Lone Star Steak House, 4045 Hammond Avenue, Waterloo 50701 / 319-232-3233 / Open Sunday–Thursday, 11AM–10PM; Friday and Saturday until 11PM / Mesquite-grilled steaks

Perkins Restaurant, 3280 University Avenue, Waterloo 50701 / 319-235-6595 / Open 24 hours daily / Complete menu

Southtown Lounge & Restaurant, 2026 Bopp Street, Waterloo 50702 / 319-236-9112 / Open Monday–Saturday, 7AM–11PM; bar open until 2AM; closed Sunday / Features chicken and pork tenderloins

VETERINARIANS

Den Herder Veterinary Hospital, 974 Home Plaza, Waterloo 50702 / 319-232-5292

SPORTING GOODS

Scheels Sport Shops, 2060 Crossroads Boulevard, Suite 126, Waterloo 50702 / 319-234-7534

K-Mart, 1645 East San Marnan Drive, Waterloo 50702 / 319-235-1426

AUTO REPAIR

Rydell Chevrolet, 1325 East San Marnan Drive, Waterloo 50702 / 319-234-4601

Dick Witham Ford, 2033 Laporte Road, Waterloo 50702 / 319-234-4200

AUTO RENTAL

Avis / 800-831-2847; **Hertz** / 800-654-3131; **National** 800-227-7368 / All located at airport

AIRPORT

Waterloo Airport, 2790 Airport Boulevard, Waterloo 50703 / 319-291-4483 / Airlines: United Express, Northwest Airlink, TW Express

MEDICAL

Covenant Medical Center, 3421 West 9th Street, Waterloo 50702 / 319-272-8000

FOR MORE INFORMATION

Waterloo Chamber of Commerce
620 Mulberry Street #102
Waterloo, IA 50703
319-233-8431

Des Moines
Greene, Boone, Story, Polk, and Dallas Counties

County Population:
Greene–10,045
Boone–25,186
Story–74,252
Polk–327,140
Dallas–29,755
County Area:
Greene–572 sq. mi.
Boone–574 sq. mi.
Story–574 sq. mi.
Polk–592 sq. mi.
Dallas–591 sq. mi.

Des Moines. Population–193,187
Annual Precipitation–33"
November Temperature–39°
CRP Acres:
Greene–2,961
Boone–2,983
Story–3,508
Polk–3,192
Dallas–5,164

Although this five-county area contains Des Moines, Iowa's largest city, and has a total population of nearly half a million, it also has quite good hunting opportunities for pheasants, turkeys, and waterfowl. Greene County and the western portions of Boone and Dallas Counties generally have the best pheasant hunting, mostly on private ground. Turkey and waterfowl hunting can be very good along the Des Moines River, especially in Boone County, where the 11,000-acre Saylorville Area extends well upstream from the town of Boone. Hendrickson Marsh (800 acres) in Story County and Dunbar Slough (1,300 acres) in Greene County are both quite good for waterfowl and pheasants.

Des Moines obviously has excellent facilities. We have selected accommodations on the north and west sides of the metropolitan area for easier access to hunting without fighting city traffic. Should you prefer smaller cities, Ames in Story County and Boone in Boone County both have good facilities as well, and are conveniently close to Des Moines. However, motel rooms can be hard to come by in either town when Iowa State University has a home football game.

UPLAND BIRDS
Pheasants, Hungarian Partridge, Woodcock, Wild Turkeys

WATERFOWL
Ducks and Geese

ACCOMMODATIONS
Comfort Inn, 5900 Sutton Drive, Urbandale 50322 / 515-270-1037 / 60 rooms, smoking and nonsmoking / No dogs / $$
Days Inn, 4845 Merle Hay Road, Des Moines 50310 / 515-278-5511 / 80 rooms, smoking and nonsmoking / No dogs / $$

How to dispatch a crippled rooster quickly and cleanly. Grab the bird on either side of the backbone, above the wings, and squeeze. This cuts off the blood supply.

Super 8 Lodge, 4755 Merle Hay Road, Des Moines 50310 / 515-278-8858 / 152 rooms, smoking and nonsmoking / Dogs allowed ($20 refundable deposit) / $$

Motel 6, 4817 Fleur Drive, Des Moines 50315 / 515-287-6364 / 98 rooms, smoking and nonsmoking / No dogs / $

CAMPGROUNDS

Adventureland Campground / 515-265-7384 / 310 sites, 280 full hookups, 83 pull-thrus / Open all year

KOA-Des Moines West / 800-KOA-2181 / 100 sites, 28 full hookups, 48 water and electric, 1 electric, 76 pull-thrus / Open all year

Walnut Woods State Park, From jct I-135 and Hwy 5, go 1 mile east on Hwy 5, then 2 miles northeast on CR / 515-285-4502 / 28 sites, 21 ft. maximum RV length, 8 electric, non-flush toilets / Open all year

RESTAURANTS

Best Steak House, 1568 East Euclid Avenue, Des Moines 50313 / 515-266-9033 / Open Sunday–Thursday, 11AM–9PM; Friday and Saturday until 10PM

Christopher's, 2816 Beaver Avenue, Des Moines 50310 / 515-274-3694 / Open Monday–Thursday, 5–10PM; Friday and Saturday until 10:30PM; closed Sunday

Country Kitchen, 5030 NE 14th Street, Des Moines 50313 / 515-262-9802 / Open 24 hours daily / Complete menu

Hostetler's BBQ, 4875 Merle Hay Road, Des Moines 50322 / 515-276-0071 / Open Sunday–Thursday, 11AM–9PM; Friday and Saturday until 10PM

Perkins Restaurant, 4601 Merle Hay Road, Des Moines 50322 / 515-278-0468 / Open 24 hours daily / Complete menu

VETERINARIANS

Avondale Animal Hospital, 4318 East Army Post Road, Des Moines 50320 / 515-262-6111

West-side Veterinary Clinic, 3100 Merle Hay Road, Des Moines 50310 / 515-276-5972

SPORTING GOODS

Des Moines Sports, 9350 Hickman Road, Des Moines 50325 / 515-276-2764

Floyds Sporting Goods, 4359 Merle Hay Road, Des Moines 50310 / 515-276-3498

K-Mart, 1200 SE Army Post Road, Des Moines 50315 / 515-287-3815

Wal-Mart, 5101 SE 14th Street, Des Moines 50320 / 515-287-7725

AUTO REPAIR

All Pro Servicecenter, 5904 Meredith Drive, Urbandale 50322 / 515-278-2059

Tuffy Auto Service, 5701 Douglas Avenue, Des Moines 50310 / 515-276-4989

AUTO RENTAL

Alamo / 800-327-9633; **Avis** / 800-831-2847; **Budget** / 800-527-0700; **Hertz** / 800-654-3131; **National** / 800-227-7368 / All located at airport

AIRPORT

Des Moines International Airport, Fleur Drive & Army Post Road, Des Moines 50321 / 515-256-5100 / Airlines: United, American, Northwest, Delta, TWA, Air Midwest, US Air, America West, American Eagle

MEDICAL

Des Moines General Hospital, 603 East 12th Street, Des Moines 50309 / 515-263-4200

FOR MORE INFORMATION

Greater Des Moines Chambers of Commerce Federation
601 Locust Street, Suite 100
Des Moines, IA 50309
515-286-4950

Iowa Guides
and Hunting Lodges

Guided bird hunting is a relatively new phenomenon in Iowa, and compared to other states, there are not a lot of guide services. Also, the Iowa DNR does not license guides nor does it maintain a listing of guide services. Guides we have listed first in this book are generally those who advertise in hunting magazines and who responded to our request for further information. We suggest that you call or write a guide service—preferably well in advance of your planned hunt, because many book up early—and ask for references.

Included in our list, you will find a broad range of guide services. These range from simply providing access to private land on which to hunt, to bed and breakfast with a host landowner, to accompanying you on the hunt and providing dogs, to a full-service hunt including all meals and lodging. You should be able to find a guide who meets your particular needs.

As a former guide myself, I suggest that you ask the following questions (in addition to the obvious ones—cost and dates available) before committing yourself to a guide service:

- Is an advance deposit required? If so, is it refundable if I must cancel prior to the hunt?
- Will I be hunting only with the group I bring with me, or will we be included into a larger hunting party?
- What kind of dogs do you have (pointing, flushing)?
- What kind of cover do you hunt most of the time—CRP ground, crop ground, public areas??
- Will I be hunting strictly wild birds, or do you release pen raised birds as well?
- How many years has your service been in business?
- How much of your business is from hunters you have guided in previous years?
- Will we be hunting on leased private ground to which you have exclusive access?

Good hunting!

Randy's Guide Service
838 North 21st Street
Fort Dodge, IA 50501
515-573-4076
Contact–Randy Risetter
Land–3,000 acres
Game–pheasant, quail, ducks, geese
Personal Guides–Available
Dogs–Available; hunters' dogs welcome
Extras–Airport pickup, lunch, bird
    cleaning

Pheasants Galore
323 East 4th Street
Villisca, IA 50864
712-838-4890; 515-322-4202 evenings
Contact–Darwin Linn
Land–300,000 acres
Game–pheasant, quail, Huns, ducks,
    geese
Personal Guides–Available
Dogs–Available; hunters' dogs welcome
Extras–Lodging with host farmers

Alan Worth Guiding Service
2550 170th Street
Prescott, IA 50859
515-335-2330
Contact–Alan Worth
Land–13,000 acres
Game–pheasant and quail
Personal Guides–available
Dogs–available; hunters' dogs welcome
    (kennels provided)
Extras–bed and breakfast; bird cleaning;
    video tape of hunt

Iowa Pheasants 'n More Hunting Lodge
1704 8th Avenue
Belle Plaine, IA 52208
319-444-3912
Contact–Dale Fisher
Land–13,000 acres
Game–pheasant, ducks, geese, turkey
Personal Guides–Available

Dogs–Available; hunters' dogs welcome;
    kennels provided
Extras–bed and breakfast

Quills Inc.
2786 Oak Avenue
Guthrie Center, IA 50115
800-524-5389
Contact–Larry Sleister
Land–70,000 acres
Game–pheasant, quail, turkey, geese
Personal Guides–Available
Dogs–Available; hunters' dogs welcome
Extras–Bed and breakfast; bird cleaning

Shivvers Farms
RR1, Box 119A, Corydon, IA 50060
515-872-1803
Contact–Doug Shivvers
Land–1,700 acres
Game–pheasant and quail
Other Information: No guides, dogs,
    lodging available; access to private
    ground only for a trespass fee

Sure Shot Guide Service
1210 Gordon Drive
Okoboji, IA 51355
712-332-9107
Contact–Don Nolan
Land–4,000 acres
Game–pheasant, Huns, quail, ducks,
    geese
Personal Guides–Available
Dogs–Available; hunters dogs welcome
Extras–Airport pickup; field lunches;
    bird cleaning

Mark's Guide Service
417 100th Avenue
Norwalk, IA 50211
515-961-4734
Contact–Mark Stogdill
Land–1,500 acres
Game–pheasant, quail, turkey, geese
Dogs–Available; Hunters dogs welcome
Extras–bird cleaning

Randall and Kitty Strand
P.O. Box 196
Clarinda, IA 51632
712-542-5060
Contact–Randall Strand
Land–1,000 acres
Game–pheasants and quail
Personal Guides–Fully guided hunts
Dogs–Available; hunters' dogs welcome
Extras–Lodging and meals with hosts;
    bird cleaning; airport pickup

Trail's End Ranch and Lodge
RR 1
Allerton, IA 50008
515-873-4470
Contact–Jim Jones
Land–2,000 acres
Game–pheasants, quail, turkeys
Extras–Modern lodge

Other Iowa Guides

Russel Guide Service
Perry and Dana Russell
1123 North 5th Street
Estherville, IA 51334
712-362-4251

Hawkeye Whitetail Deer, Turkey,
    Pheasants
RR 2, Box 146
Chariton, IA 55049
515-766-6411; 515-877-2009

Finn Wing Ent. Guide Service
1732 175th Street
Gravity, IA 50848

South West Iowa Bed & Breakfast
Deer and Pheasant Hunting
Clude Belding
1318 Oregon Avenue
Lenox, IA 50851
515-333-4338

Lexington Hunt Club
206 Main Street
Bedford, IA 50833
712-523-2177; 712-523-3120

Ringneck Country Hunting Lodge
Dave Gray
2365 South Lakeshore Drive
Brooklyn, IA 52211
888-531-3283

Safari Iowa Hunting Farms
Parnell, IA 52325
319-664-3472

Iowa Wild Bird Deluxe
Near Des Moines, IA
Booked through Cabela's

Kojac Kennels and Guide Service
Jerry Jorden
3303 56th Street Trail
Center Point, IA 52213
319-443-2604

Bill Reed
515-333-2539

Stan Knox
1680 Vail Avenue
Clearfield, IA 50840
515-336-2388

Oakwood Hunting Ranch
Bill Kuntz
RR2, Box 69
Sigourney, IA 52591
800-432-3290

White Thorn Kennel and Guide Service
Richard, Terry, Keith Lindsey
611 D Avenue
Vinton, IA 52349
319-472-2891

Bob Burchett
1758 295th Street
Argyle, IA 52619
319-838-2822

Tony McGrane
Waterloo, IA
319-234-0498

L.J. Kennels
Lawrence Ficeck
Grinnell, IA
515-236-1057

Wayne Davis
1763 53rd Street
Mount Auburn, IA
319-475-2209

Iowa Trophy Hunting
John Hambleton
2462 160th Road
Guthrie Center, IA 50115
800-842-0574; 515-747-2621
Turkey and Deer

Sportsmans Lodge
Clarke Perkins
RR1, Box 100A
Lamoni, IA 50140
515-787-8770

Heartland Outfitters of Iowa
Steve and Fran Ross
P.O. Box 306
Carlisle, IA 50047
515-989-9985

Prairies Edge Goose Club
308 SW Park Avenue
Des Moines, IA 50315

Iowa's Public Hunting Areas

Iowa's Department of Natural Resources manages 340 wildlife areas, totaling more than 270,000 acres and containing a variety of habitats, including wetland, grassland, timber, and agriculture. These areas are managed to provide not only food, winter cover, and secure nesting habitat for resident and migratory wildlife species, but to provide public hunting opportunities.

Public Hunting Areas

The boundaries of DNR wildlife areas are posted every one-eighth mile with green and white "Public Hunting Area" signs. These areas provide all users equal access to public lands but include few, if any, public use facilities such as restrooms, drinking water, hiking trails, and other conveniences. Lands adjacent to public wildlife areas are privately owned and require landowner permission for access. Please respect private property.

Directions in the public lands listing starting on page 219 refer to the city nearest the area and then direct you along federal, state, and county roads. Brown and white signs, displaying a duck or duck and fish, are posted along these roads and will direct you to the nearest parking lot.

Although hunting and trapping are the primary recreational activities available on these areas, bird watching, hiking, mushrooming, and nature study are allowed, preferably when hunting and trapping seasons are closed.

Wildlife Refuges

Certain wildlife areas and portions of some areas have been posted as wildlife refuges by the DNR. Wildlife refuge signs are yellow with black letters. It is unlawful to hunt, pursue, kill, trap, or take any wild animal, bird, or game on these areas. All firearms are prohibited within refuge areas. Additionally, it is unlawful to trespass in any manner on wildlife refuges, where posted, between the dates of September 10 and December 25 of each year, both days inclusive.

Open Water Refuges

Certain natural lakes have been designated as "Open Water Refuges." Hunting on these natural lakes is limited to a zone extending 50 yards into the lake from the ordinary high water mark, rooted vegetation, or islands, unless posted otherwise. Beyond this zone is a wildlife refuge.

Controlled Waterfowl Hunting Areas

Daily permits are required to hunt portions of the Riverton, Forney Lake, and Odessa Wildlife areas during the waterfowl season. Hunters receive their permits at check stations and are required to check their bags at the check stations before leaving the area. Drawings are held approximately 90 minutes before shooting time for the purpose of selecting blinds or stake sites. For information about reservations, contact the area office: Riverton and Forney Lake at 712-374-3133, and Odessa at 319-523-8319.

Wildlife Area Restrictions

- **Motorized Vehicles:** The use of motorized vehicles is prohibited on all wildlife areas except on designated roads and parking lots. Handicapped persons may be authorized to use certain motorized vehicles on designated roads after first obtaining a permit from the DNR.
- **Blinds:** Blinds may be constructed on wildlife areas, provided they are constructed using only the natural vegetation found on the area. No trees or parts of trees, other than willows, may be cut for the construction of the blind, and construction of a blind does not give that person proprietary right to use the blind. Nails, spikes, pins, or any other objects, metal or otherwise, may not be driven into any tree for the purpose of constructing a blind or to facilitate access to a blind or hunting location above ground. No sawed lumber, wire, nails, bolts, posts, pipes, metal cable, or hardware of any type can be used to build a blind on wildlife areas. Portable blinds and self-contained units that are readily movable are allowed; however, portable blinds and decoys are prohibited between the hours of one hour after the close of legal shooting time and midnight during the open waterfowl season. A portable blind constructed on a boat is considered removed when the boat supporting the blind is tied up or moored at an approved access site.
- **Nontoxic Shot:** Only steel shot, copper-coated or nickel-coated steel shot, or bismuth-tin shot may be used to hunt migratory game birds (except woodcock) on any lands or waters of the state of Iowa.
- **Dog Training:** Dogs are prohibited on all wildlife areas from March 15 through July 15. Field and retriever training are allowed on designated training areas only and require a permit from the DNR.
- **Field Trials:** Field trials are prohibited on wildlife areas except at designated areas and during times that do not conflict with established hunting and trapping seasons. A permit is required for all field trials. Applications can be obtained by contacting the DNR in Des Moine at 515-281-8688.
- **Secondary Uses:** The use of horses and snowmobiles are prohibited on all wildlife areas except where designated trails have been established according to IAC 571-67. DNR area managers may limit or suspend the use of trails in the event that natural or unnatural events degrade the trail beyond acceptable limits.

Descriptions and maps of selected larger public hunting areas are listed next, and after that is a complete listing of Iowa's public hunting areas.

Waterfowl Production Areas

Iowa has 12,585 acres designated as Waterfowl Production Areas, located in 18 counties. Waterfowl Production Areas are smaller than wildlife refuges and range in size from just over 100 acres to over 3,700 acres in Iowa. They provide ideal nesting habitat for waterfowl and good cover for upland birds. WPAs are typically small potholes, but any of them can draw in good numbers of ducks and geese. Hunters will also find great upland bird shooting, mostly on lands bordering the WPAs. Hunters can recognize WPAs by the distinctive green sign that is posted on the border of each. The refuges and Wetland Management Districts have maps and a list of the WPAs in their district.

RATHBUN WILDLIFE MANAGEMENT AREA

17,000 acres
Iowa Department of Natural Resources
Agricultural Building
RFD 2, Box 310
Chariton, IA 50049
515-774-4918

The area around Rathbun Reservoir provides good hunting for turkeys, pheasants, quail, and waterfowl. However, it is a partial refuge, and Canada goose hunting is prohibited on the entire area.

The best upland habitat is found in the two arms of the area extending back and west of the reservoir's main pool.

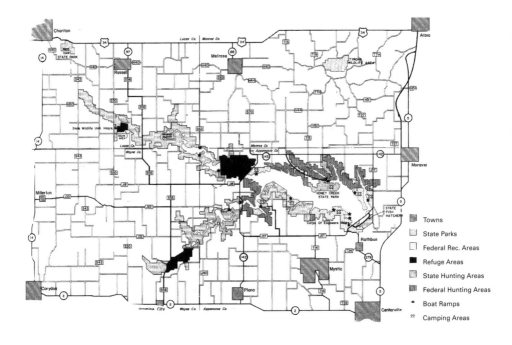

RED ROCK WILDLIFE MANAGEMENT AREA

25,500 acres

Extending west of the Highway 14 bridge along the Des Moines River, Red Rock has good hunting for turkeys, pheasants, and waterfowl. Hunters may also encounter an occasional covey of quail. Red Rock is a partial refuge.

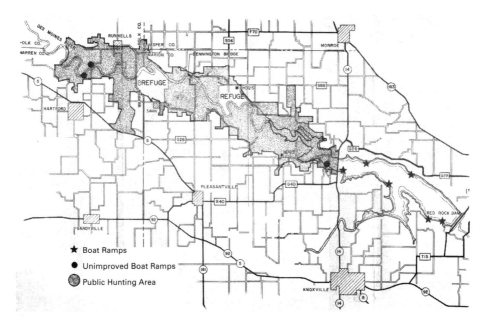

SAYLORVILLE WILDLIFE MANAGEMENT AREA

11,000 acres
Park Manager, US Army Corps of Engineers
Saylorville Lake, RR 3
Johnston, IA 50131
515-276-4656

The Saylorville Area extends from the Saylorville Dam, just north of the city of Des Moines, and follows the Des Moines River to the Boone County town of Fraser. Parts of the area are recreation areas or refuge and are closed to hunting; other areas are restricted to bow hunting only. There are good numbers of turkeys in the timber along the river, some pheasants where the area borders agricultural ground, and woodcock that migrate down the river in late October to early November. Waterfowling is also quite good.

Upper Reach

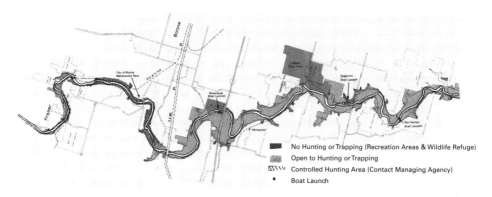

Lower Reach

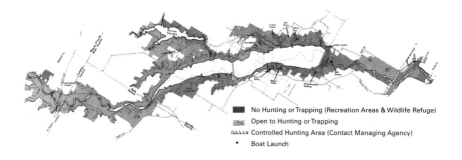

UPPER MISSISSIPPI RIVER
NATIONAL WILDLIFE AND FISH REFUGE

200,000 acres
319-873-3423 or 507-452-4232

Most of this enormous area, extending across the two- to five-mile wide river bottom and running from Iowa's northern border to Scott County, is open to hunting in accordance with federal refuge regulations. The refuge offers mainly waterfowl shooting, especially for ducks, and the hunting can be very good. There are also opportunities for take migrating woodcock and wild turkeys.

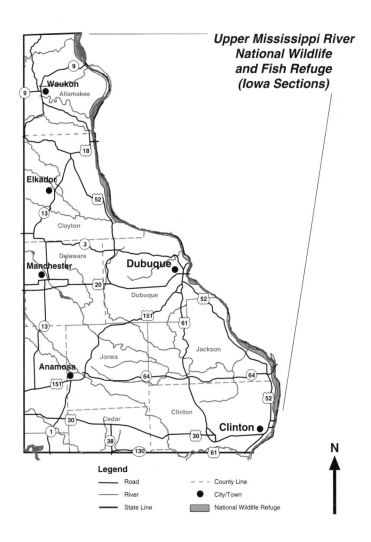

FORNEY LAKE

1,128 acres
Iowa Department of Natural Resources
Forney Lake Area
Thurman, IA 51654
712-628-3155

Forney is one of the state's premier public waterfowl areas. Hunting is done from assigned blinds allotted by drawing. Blind reservations will be accepted by mail. The area is a partial refuge.

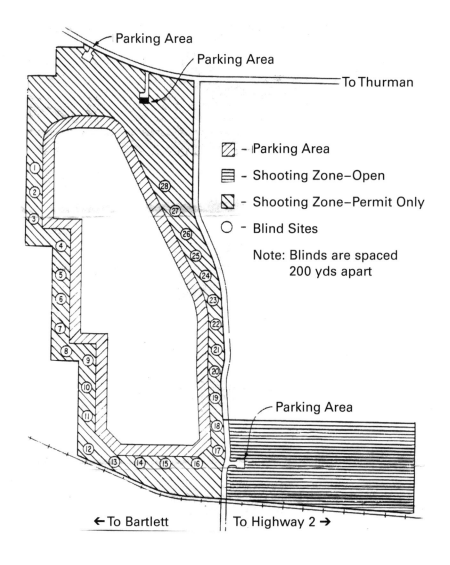

RIVERTON AREA

2,720 acres
Iowa Department of Natural Resources
Riverton Wildlife Area
Riverton, IA 51650
712-374-2510

Riverton, like Forney, is a controlled waterfowl hunting area with essentially the same special regulations. However, it does have a larger adjacent area open to unrestricted access. Like Forney, Riverton is a partial refuge.

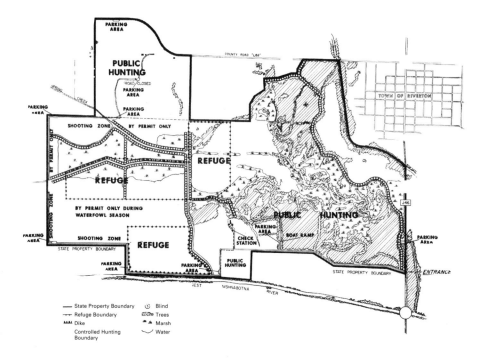

YELLOW RIVER STATE FOREST
PAINT CREEK UNIT

4,500 acres
Iowa Department of Natural Resources
729 State Forest Road
Harpers Ferry, IA 52146
319-586-2254

The Paint Creek Unit is the largest segment of the 7,500-acre Yellow River State Forest. Road access is fairly limited. However, a good network of hiking trails will allow hunters to reach some very good hunting for wild turkeys, ruffed grouse, and woodcock. Hunting is permitted on the entire area with the exception of a few designated sites, primarily camping areas.

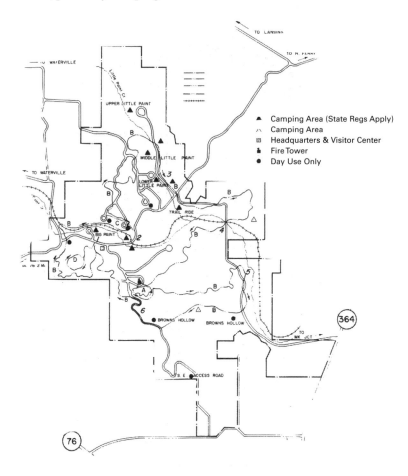

HAWKEYE WILDLIFE AREA

13,500 acres

This large area surrounding the upper end of the Coralville Reservoir has good hunting for waterfowl (including snipe and rail) around the lake and marsh portions, a good number of wild turkeys in the timber, and pheasants in the upland areas. It is a partial refuge.

LAKE ODESSA WILDLIFE MANAGEMENT AREA

3,800 acres
Iowa Department of Natural Resources
Lake Odessa Unit
RR 1
Wapello, IA 52653
319-523-8319

Lake Odessa, an old Mississippi River oxbow, is another of the state's controlled waterfowl hunting areas. Blinds are assigned by drawing, and a $2 daily use fee (or $25 season ticket) is also required.

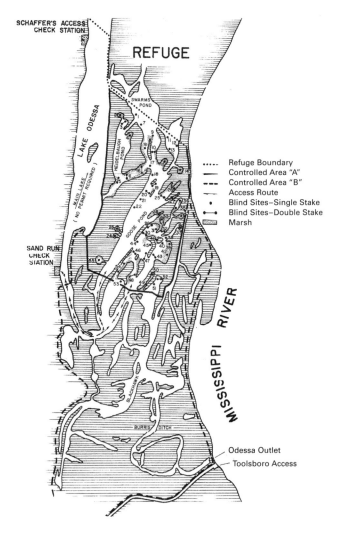

VOLGA RECREATION AREA

5,400 acres
Iowa Department of Natural Resources
10225 Ivy Road
Fayette, IA 52142
319-425-4161

The Volga Area has very good wild turkey, ruffed grouse, and woodcock hunting in the timber, and fair pheasant hunting in the upland habitat, which is mostly located around the area's perimeter. Road access on the area is very limited. However, a good network of horseback trails will permit an energetic hunter to reach its most remote corners.

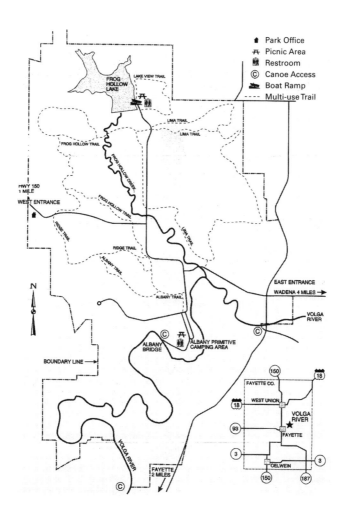

BRUSHY CREEK RECREATION AREA

6,700 acres
Iowa Department of Natural Resources
3175 290th Street
Lehigh, IA 50557
515-543-8298

Brushy Creek, containing one of the larger stands of timber in this region of the state, has good numbers of wild turkeys. Woodcock also use Brushy on their southward migration. There are some decent pheasant hunting opportunities in the upland habitat, mostly around the area's perimeter.

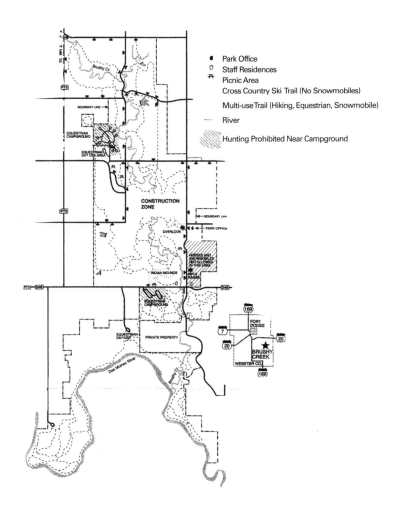

Iowa Public Hunting Areas by County

Area	Game	Description	Directions
Adair County			
Adair	T	350 A; ½ timber, ½ upland	2.5 mi W of Fontanelle on Hwy 92
Meadow Lake	W, P	320 A; ¼ lake, ¾ upland	6 mi N of Greenfield on Hwy 25, .75 mi E on 180th St
Adams			
Lake Icaria*	W, P	1,945 A; ⅓ lake, ⅔ upland	4.5 mi N of Corning on Hwy 148, .5 mi E on Hwy 951
Allamakee			
Blackhawk Point	T, G	308 A; ¾ timber, ¼ upland	1.7 mi S of New Albin on Hwy 26
Clear Creek	T	438 A; ¾ timber, ¼ upland	11.4 mi N of Waukon on Hwy 76, 5.8 mi E on A26, .8 mi N on X6A, E on gravel road
Fish Farm Mounds	T, G	576 A; timber	3 mi S of New Albin on Hwy 26
French Creek	T, G	1,338 A; ¾ timber, ¼ upland	4.5 mi NE of Waukon on Hwy 9, 7.6 mi N on X20, 1.4 mi SE on X6A
Kains Lake	W	200A; ½ marsh, ½ bottom timber	4 mi S of New Albin on Hwy 26
Lansing	T, G	1,955 A; ¾ timber, ¼ upland	3 mi N of Lansing on Hwy 26, .3 mi W on gravel road
New Albin Big Lake	W	200 A; ¾ lake, ¼ marsh	2 mi SE of New Albin

Key: T = Turkey; P = Pheasant; G = Grouse; W = Waterfowl; Q = Quail.
* Indicates portions of the area established as a wildlife refuge. Where posted, there is no trespassing allowed between September 10 to December 25 of each year.
† Indicates a natural lake established as an open water refuge. Hunting is restricted to a zone extending 50 yards into the lake from the shoreline, rooted vegetation or islands. Beyond this zone is a wildlife refuge.

Area	Game	Description	Directions
Pine Creek	T, G	626 A; ¾ timber, ¼ upland	1.4 mi S of Highlandville on A24, 3.5 mi E on A26, 2 mi S on W60
Pool Slough	W	555 A; floodplain marsh	East side of New Albin
Waukon Jct Access	W	203 A; floodplain marsh	Waukon Junction
Yellow River State Forest	T, G	160 A; timber	2 mi N, 3.5 mi W of Marquette
Luster Hts. Unit	T, G	712 A; timber	1 mi S of Waukon Jct. on Hwy 364
Mud Hen Unit	W	196 A; river timber	East of Waukon Jct
North 80 Unit	T, G	80 A; timber	3 mi W of Harper's Ferry
Paint Creek Unit	T, G	4,568 A; timber	4.8 mi SW of Harper's Ferry on B25
Paint Rock Unit	T, G	714 A; timber	1 mi S of Harper's Ferry, Hwy 364
Waukon Junction	T	195 A; timber	North edge of Waukon Jct
Yellow River Unit	T, G	1,062 A; timber	5 mi NW of Marquette
Appanoose			
Rathbun*	W, P, Q	15,970 A; ¼ lake, ¼ timber, ½ upland	6 mi N of Plano on Hwy 142
Stephens Forest (Unionville Unit)	T	2,657 A; timber	1 mi N of Unionville on T61
Benton			
Dudgeon Lake	W, P	1,735 A; ¼ upland, ¼ marsh, ½ timber	.5 mi N of Vinton on Hwy 150
Minne Estema	W	63 A; ¼ marsh, ¼ timber	4 mi N of Vinton on Hwy 150, 2.75 mi N on 24th Ave
Red Fox	W, P	196 A; ¼ marsh, ¼ timber, ½ upland	4 mi N of Vinton on Hwy 150, 1.25 mi W on 55th St
Black Hawk			
Falls Access	T	269 A; timber	2 mi NW of Cedar Falls on Union Road

Area		Size / Type	Location
Boone			
Harrier Marsh	W, P	385 A; ¼ marsh, ¾ grassland	1 mi S of Ogden on Hwy 169, .5 mi E on 230th St
Holst Forest	T	313 A; forest	.5 mi S of Fraser on Kale Rd, .5 mi NW on 168th Lane
McCoy	T	329 A; ¾ timber, ¼ upland	2 mi N of Luther on Hwy 17, 3.5 mi W on E52, .5 mi S on P Ave, 1 mi W on 255th St
Saylorville	T, W	10,904 A; ½ timber, ¼ upland, ¼ reservoir	Des Moines River Valley from Hwy 17 in Polk Co. N to Fraser in Boone Co.
Bremer			
Aldo Leopold Wetland	W, P	927 A; marsh, upland	3 mi E of Readlyn on Hwy 3, 2.25 mi S on Timber Rd, .5 mi E on 252nd St
Sweet Marsh*	W	2,267 A; ½ marsh, ¼ timber, ¼ upland	1.5 mi E of Tripoli on 170th St, 3 mi NE of Tripoli on Hwy 93, 1 mi S on Quail Rd; OR 4 mi NE of Tripoli on Hwy 93, 1 mi S on Reed Rd
Buchanan			
Troy Mills	W	324 A; ½ timber, ¼ marsh, ¼ upland	2 mi N of Walker on W35, 1 mi E on 330th St, .5 mi N on Quonset Ave, 1.5 mi E on 325th St.
Buena Vista			
Grau Wildlife Area	P, W	64 A; ⅒ marsh, ⁹⁄₁₀ upland	10 mi E of Storm Lake on County Rd C49
Little Storm Lake	W, P	312 A; ⅔ marsh, ⅓ upland	West edge of Storm Lake on Hwy 110
Pickerel Lake	W	176 A; lake	3 mi E of Marathon on Hwy 10, 4 mi N on 180th Ave
Storm Lake†	W	3,367 A; lake and access	South edge of Storm Lake
Butler			
Big Marsh*	W, P	209 A; ⅓ each marsh, timber, upland	6 mi N of Parkersburg on Hwy 14
Calhoun			
North Twin Lake†	W	574 A; lake	5 mi N or Rockwell City on N57

Area	Game	Description	Directions
South Twin Lake*	W	600 A; lake	1 mi W of Rockwell City on Hwy 20, 4 mi N on Hwy 4, .5 mi E on 230th St
Carroll			
Towhead Lake	P	195 A; upland	5 mi S of Fonda on N28, 2 mi E on D15
Cedar			
Artesian Lake	W	42 A; ⅔ marsh, ⅓ timber	1.5 mi S of Lanesboro on Walnut Ave, 1.5 mi E on Voyager Ave
Mink Run	G	75 A; ⅔ upland, ⅓ timber	.5 mi E of Lisbon on Hwy 30, 2.25 mi S on Adams Ave, .25 mi E on 145th St
Cerro Gordo			
Clear Lake†	W	3,643 A; lake	South side of Clear Lake
McIntosh	W, P	219 A; ⅒ timber, ⅒ marsh, 8/10 upland	Northeast corner of Ventura on N Shore Drive
Sandpiper Hills	W, P	125 A; ⅒ marsh, 9/10 upland	8 mi N of Ventura on S14, .25 mi W on B14
Union Hills	W, P	751 A; ⅕ marsh, ⅘ upland	4 mi N of Thornton on Hwy 107, 2 mi W on B55
Ventura Marsh	W, P	782 A; ½ marsh, ½ upland	South edge of Ventura on S13
Wild Goose Marsh	W, P	1600 A; ⅓ marsh, ⅔ upland	4 mi N of Ventura on S14, .25 mi E on 290th St
Clay			
Dan Green Slough	W, P	490 A; ⅔ marsh, ⅓ upland	3 mi N of Spencer on Hwy 71, 7 mi E on B17
Deweys Pasture Wetland Complex*	W, P	5,874 A; 2/5 lakes, 2/5 marsh, 1/5 upland	.5 mi W of Ruthven on Hwy 18, 4 mi N on N18
Dry Mud Lake	P	252 A; upland	4 mi E of Webb on B63, 1 mi S on 330th Ave
Elk Lake Complex	W, P	522 A; ½ lake, ¼ marsh, ¼ upland	2 mi W of Ruthven on Hwy 18, 3 mi S on 330th Ave
Fen Valley	P	160 A; upland	1 mi E of Gillett Grove on M54

Name	Type	Size/Habitat	Location
Hawk Valley	T, W	330 A; ¼ marsh, ¼ timber, ½ upland	4 mi E of Spencer on Hwy 18
Little Sioux	T	213 A; river access, timber	7 mi S of Spencer on Hwy 17, 5 mi E on 420th St
Ocheyedan	P	316 A; ½ timber, ¼ marsh, ¼ upland	5 mi W of Spencer on W 4th St
Reiter	P	54 A; timber	1 mi N of Spencer on 4th Ave
Tuttle Marsh	P	137 A; ⅓ marsh, ⅔ upland	1 mi N of Spencer on Hwy 71, 6 mi W on Hwy 18, 2 mi N on 160th Ave
Clayton			
Bloody Run	T, G	526 A; timber	.5 mi W of Marquette on Hwy 18, 1 mi W on 128th St (limited access via county, private property)
Joy Springs	T	71 A; timber	2 mi W of Strawberry Point on Hwy 3, 1 mi S on Alpha Ave (access by crossing County Conservation Board property)
Mosey Glen	T	80 A; timber	1.5 mi W of Edgewood on Hwy 3, 4 mi N on Eagle Ave
Sny Magill/ North Cedar	T, G	1,635 A; timber	6 mi S of McGregor on X56, 3 mi NW on Keystone Rd
Clinton			
Barber Creek	T, W	600 A; ¾ timber, ¼ crop, upland	2 mi W of DeWitt on Hwy 30, S on 260th Ave, .5 mi W on 255th St, 1 mi S on 252nd Ave, .5 mi W on 270th St, 1 mi S on 247th Ave
Goose Lake	W, P	936 A; ¾ marsh, ¼ timber, upland	1 mi W of Goose Lake on Hwy 136
Syracuse	D, W	695 A; ¾ timber, ¼ upland	1.5 mi W of Calamus on Hwy 30, .5 mi NW on old Hwy 30 (235th St)
Wapsi	T, W	86 A; ½ grass, ½ timber, lake	1 mi S of DeWitt on old Hwy 61 (285th Ave), 1 mi W on 270th St, 1.5 mi S on 270th Ave

Area	Game	Description	Directions
Crawford			
Schrader	P	190 A; upland	2 mi E of Vail on Hwy 30, 3 mi N on 360th St
Dallas			
Beaver Lake	P	380 A; 1/4 lake, 3/4 upland	1.75 mi N of Dexter on gravel road
Pleasant Valley	T	145 A; timber	6 mi W of Adel on Hwy 6, 1 mi S on Panther Creek Rd, .5 mi W on 315th St, 1 mi S on Indian Trail
Saylorville	T, W	10,904 A; 1/2 timber, 1/4 upland, 1/4 reservoir	Des Moines River Valley, Hwy 17 in Polk Co. north to Fraser in Boone Co. *(portions in Boone and Polk Counties)*
Davis			
Eldon	T, Q	1,312 A; 1/4 upland, 3/4 timber	4 mi E of Floris on J15, 1 mi N
Soap Creek	T, Q	519 A; timber	4 mi S of Blakesburg on T61, 2 mi SE
Stephens State Forest	T	1,879 A; timber	3 mi NE of Unionville on T61A; 2 mi E
Decatur			
Dekalb	T, Q	1,995 A; 3/4 timber, 1/4 upland	5.5 mi W of Grand River on J20, .75 mi N on gravel road
Little River	W, P, Q	2,000 A; 1/3 lake, 2/3 upland	1 mi W of Leon on Hwy 2, 1 mi N on blacktop road
Sand Creek	T, Q, P	2,580 A; 3/4 timber, 1/4 upland	3 mi N of Grand River on R15, 1 mi W on gravel road
Delaware			
Backbone State Forest	T	186 A; timber	1 mi S of Strawberry Point on Hwy 3, 1 mi W and 1 mi S on Hwy 410
Ram Hollow	T, G	480 A; timber	2 mi E of Colesburg on Voyager Rd
Des Moines			
Augusta	T	111 A; 3/4 timber, 1/4 upland	North edge of Augusta on Hwy 394
Blackhawk Bottoms	W	587 A; 3/5 timber, 1/5 marsh, 1/5 upland	4 mi S of Burlington on Hwy 61, .75 mi NE on X62, .25 mi SE on Spring Lake Rd

Dickinson

Area	Type	Description	Location
Cayler Prairie	P	160 A; virgin prairie	6 mi W of Spirit Lake on Hwy 9, 2 mi S on 170th Ave
Center Lake Complex	W, P	649 A; lake bordered by timber, grass, marshes	1 mi W of Spirit Lake on Hwy 9, .5 mi W on 155th St, .5 mi S on 220th Ave
Cory Marsh	W, P	121 A; ¼ marsh, ¾ upland	2 mi E of Lake Park on Hwy 9, 2 mi N on 150th Ave
Diamond Lake	W, P	598 A; shallow lake, bordered by timber, grass	3 mi W of Spirit Lake on Hwy 9, 3 mi N on Hwy 86
Dugout Creek	W, P	638 A; ¼ marsh, ¾ upland	1 mi E of Lake Park on Hwy 9, 1 mi S on 140th Ave
East Okoboji Lake†	W	1,873 A; lake	East edge of Spirit Lake on Hwy 9
East Okoboji Slough	W, P	20 A; marsh	.5 mi N of Spirit Lake on Hwy 276
Garlock Slough Complex	P, W	426 A; ½ marsh, ½ upland prairie	1 mi N of Milford on Hwy 71, 1.5 mi W on Hwy 86
Hale's Slough	W, P	85 A; marsh (borders Spirit Lake)	2 mi N of Orleans on Hwy 327/M56
Jemmerson Slough Complex	W, P	855 A; ⅓ marsh, ⅔ upland	1 mi NW of Spirit Lake on Hwy , .5 mi E on 153rd St
Kettleson Hogsback Complex*	W, P	1,681 A; marsh, upland, timber, prairie	3 mi N of Spirit Lake on Hwy 276, then 1 mi west on 125th St (includes Hottes, Marble, McBreen Marsh, Grovers, Sunken Lakes)
Korey Halbur	W, P	82 A; ⅓ marsh, ⅔ upland	2 mi E of Milford on A34, 1.5 mi N on 240th St
Little Spirit Lake	W	214 A; lake	5 mi N of Spirit Lake on Hwy 276
Lower Gar Lake	W, P	317 A; lake, upland	1 mi N of Milford on Hwy 71, 1 mi E on 210th St
Minnewashta Lake†	W	122 A; lake	East edge Arnolds Park on Hwy 71
Silver Lake†	W	1,113 A; lake bordered by timber	1 mi W of Lake Park on Hwy 9
Spirit Lake†	W	5,684 A; lake	North edge Orleans on Hwy 276
Spring Run Wetland Complex	W, P	2,522 A; ⅓ lake/marsh, ⅔ upland	3 mi E of Spirit Lake on Hwy 9, 2.5 mi S on 280th Ave (includes Lily, Pleasant, and Prairie Lakes)

Area	Game	Description	Directions
Swan Lake/ Christopherson Slough Complex	W, P	930 A; ⅔ shallow lake marsh, ⅓ upland grass, timber	2 mi N of Superior on N16
Trickle Slough	W, P	19 A; marsh, upland	4 mi NE of Orleans on Hwy 327/M56, .5 mi W on 100th St
Twin Forks	P	70 A; river bottom timber, grassland	6 mi W of Spirit Lake on Hwy 9, 1 mi S on 170th Ave
Welch Lake	W	75 A; shallow lake	2.5 mi W of Spirit Lake on Hwy 9, 2 mi N on Hwy 86, .5 mi E on 130th St
West Okoboji Lake†	W	3,949 A; lake	West edge of Arnolds Park on Hwy 71
Yager Slough	W, P	56 A; marsh	3 mi S on M34
Dubuque			
White Pine Hollow	T, G	903 A; ⁹⁄₁₀ timber, ¹⁄₁₀ upland	2 mi W of Luxemburg on Hwy 3, 1.5 mi N on White Pine Lane
Emmet			
Anderson Prairie	P	360 A; ¾ upland grassland, ⅓ timber and native prairie	1 mi W of Estherville on Hwy 9, 2 mi N on 360th Ave
Birge Lake	P	137 A; drained lakebed, ¾ upland, ¼ timber	7 mi W of Armstrong on Hwy 9, 6 mi N on N52, 3 mi W on A13
Burr Oak Lake	W, P	321 A; ¼ marsh, ½ upland, ¼ timber	3 mi E of Wallingford on A34, 2 mi S on 430th Ave
Cheever Lake	W, P	515 A; ½ marsh, ¼ upland, ¼ timber	1 mi S of Estherville on Hwy 4, 3 mi W on 190th St
Eagle Lake	W, P	312 A; ¾ marsh, ¼ timber and upland	5 mi N of Estherville on Hwy 4, .5 mi W on 110th St

Area	Access	Size / Habitat	Directions
East Des Moines River Access	P, T	45 A; river access, timber	2 mi S of Armstrong on Hwy 15, 1.5 mi E on 200th St
East Swan Lake	P	724 A; drained lakebed, ¾ upland, ¼ timber	6 mi W of Armstrong on Hwy 9, 1.5 mi S on 500th Ave
Four Mile Lake	W, P	691 A; ½ marsh, ½ upland	3 mi W of Estherville on Hwy 9, 1.5 mi S on 340th Ave
Grass Lake	P	171 A; drained lakebed, ¼ timber, ¾ upland	2 mi E of Estherville on Hwy 9, 5 mi N on N32, 1 mi E on 120th St
Ingham-High Wetland Complex*†	W, P	397 A; ⅔ lake marsh, ⅓ timber, uplands	5 mi E of Wallingford on A 34
Iowa Lake	W, P	526 A; ½ shallow lake, ½ upland timber	7 mi N of Armstrong on Hwy 15, .5 mi W on 110th St
Ryan Lake	P	360 A; drained lakebed, ½ timber, ½ upland	4 mi E of Estherville on Hwy 9, 2.5 mi S on 430th Ave
Tuttle Lake Wetland Complex†	W, P	1,378 A; ⅔ shallow lake/marsh, ⅓ upland, prairie, timber	7 mi W of Armstrong on Hwy 9, 6 mi N on N52, 2 mi E on A13
Twelve Mile Lake	W, P	443 A; ⅔ shallow lake/marsh, ⅓ upland	2 mi S of Wallingford on Hwy 4, 4 mi W on 250th St
West Swan Lake	W, P	1,345 A; ¾ shallow lake/marsh, ¼ upland timber	4.5 mi E of Estherville on Hwy 9, 4 mi S on N40, 1.5 mi E on A33, .5 mi N on 200th St
Fayette			
Grannis Creek	T	179 A; timber	2.5 mi SE of Fayette on C 24, 1.5 mi E on Grannis Rd
Volga Recreation	T, P	5,400 A; ¾ timber, ¼ upland	3.5 mi S of West Union on Hwy 150, 1 mi E on 175th St
Floyd			
Idewilde	T	254 A; timber	3 mi N of Floyd on Hwy 218, 1 mi W on 130th St, 2.5 mi N of Floyd on Quarry Rd
Restoration Marsh	W, P	117 A; ⅓ marsh, ⅔ upland	3 mi N of Floyd on Hwy 218, 1 mi E on 130th St, 1.5 mi N on Quail Ave

Area	Game	Description	Directions
Franklin			
Beeds Lake	W, P	30 A; 1/3 marsh, 1/3 timber, 1/3 upland	1 mi N of Hampton on Hwy 65, 1.5 mi W on C31
Whitetail Flats	W, P	391 A; 1/4 marsh, 1/4 timber, 1/2 upland	2 mi S of Dows on S13, .5 mi S on gravel (Apricot)
Fremont			
Bartlett Lake	W, P	57 A; 2/3 lake, 1/3 upland	.5 mi W of Bartlett on J10, .25 mi N on L31
Forney Lake*	W, P	1,128 A; 1/2 marsh, 1/2 upland	2 mi N of Thurman on L44, .5 mi W
Green Hollow	T	341 A; 3/4 timber, 1/4 upland	.75 mi NE of Thurman on J18, 1.75 mi N
Lake Shawtee	P, Q	680 A; upland	3 mi E of Randolph on Hwy 184, 1.5 mi S
McPaul	W, P	166 A; 1/4 lake, 3/4 upland	2 mi N of Thurman on L44, 2 mi W
O.S. Wing	T	140 A; 1/2 timber, 1/2 upland	1.5 mi SE of Hamburg on Hwy 275
Percival	P, W	80 A; 1/3 lake, 2/3 upland	.5 mi W of Percival on J26, 1.25 mi N on L31
Riverton*	W, P	2,720 A; 1/2 marsh, 1/2 upland	2 mi N of Riverton on L68
Scott	W	80 A; 1/3 lake, 2/3 timber	2 mi S of Bartlett on L31
Waubonsie Access	W	52 A; 1/2 lake, 1/2 timber	1 mi E of Missouri River on Hwy 2
Greene			
Dunbar Slough*	W, P	1,350 A; 1/2 marsh, 1/2 upland	3 mi S of Scranton on Hwy 25, 3 mi W on 270th St, .5 mi N on "B" Ave
Finn Pond	W, P	56 A; 1/2 marsh, 1/2 upland	2 mi W of Jefferson on Hwy 30
Goose Lake	W	456 A; marsh	5 mi N of Jefferson on Hwy 4, 1 mi W on 170th St
Snake Creek	W, P	400 A; 1/4 marsh, 3/4 upland	1.5 mi N of Rippey on P46
Guthrie			
Bays Branch*	W, P, Q	842 A; 1/4 lake, 3/4 upland	2 mi N of Panora on Hwy 4, 2.5 mi E on 190th St
Elk Grove	T	1,600 A; timber	7.5 mi S of Coon Rapids on N46, .5 mi E on 165th St

Area	Type	Size/Description	Location
Lakin Slough	W, P	350 A; ¾ marsh, ¼ upland	1.5 mi E of Yale on F25 (160th Rd)
Lennon Mills	T	555 A; timber	.5 mi SW of Panora on Soldier Trail, 1 mi S on Toy Lane
Marlowe Ray	T	187 A; timber	6 mi S of Panora on P28, .5 mi E on 268th St, 1 mi N on Winding Trace
McCord Pond	W, P	112 A; ½ marsh, ½ upland	2.5 mi W of Bayard on 141, .5 mi S on Hickory Ave
Hamilton			
Boone Forks	T, P	3,210 A; ¾ timber, ¼ upland, river access	4 mi N of Stratford on R21, .5 mi W on 318th St
Little Wall Lake	W	273 A; shallow lake	2 mi S of Jewell on Hwy 69
Tunnel Mill	T	115 A; timber	7 mi S of Webster City on R27
Hancock			
Crystal Hills	W, P	320 A; ⅓ marsh, ⅔ upland	2 mi E of Crystal Lake on 320th St
Crystal Lake	W, P	390 A; ⅓ upland, ⅔ lake	North edge of town of Crystal Lake
Eagle Flats	W, P	406 A; ½ marsh, ½ upland	3mi E of Britt on Hwy 18, 3.5 mi N on Lake Ave
Eagle Lake	W,P	919 A; marsh	6.5 mi W of Garner on Hwy 18, 1.5 mi N on Lake Ave
Eagle Lake Flats	P, W	417 A; ⅓ marsh, ⅔ upland	6.5 mi W of Garner on Hwy 18, 3.5 mi N on Lake Ave
East Twin Lake	W, P	493 A; ⅔ marsh, ⅓ timber/grassland	4 mi E of Kanawha on 120th St
Eight Mile Pits	P	202 A; ⅔ upland, ⅓ pits	5.5 mi W of Forest City on B14
Gabrielson	T, P, W	592A; ⅔ marshy timber, ⅓ upland	3.5 mi E of Forest City on B14
Goodell	T	71 A; timber	3 mi E of Goodell on B63, 1 mi N on R66
Meredith Marsh	W, P	314 A; ⅓ marsh, ⅔ upland	3 mi W of Forest City on B14
Schuldt Wildlife Area	P	80 A; upland	5 mi S of Garner on Hwy 69, .25 mi W on 180th St

Area	Game	Description	Directions
Harrison			
California Bend Wildlife Area	W, Q	420 A; ¼ marsh, ¾ willow/ cottonwood	Access only by river
Deer Island Wildlife Area	Q, P	710 A; ⅕ marsh, ⅘ timber	5 mi S of Blencoe on K45, 1 mi W on 120th St
Loess Hills State Forest	T, Q	3,472 A; ¾ timber, ¼ upland	*(maps available at headquarters in Pisgah)*
Noble's Lake	W, P, Q	232 A; ½ marsh, ½ upland	3 mi W of I-29 Missouri Valley Exit on Hwy 30, 3 mi S on Grover Ave
Rand Bar	Q, W	64 A; ¾ willow/cottonwood, ¼ marsh	Access only by river
Round Lake Wildlife Area	W, P	447 A; ½ marsh, ¼ upland, ¼ willow/cottonwood	North of Mondamin; 2 mi N of Hwy 127 on K45
Soldier Bend Wildlife Area	W, Q	279 A; ¾ timber, ¼ marsh	Southwest of Mondamin; .25 mi W of I-29 on Hwy 27, 5.1 mi S on Cody Ave, 2 mi W on Boone Trail
St. Johns Wildlife Area	W, P	87 A; ½ marsh, ½ willow/ cottonwood	North of Missouri Valley; N on I-29 on E side of rest area
Tyson Bend Wildlife Area	W, Q	780 A; ¼ marsh, ¾ timber	West of Modale; .5 mi S of I-29 on K45, 4 mi W on 270th
Howard			
Elma	P, W	155 A; timber, floodplain	4.3 mi W of Elma on B17
Hayden Prairie	P	240 A; native prairie	4.9 mi W of Lime Springs on A23
Turkey River Access	T	410 A; ½ timber, ½ upland	1 mi S of Cresco on V-58, .6 mi E on Kings Rd

Humboldt

Bradgate	W, P, T	124 A; ¾ timber, ¼ upland	2 mi E of Gilmore City on Hwy 3, 3 mi N on Delaware Ave, .5 mi W on C18
Ottosen Potholes	W, P	106 A; ½ marsh, ½ grassland	4 mi N of Humboldt on Hwy 169, 5 mi W on C26, 1.5 mi N on Georgia Ave, 1 mi W on 155th St
Willows Access	W, P	81 A; bottomland timber, river accesses	West edge of Bradgate, S of P19

Iowa

Hwy 21 Access	P	21 A; ½ upland, ¼ timber, ¼ marsh	1.5 mi S of Belle Plaine on Hwy 21
Randolph	T	399 A; ¾ timber, ¼ upland	3 mi S of Belle Plaine on Hwy 21, 2 mi E on Hwy 212

Jackson

Big Mill	T, G	739 A; ½ timber, ¼ upland, ¼ wetland	5 mi W of Bellevue on D57
Green Island*	W, T	3,722 A; ½ marsh, ¼ timber, ¼ upland	6 mi N of Sabula on Hwy 52, right on Green Island Rd
Little Mill	T	43 A; ¾ timber, ¼ upland	2 mi W of Bellevue on D61, 2 mi S on 216th

Jasper

Colfax	W	350 A; ¼ marsh, ¾ timber	I-80 exit 155 (Colfax), .25 mi S, 1 mi E on Orchard Ave
Rock Creek Marsh	P, W	444 A; ½ upland, ¼ timber, ¼ marsh	3 mi N of Kellogg on Hwy 224, 3 mi E on F27

Johnson

Hawkeye Wildlife Area*	W, P	13,511 A; ¼ timber, ¼ upland, ¼ lake	2 mi N of North Liberty on Hwy 965, 1.5 mi W on Swan Lake Rd, .75 mi E of Swisher on F12, 2.5 mi S on Hwy 965, .5 mi W on Amana Rd
Redbird Farm	P, T	500 A; ¼ upland, ¾ timber	4 mi SW of Iowa City on Hwy 1, 3.5 mi W on Black Diamond Rd

232 — WINGSHOOTER'S GUIDE TO IOWA

Area	Game	Description	Directions
Swan Lake	W	44 A; 1/3 lake, 2/3 marsh	2 mi N of North Liberty on Hwy 965, 2.5 mi W on Swan Lake Rd
Jones			
Indian Bluffs	T	410 A; 3/4 timber, 1/4 upland	1 mi W of Cascade, 5 mi S on Butterfield Rd
Muskrat Slough*	W, P, Q	365 A; 3/4 marsh, 1/4 upland	.5 mi S of Olin on Hwy 38, 3.5 mi W on 35th St, .25 N on 170th Ave
Pictured Rocks	T	1,138 A; 3/4 timber, 1/4 river	3 mi SE of Monticello on Hwy 38, 1 mi E on 190th St
Keokuk			
Pool	P, Q, T	60 A; 1/2 upland, 1/2 timber	2 mi W of Richland on Hwy 78
Rubio Access	T	296 A; timber (borders Skunk River)	2 mi N of Richland on W15, 2 mi E on G67, 1 mi N on gravel road
Skunk River	T	425 A; timber (borders Skunk River)	4 mi N of Richland on W15
South Skunk River Access	T, Q, P	426 A; 1/4 upland, 3/4 timber	2 mi E, 3 mi N of Martinsburg on Hwy 149, 2 mi E, 2 mi N on gravel road
Kossuth			
Goose Lake	W, P	224 A; 1/2 shallow lake/marsh, 1/2 timber upland	7 mi N of Armstrong on Hwy 15, 2 mi E on A16
Iowa Lake Marsh	W, P	325 A; 1/2 marsh, 1/2 upland	7 mi N of Armstrong on Hwy 15, .75 mi E on A16
State Line Marsh	W, P	277 A; 1/2 marsh, 1/2 upland	7 mi N of Armstrong on Hwy 15, 4 mi E on A16
Lee			
Shimek State Forest Units			
Donnellson	T	1,223 A; forest	5 mi W of Donnellson on Hwy 2
Farmington	T	2,098 A; forest	1 mi NE of Farmington on J56
Lick Creek	T	2,846 A; forest	3 mi E of Farmington on Hwy 2

Linn

Chain-O-Lakes	W, P	612 A; 1/4 upland, 1/4 marsh, 1/2 timber	1 mi E of Palo on Blairs Ferry Rd

Louisa

Cone Marsh	W, P	701 A; 1/2 marsh, 1/4 upland, 1/4 timber	3 mi W of Conesville on 220th St, 1 mi N on "V" Ave
Klum Lake	W, T	650 A; 2/3 timber, 1/3 marsh	3 mi N of Wapello on Hwy 61, 3 mi E on G56, 1 mi N on X61
Lake Odessa	W, T	3,828 A; 1/2 timber, 1/4 lake, 1/4 marsh	.5 mi E of Wapello on Hwy 99, 3.5 mi NE on G62, .25 mi N on X61

Lucas

Broadhead Woods	T	45 A; upland	2 mi W of Chariton on Hwy 34, 2 mi N on S23, 2 mi W on gravel road, .5 mi N on gravel road
Browns Slough	T, Q	155 A; 2/3 timber, 1/3 upland	4.5 mi S of Russell on S 56, 1 mi E and 1 mi S on gravel road
Colyn*	W, P, Q	770 A; 1/3 marsh, 1/3 timber, 1/3 upland	4.5 mi S of Russell on S56, .75 mi W and .5 mi S on gravel road
Rathbun	W, P, Q	15,970 A; 1/4 lake, 1/4 timber, 1/2 upland	6 mi S of Russell on S 56
Stephens State Forest Units			
Cedar Creek	T	1,377 A; timber	7 mi E of Chariton on H32, 1.5 mi N on gravel road
Chariton	T	1,395 A; timber	8 mi E of Chariton on Hwy 34, 6 mi N on gravel road
Lucas	T	991 A; timber	.5 mi W of Lucas on Hwy 34, 1 mi S on gravel road
Thousand Acre	T	1,344 A; timber	10 mi E of Chariton on Hwy 34, 7 mi N on gravel road
Whitebreast	T	4,048 A; timber	2 mi S of Lucas on Hwy 65, 2 mi W on gravel road

Area	Game	Description	Directions
Lyon			
Big Sioux River			
Kroger	T	434 A; timber, uplands, river	4 mi W of Inwood on Hwy 18
Nelson	T	244 A; timber, uplands	2 mi N of Inwood on Hwy 182, 4 mi W on 220th St
Olson	T	80 A; timber, uplands	4 mi N of Inwood on Hwy 182, 4.5 mi W on 200th St
Gitchie Manitou	P	91A; timber, prairie, river	5 mi NW of Larchwood on Hwy 9, 4.5 mi W on 100th St
Madison			
Badger Creek	P, Q, W	1,150 A; ¼ lake, ¾ upland	1 mi W of Booneville on F90, 3 mi S on Tabor Rd
Mahaska			
Hawthorn	P	1,682 A; ½ upland/ ½ timber	1 mi S of Barnes City on V13
Hull	P, Q	575 A; upland	4 mi W of Oskaloosa on SH92
Marion			
Red Rock*	W, P	25,500 A; ¼ marsh and lake, ¼ timber, ½ upland	North Access: 3.5 mi S of Monroe on Hwy 14, 7 mi W on Carpenter St; South Access: 4 mi N of Pleasantville on 40th Ave
Marshall			
Hendrickson Marsh	P, W	776 A; ⅔ upland, ⅓ marsh/lake	2.5 mi W of Rhodes on E63
Mills			
Folsom Lake	W	100 A; ½ lake, ½ marsh	3 mi W of Glenwood on Hwy 34, 2 mi N on L31, .5 mi W
Keg Lake	P, W	104 A; ½ marsh, ½ upland	3 mi SW of Glenwood on Hwy 385, 1 mi S on L31, .25 mi E
Willow Slough	W, P	599 A; ⅔ marsh, ⅓ timber	1 mi E of Hastings on Hwy 34, 4 mi N on M16, .25 mi E, .6 mi N

Mitchell

Area	Codes	Characteristics	Directions
Wapsie River Access	T, P	113 A; ¾ timber, ¼ grassland	2 mi N of McIntire on Walnut Ave, 2 mi W on 485th St

Monona

Area	Codes	Characteristics	Directions
Badger Lake*	W, P	1,027 A; ⅓ marsh, ⅔ upland	2 mi W of I-29 Whiting Exit on K42
Blackbird/Ivy Island	Q, P, W	722 A; ⅔ bottomland timber, ⅓ marsh	Public access only from the river
Blue Lake	W, Q, P	868 A; ¾ marsh, ¼ upland	2 mi W of I-29 Onawa Exit, .5 mi N on Hwy 324, 1 mi W on 225th St
Loess Hills	T, Q	2,742 A	1 mi W of Castana on L20, 3 mi N on Oak Rd
Loess Hills State Forest	T, Q, P	3,081 A; ¾ timber, ¼ prairie	9 mi E of Blencoe on Hwy E60
Louisville Bend	Q, P, T	987 A; ½ marsh, ¼ timber, ¼ upland	W of I-29 Blencoe Exit, 1 mi N on Hazel Ave, 1.5 mi W on 284th St
Middle Decatur	W, P, Q	338 A; ¾ marsh, ¼ shallow lake	2 mi W of I-29 Onawa Exit, 1.25 mi S on Cherry Ave, W on 243rd St
Upper Decatur	Q, W	534 A; ⅔ timber, ⅓ marsh	6 mi W of Onawa I-29 Exit on Hwy 175

Monroe

Area	Codes	Characteristics	Directions
Cottonwood Pits	P	55 A; ⅓ lake, ⅔ upland	.5 mi S of Albia on Hwy 5, .5 mi E, 1 mi E, .5 mi S on gravel road
LaHart	T, Q	400 A; ½ timber, ½ upland	1 mi S of Lovilia on Hwy 5, 3 mi SW on T19
Miami Lake	T, Q	766 A; ¼ lake, ¼ upland, ½ timber	2 mi N of Albia on Hwy 137, 1.5 mi W on H33, 2 mi N on T31, .5 mi W and 1.5 mi N on gravel road
Tyrone	T	1,020 A; ¼ upland, ¾ timber	7 mi S of Albia on Hwy 34, 2 mi S on T19, 1 mi E on gravel road

Area	Game	Description	Directions
Muscatine			
Red Cedar	T, W	773 A; ⅘ timber, ⅕ upland/marsh	1.25 mi E of Nichols on Hwy 22, 1.25 mi S on Elder Ave, .5 mi E on 195th St
Wise Slough	W	1,707 A; ⅘ timber, ⅕ marsh	2.5 mi E of Atalissa on Hwy 6
O'Brien			
Waterman Creek	W, P	145 A; stream, uplands	6 mi S of Hartley on M12, 1 mi E on 390th St
Waterman Prairie	P, T	532 A; prairie, timber, stream	3.5 mi SE of Sutherland on Hwy 10, 2 mi N on Wilson Ave
Osceola			
Iowa Lake	W	114 A; shallow lake, marsh	1 mi W of Harris on Hwy 9, 5 mi N on White Ave
Rush Lake	W, P	336 A; shallow lake, marsh	2 mi E of Ocheyedan on Hwy 9
Palo Alto			
Blue Wing Marsh	W, P	570 A; ⅓ marsh, ⅔ upland	2 mi N of Ruthven on 350th Ave, .5 mi E on 340th St, .5 mi N on 355th Ave
Deweys Pasture Wetland Complex	W, P	5,874 A; ⅖ lakes, ⅖ marsh, ⅕ upland	.5 mi W of Ruthven on Hwy 71, 4 mi N on N18 (Barringer Slough, Trumbull and Round Lakes, DU Marsh)
Fallow Marsh	W, P	242 A; ⅓ marsh, ⅔ upland	3 mi S of Graettinger on Hwy 4, 2 mi W on 320th St
Five Island Lake*	W, P	1,104 A; lake, marsh	North side of Emmetsburg, along W side of N48
Perkins Marsh	W, P	24 A; ½ marsh, ½ upland	3 mi S of Graettinger on Hwy 4, 2 mi W on 320th St
Rush Lake	W, P	522 A; marsh	7 mi N of Laurens on N28, .5 mi W on B63
Silver Lake†	W	684 A; lake	2 mi W of Ayrshire on 420th St
Virgin Lake	P, W	432 A; ¾ lake, ¼ upland	.5 mi W of Ruthven on Hwy 18, 2 mi S on N18, .5 mi E on 380th St

Plymouth			
Dear Creek	P	1,018 A; lake, upland	5 mi N of Sioux City on Hwy 12, 5 mi NE on K18, 1 mi W on Butcher Rd
Pocahontas			
Kalsow Prairie	P	160 A; native prairie	3 mi N of Manson on N56, 1 mi W on 630th St
Leo Shimon Marsh	W, P	345 A; 1/3 marsh, 2/3 upland	1 mi W of Fonda on Hwy7, 2 mi N on 120th Ave
Little Clear Lake	W	187 A; shallow lake, marsh	10 mi W of Pocahontas on Hwy 3
Lizard Lake	W	348 A; 3/4 marsh, 1/4 timber	3 mi W of Gilmore City on Hwy 3, 4 mi S on 320th Ave
Sunken Grove	W, P	371 A; 1/2 marsh, 1/2 timber	2 mi W of Fonda on Hwy 7, 2.5 mi N on 110th Ave
Polk			
Big Creek*	W, P	3,100 A; 1/3 lake, 2/3 upland	1 mi N of Polk City on Hwy 415
Cottonwood	P	60 A; upland	2 mi SW of Bondurant on Hwy 65
Paul Errington Marsh	P, W	193 A; 1/3 marsh, 2/3 uplands	4 mi E of Ankeny on NE 94th Ave, 2 mi N on NE 56th St
Saylorville	T, W	10,940 A; 1/2 timber, 1/4 upland, 1/4 reservoir	Des Moines River Valley, Hwy 17 in Polk Co. N to Fraser in Boone Co.
Pottawattamie			
Wilson Island Recreation Area	T	577 A; timber	4 mi S of Missouri Valley on I-29, 5.5 mi W on Hwy 362
Ringgold			
Fogle Lake	P, W, Q	200 A; 1/4 lake, 3/4 upland	.5 mi W of Diagonal on J23
Mount Ayr Wildlife Area	T, P, Q	1,158 A; 1/2 timber, 1/2 upland	2 mi W of Mount Ayr on Hwy 2/169, 2 mi S on Hwy 169, 2 mi W on T43
Ringgold	Q, P, T	1,200 A; 1/4 timber, 3/4 upland	6 mi E of Mount Ayr on Hwy 2, 8 mi S on P64, 1 mi W on gravel road

Area	Game	Description	Directions
Sac			
Black Hawk Lake†	W	9,252 A; lake	East edge Lake View
Black Hawk Marsh*	W, P	975 A; ½ upland, ¼ marsh, ¼ timber	1.5 mi W of Carnarvon on D59, 1 mi N on M68
Burrow's Pond	P, W	292 A; upland	2 mi W of Nemaha on D15, 1 mi S on Lee Ave
Kiowa Marsh	P, W	578 A; ¼ marsh, ¾ upland	2 mi E of Early on D27
Tomahawk Marsh	W, P	405 A; ½ marsh, ½ upland	2 mi W of Sac City on Hwy 20, 4 mi S on M68
Whitehorse Access	P	206 A; ⅔ timber, ⅓ upland, river access	4 mi E of Lake View on Hwy 71/175, 2 mi E on 330th St, .5 mi on Wadsley Ave, 1 mi E on 335th St
Scott			
Lost Grove Lake	P	1,538 A; ¾ crops/upland, ¼ timber	6 mi N of Davenport on Utica Ridge Rd or 215th Ave
Princeton*	W, T	1,190 A; ¾ wetland, ¼ timber/crops	.5 mi N of Princeton on Hwy 67, 1mi N on 285th Avenue, E on 266th St
Shelby			
Peterson	P, Q	432 A; upland	2 mi S of Manilla on Quince Rd
Sioux			
Big Sioux River-Groth	T	93 A; timber, upland, river	6 mi W of Rock Valley on Hwy 18, 2.5 mi W on 310th St
Story			
Doolittle Prairie	P	26 A; prairie	2 mi S of Story City
Hendrickson Marsh	W, P	776 A; ⅓ marsh, ⅔ upland	2 mi W of Rhodes on E63, .5 mi N on gravel road
Pyle Marsh	P, W	80 A; ½ upland, ½ marsh	2 mi W of Story City on E15, 1 mi N on gravel road, .5 mi W on 400th St

Tama			
Otter Creek Marsh*	W, P, T	3,400 A; ½ marsh, ¼ timber, ¼ upland	1 mi NW of Chelsea on E66
Salt Creek	T	114 A; timber	1 mi E of Vining on "V" Ave
Union Grove	P, W	108 A; ¾ upland, ¼ lake	4 mi S of Gladbrook on T47, 1 mi W on 230th St
West Salt Creek	P	80 A; upland	.5 mi SW of Vining on "T" Ave
Union			
Mitchell Marsh	W, P	160 A; ¼ marsh, ¾ upland	1 mi N of Creston on Hwy 186
Three Mile Lake*	W, P, T	3,100 A; ¼ lake, ¼ timber, ½ upland	3.5 mi N of Afton on P53, 1 mi W on 150th St
Twelve Mile Lake	W, P	1,500 A; ⅓ lake, ⅔ upland	4 mi E of Creston on Hwy 34, .75 mi N
Van Buren			
Lake Sugema*	Q, T	3,618 A; ¾ upland, ¼ timber	4 mi S of Keosauqua through Lacey Keosauqua Park; or 5 mi W of Keosauqua on J40, 1 mi S
Shimek Forest (Keosauqua Unit)	T, Q	898 A; timber	5 mi W of Keosauqua on J40, 1 mi S and .5 mi E
Van Buren	T	440 A; timber	1 mi N of Douds on Hwy 98, 1.5 mi E on Hwy 16, 1 mi S on gravel road
Wapello			
Fox Hills	T, Q	1,297 A; timber	1 mi SE of Agency on Alpine Rd, 1 mi S on 70th Ave
Warren			
Hooper	P	400 A; ½ timber, ½ upland/lake	5.5 mi S of Indianola on Hwy 65-69, 1 mi W on Pershing St

Area	Game	Description	Directions
Wayne			
Railroad Right-of-Way	P	14 A; abandoned railroad, trail	1 mi N of Humeston on Hwy 65, .75 mi E on Vail Rd
Rathbun*	W, P, Q	15,970 A; ¼ lake, ¼ timber, ½ upland	2 mi N of Promise City on S56
Webster			
Boone Forks	T, P	3,210 A; ¾ timber, ¼ upland, river access	4 mi W of Stratford on Hwy 175, 1 mi N on gravel road
Brushy Creek	T, P	6,682 A; 2/3 upland, ⅓ timber	3 mi E of Lehigh on D46
Deception Hollow	T	43 A; timber, river access	1.5 mi S of Lehigh on P73, 1.5 mi E on gravel road
Lizard Creek	T	103 A; ¼ water, ½ timber, ¼ upland	2 mi W of Fort Dodge on Hwy 7, 2 mi S on gravel road and D22
Winnebago			
Harmon Lake	W, P	483 A; ½ marsh, ½ upland	5 mi W of Lake Mills on Hwy 69, 2 mi W on A30, 3 mi N on R50, 1 mi W on 480th St
Hogsback	W, T, P	203 A; ⅔ marsh, ⅓ upland	2 mi N of Lake Mills on R74, 1 mi W on A16
Myre Slough	W, P	430 A; ⅔ marsh, ⅓ timber/grassland	7 mi W of Forest City on A42, .5 mi N on 100th Avenue
Pilot Knob Recreation Area	T, W, P	160 A; ⅔ timber, ⅓ prairie potholes	4 mi E of Forest City on Hwy 9, .5 mi S on 210th Avenue, north edge of Pilot Knob State Park
Rice Lake*	W, P, T	1,831 A; ¾ lake, ¼ timbered grasslands	1 mi W of Lake Mills on 445th St, 1 mi S on 235th Ave
Wood Duck Marsh	W, P	193 A; ⅓ marsh, ⅓ upland, ⅓ timber	1 mi SW of Lake Mills on 12th Ave South

Winneshiek			
Bluffton Fir Stand	G, T	131 A; timber, Upper Iowa River	Adjacent to Bluffton
Canoe Creek	T, G	293 A; timber, Canoe Creek/Upper Iowa River	9 mi NE of Decorah on A6W, 1.5 mi ENE on gravel road
Cardinal Marsh	W, G	1,165 A; ½ timber, ¼ upland, ¼ marsh	1 mi NW of Ridgeway on Hwy 9, 3.5 mi W on Madison Rd
Coldwater Creek	T, G	232 A; ¾ timber, ¼ upland	.5 mi N of Bluffton on Bluffton Hill Rd, 2.1 mi NW of Bluffton Rd, 1 mi W on Coldwater Rd
Coon Creek	T, G	950 A; ¾ timber, ¼ upland	4.3 mi NE of Freeport on River Rd, .2 mi E on 143rd Ave, 1.3 mi NE on Coon Creek Rd
Falcon Springs	T, G	241 A; ¾ timber, ¼ upland	2 mi N of Jct. Hwy 9 & 52, 4.7 mi NW on Pole Line Rd
Malanaphy Springs	T	64 A; timber, Upper Iowa River	2mi N of Jct. Hwy 9 & 52, 2.2 mi NW on Pole Line Rd, .7 mi NW on Bluffton Rd
North Bear Complex	T, G	571 A; ¾ timber, ¼ upland	3.1 mi E of Highlandville on Quandahl Rd
South Bear Complex	T, G	845 A; ¾ timber, ¼ upland	West edge of Highlandville
Trout River	T	170 A; ½ timber, ½ upland	6.5 mi E of Decorah on Hwy 9, 1.7 mi N on 133rd Ave
Upper Iowa Accesses	T, G	3,961 A; Upper Iowa River, adjacent uplands	Several accesses along A6W west of Decorah
Woodbury			
Brown's Lake IPS	Q, W, P	1,311 A; ¼ timber, ½ upland, ¼ marsh	2.25 mi W of I-29 Salix Exit on Port Neal Rd
Dakota Bend	Q, P	109 A	Access by river only
Mile-Long Island	Q, P	230 A; ¾ bottomland timber, ¼ upland	1.25 mi W of I-29 Port Neal Rd Exit, W on 235th St to Allison Ave, S to 240th St, .75 mi W
Sioux Bend	Q, T, P	64 A; ⅔ bottomland timber, ⅓ upland	.5 mi W of Correctionville, S side of Hwy 20

Snyder-Winnebago Bend*	W, P, Q	2,865 A; ⅓ timber, ⅓ upland, ⅓ marshland	1.5 mi W of I-29 Salix Exit on K42, 1.5 mi S on Snyder Bend Rd; or .25 mi W of I-29 Sloan Exit, 1mi S on K42, 5 mi W on 340th St
Worth			
Bright's Lake	P, T	186 A; ¾ drained lakebed, ¼ timber	1 mi S of Emmons on Apricot Ave, .5 mi E on 500th St
Elk Creek Marsh*	W, P, T	2,532 A; ⅓ marsh, ⅓ upland, ⅓ timber	4 mi E of Lake Mills on Hwy 105, .5 mi S on Dogwood Ave
Peterson's Potholes	P, W	45 A; ¼ marsh, ¾ upland	2.5 mi E of Lake Mills on Hwy 105, 1.5 mi N on Bluebill Ave, 1 mi E on 465th St
Silver Lake/Silver Lake Marsh	W, T	447 A; ¾ lake, ¼ marsh	6 mi E of Lake Mills on Hwy 105, 3.5 mi N on Finch Ave, 1 mi W on Silver Lake Rd
Wright			
Big Wall Lake	W	988 A; marsh	5 mi E of Clarion on Hwy 3, 8 mi S on Hwy 69
Elm Lake	W	466 A; marsh	6 mi S of Belmond on Hwy 69, 2.5 mi W on 200th St
Morse Lake	W, P	235 A; ½ lake, ¼ upland, ¼ marsh	1 mi S of Belmond on Hwy 69, 3.5 mi W on 150th St

Iowa's Wildlife Management Units

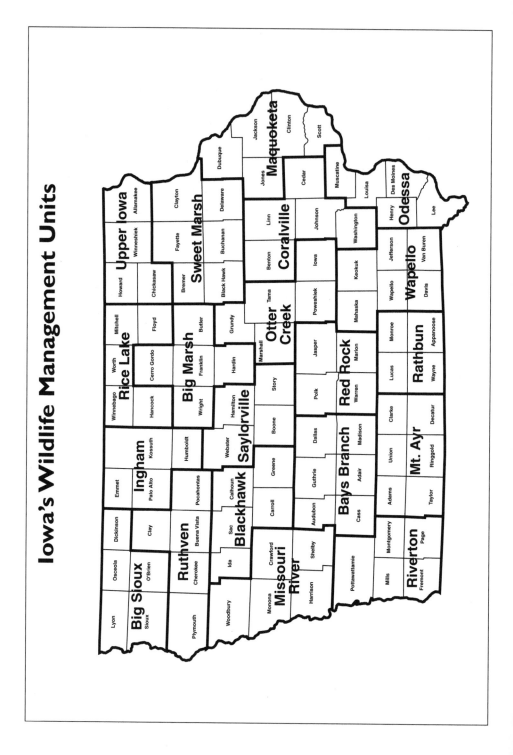

Iowa's Wildlife Management Units and Biologists

The wildlife biologists listed below are responsible for state-owned lands on their management units. There are 20 units as well as the Mississippi River.

Doug Harr
Big Sioux Unit
301½ 1st Avenue
Rock Rapids, IA 51246
712-472-3751

Ron Howing
Ingham Unit
2109 Murray Road
Estherville, IA 51334
712-362-2091

Greg Hanson
Rice Lake Unit
1604 Central Avenue
Northwood, IA 50495
515-3234-2431

Bob Kurtt
Upper Iowa Unit
903 Commerce Drive
Decorah, IA 52101
319-382-4895

Tom Neal
Ruthven Unit
1900 North Grand 84056
Spencer, IA 51301
712-262-4177

Doug Janke
Big Marsh Unit
115 2nd Avenue NW
Hampton, IA 50441
515-456-3730

Bob Dolan
Sweet Marsh Unit
501 17th SE
Independence, IA 50644
319-334-9191

Ed Weiner
Missouri River Unit
RR 2, Box 15a
Onawa, IA 51040
712-423-2426

Mike Mahn
Black Hawk Unit
Box 619
Lake View, IA 51450
712-657-2639

Scott Petersen
Saylorville Unit
1327 SE Marshall
Boone, IA 50036
515-432-2235

Rick Trine
Otter Creek Unit
2502 South Center #L
Marshalltown, IA 50158
515-752-5521

Tim Thompson
Coralville Unit
238 Stevens Drive
Iowa City, IA 52240
319-354-8343

Bob Sheets
Maquoketa Unit
201 West Platt
Maquoketa, IA 52060
319-652-3132

Ken Herring
Bays Branch Unit
1918 Gren #2
Adel, IA 50003
515-993-3911

Chuck Kakac
Red Rock Unit
Box 423
Indianola, IA 50125
515-961-0716

Carl Priebe
Riverton Unit
RR 1, Box 31
Sidney, IA 51652
712-374-3133

Mel Moe
Mt. Ayr Unit
RR 3
Mt. Ayr, IA 50854
515-464-2220

Sara Berg
Rathbun Unit
RR 5, Box 119aa #5
Chariton, IA 50049
515-774-4918

Chuck Steffen
Wapello Unit
700 Farm Credit Drive
Ottumwa, IA 52501
515-682-3552

Bill Ohde
Odessa Unit
220 South Second
Wapello, IA 52653
319-523-8319

Mike Griffin
Mississippi River Unit
206 Rose Street
Bellevue, IA 52031
319-872-5495

Appendix I
Pheasant Hunting Tips

Nearly all nonresident wingshooters who come to Iowa are here to hunt pheasants. The following tips will help make your pheasant hunting trip more successful:

- **When to come.** Because of the crowds of once-a-year resident hunters and the possibility of a late crop harvest, opening weekend is NOT the best time to plan an Iowa pheasant hunt. Also, without advance arrangements with a guide or local contact, you will not be able to get access to decent hunting ground. Plan your trip for after November 10 or so, by which time most of the corn should be harvested, and most of the casual hunters will have retired to their living rooms. You will always encounter less hunting pressure if you avoid weekends and holidays.
- **Where to hunt.** Compared to virtually every other state in the nation, you will find some good hunting in each of Iowa's 99 counties. While I would not recommend planning a trip to a part of the state ranked "poor," those areas rated "fair" can be very good indeed where you find good habitat. The tradeoff is that, in general, you will encounter less competition and, therefore, easier access to private land in the "fair" areas compared to those rated as "good."
- **Getting permission to hunt private land.** A small party of two or three hunters stands a much better chance than a larger group of half a dozen or more of securing permission to hunt. Often, the hardest part is determining land ownership—hence the value of the plat book—and finding the owner at home. I do not recommend that you call a landowner without having met him or her first. Most like to look you in the eye and "size you up" before giving the go-ahead. Once I have hunted a particular farm a couple of times and gotten to know the owner, however, I won't hesitate to call in advance. Offering the owner a dressed bird or two after the hunt or some other small gift (a Wisconsin friend of mine always brought rounds of cheese to give away) is a good way to say thanks. The practice of asking for a "trespass fee," almost standard procedure in many states, is still relatively uncommon in Iowa. I'd recommend waiting for the owner to bring up the subject of money.
- **Public vs. private land.** Iowa has relatively little public land, especially with good pheasant habitat, and the public areas tend to get hunted quite hard early in the season. However, because public areas tend to have very heavy cover, they can be good places to hunt late in the season, after the harvest is over and colder weather has set in. Because of all the cover, public areas are poor choices for dogless hunters.

Important and/or Unusual Regulations for Pheasant Hunters
1. It is legal to hunt in road ditches but not within 200 yards of a building occupied by humans or livestock. If you shoot a bird that drops onto private property, you may trespass to retrieve the bird, but you must leave your gun behind.

2. In a vehicle, shotguns must be unloaded and cased, with the case fully closed (zipped or tied shut) at all times. As an option, the gun may be broken down. If you are working a "drive and block," where you end up being picked up by a vehicle that does not have your gun case, a good solution is to carry one of the cheap, tie-shut gun slips in your coat or vest.

3. When transporting dressed pheasants, you must leave a part of the bird attached (head, wing, or leg) that will identify it as a rooster. I find that the leg is the easiest. You can even freeze the bird with the leg attached, allowing you to identify it by spur length as a bird of the year (tender) or an old survivor (tough) before preparing it for the table.

4. "Party shooting"—where members of a group pay little attention to who has shot how many birds until they reach their collective bag limit—is theoretically illegal in Iowa. In practice, however, whether your group party shoots is a question of personal ethics. To avoid potential problems with game wardens, never carry more than your own three-bird limit in your game pouch.

Appendix II
Conditioning, Equipment, and Vehicles

The following guidance is aimed mainly at pheasant hunters:

Iowa terrain, in general, is neither rugged nor remote. However, if you are a first-time visitor to the state, you will probably find that most farm fields are not as flat as you expect them to be. The best pheasant areas in the state feature rolling terrain with a lot of up and down, and some of the streams and draws can be quite steeply sloped.

You and your dog will likely be covering a lot of ground in the course of a day. Relatively few Iowa farms are large enough to permit a several-hour hunt in one place. A more typical pattern would be a hunt of anywhere from one hour to three hours' duration, followed by a break, followed by another hunt or two of similar length. By the time you are done, you may well have walked 10 miles or so. Conditioning, both for you and your dog, is necessary if you expect to have an enjoyable and successful experience.

Conditioning for the Hunter

Your own conditioning program should focus on the legs and on aerobic exercise for your heart and lungs. Walking, bicycling, and swimming are all excellent forms of exercise—if you go at them hard enough. Unfortunately, all can be done in such a casual manner that exercise value will be minimal.

Walking should be done between a 3.5- to 4-mile-per-hour pace. Likewise, if you bike or swim, do so with enough intensity to raise your heart rate significantly. Your workouts should last for at least half an hour, and you should exercise a minimum of three times a week.

Except for people with bad knees or other physiological problems, running is probably the best exercise of all. It gets a bad rap, mainly from people who aren't motivated enough to do it or who imagine that it will result in injury. Because I've spent over 30 years in the Army Reserve, I've had to maintain a running program. I've also run competitively for nearly 15 years, in races up to a marathon (26.2 miles). I'm on the wrong side of 50, still run regularly, and the worst injury I've ever sustained was a stress fracture. That only caused me to stop running temporarily, and it had no impact at all on my hunting that year.

The beauty of running is that, unless you are a top-flight competitor, there is no way to do it so slowly that it isn't good exercise. Although fast walking can be almost as good, the comparative benefit is based on the distance you cover, not the time involved. Thus, even at a slow jog (10-minute miles), you will cover a lot more ground in an hour than you would at a fast walk (15-minute miles).

If you are over 40, overweight, or have a history of heart disease in your family, you should always consult a physician before beginning any kind of strenuous exercise program. An electrocardiogram is always a wise precaution, and if it shows any abnormalities, you should then take a treadmill (stress) test.

Conditioning the Dog

Some people suggest working a dog into your own exercise program. In our busy, clock-oriented society, this may be a good way to save time, but it's a poor way to condition a dog. Your walking pace is ultra-slow for Rover. As for the "experts" who say that it's too much strain on a dog to jog along with its owners, they must be thinking of lap pooches. My jogging pace equates to little more than a very fast walk for my dogs. Although biking will push your dog to keep up, it usually takes place around cars and is thus unsafe for the dog.

A good starting point for a dog is to help it maintain an acceptable weight. Too many are allowed to get fat and lazy over the summer.

In mid- to late August, I start a program of hunting my dogs into condition. I work them in the same kind of cover—knee-high grass—where they're going to be spending much of their time looking for birds in a couple of months. In hot weather, I limit these training hunts to 15 or 20 minutes in the coolest part of the day—early in the morning or just before dark. I also make sure the dogs get plenty of water. If it's too hot to run them in bird cover, swimming is also a good exercise.

Throughout September, I gradually increase their time afield to an hour or more and may work in a preserve hunt or two before the native bird seasons open. After hunting grouse and woodcock in Iowa or the lake states for a couple of weeks or so, they are in top shape—and pretty sharp on birds as well—by the time the pheasant opener rolls around.

Clothes

The Iowa pheasant season opens in late October, when the average temperature is still quite warm. Splitting the difference between the extremes, however, derives average. I've seen opening days when I've been hot in just a cotton shirt and light vest and others when I've needed heavy chamois or wool under a hunting coat. Early season temperatures, however, will rarely be above 70° or below freezing.

The Iowa pheasant hunter needs at least two pairs of boots, and one of those has to be rubber-bottomed, if not all rubber. The other pair should be lightly lined, waterproof upland boots of Goretex or leather. Neither pair should have Vibram or other heavy lug soles—they will accumulate Iowa gumbo to the point where each foot will weigh about 10 pounds.

If you carry both a vest and a hunting coat, you'll be ready for either warm or cold weather. The game pouch on each needs to be big enough to accommodate at least a brace of roosters. (A surprising number scarcely have room for one!)

Most of what will stick you in Iowa—plants such as multiflora rose—can be avoided. However, hunting pants or chaps will help keep your legs dry while walking in wet grass and will offer some protection and insulation from snow later in the season.

Other items of clothing I always carry in my hunting bag: caps of various weights, all in blaze orange (even though Iowa has no blaze orange requirement); several pairs of gloves for temperatures from 70° above to 20° below ; and a complete change of clothing in case of rain.

Equipment

I never go afield without the following: on a dog tag chain around my neck, a spare truck key and a compass; in my pocket, a Swiss Army knife; in my vest or coat, a pair of needle-nose pliers, a dog lead, and a gun slip. I'm also never without a dog whistle. Most of the time, I also carry one of the small, fully automatic, 35mm cameras.

In my bag, in addition to usual items such as extra shells, first aid items for man and dog, and the above-mentioned change of clothes, I also include: an extra dog whistle; an extra collar and spare bells for the dogs; appropriate batteries and/or turn-on plugs, depending on what kind of electronic collar I have; game shears; and various small items, such as matches, flashlight, and plastic bags (small for birds, large for trash). Usually, unless we are in the midst of a drought, water for dogs is not a problem in Iowa. I am about as likely to carry a bottle for myself on a warm day as I am for the dog. There is almost always a stream or pond where the dog can get a drink and take a cool dip on a hot day. However, I always carry a gallon or two of water in the truck, as well as some Gaines Burgers for midday canine energy boosters. On cold or wet days when the dogs might get chilled, I towel them off and give them a shot of a concentrated, high energy food supplement called Nutri-Cal, which comes in a tube. They'll eat it right from the tube, on a Gaines Burger, or on their regular ration. It is available from many veterinarians and pet supply stores.

Compared to many hunting destinations, there is not a lot in Iowa that can harm your dog. We have no porcupines, and while an encounter with a skunk will be memorable, it is not really dangerous. There are plenty of burrs that will end up stuck in a longhaired dog's coat but few that will really hurt the animal. A dog that isn't careful around fences, however, can get barbed wire cuts ranging anywhere from minor to requiring stitches.

Traps and snares pose one of the most serious problems to dogs hunting in Iowa. Make sure you know how to extract a dog from a leghold or conibear trap, or from a snare. A stout pair of pliers or a tool with a wire cutter, such as a Leatherman, will help with snares in particular. Fortunately, most encounters with traps tend to result in temporary trauma rather than in permanent injury. All my dogs have had a toe pinched in a muskrat trap, but after a little yelping, they go back to hunting as soon as I release them.

If you have an especially nervous dog, you may want to muzzle it with a belt or bandana before trying to release it from a trap. A friend's pointer once punched a nice hole in my thumb when she thought I was part of the problem instead of the solution.

Vehicles

For the most part, as long as you're willing to sacrifice the back seat to your dogs, you can use the family sedan for hunting in Iowa. Almost all secondary roads are gravel and are passable for two-wheel drive vehicles in all kinds of weather except very deep snow. Those that aren't secondary roads are marked "Minimum Maintenance," which means dirt rather than gravel. These roads are not plowed in the winter, and they turn to mud after more than a few sprinkles. Fortunately, all inhabited farms can be accessed from gravel roads. Don't be brave and try the dirt roads just because they'll save you a couple of miles unless you have four-wheel drive.

Road maintenance around some of the large Public Hunting Areas, where there may be no working farms, varies from erratic to nonexistent. Especially in winter or in wet weather, these roads can require a 4x4.

While you can hunt from the family car, there are better options. I've tried station wagons, sport utility vehicles (SUVs), and pickups. All have their pros and cons.

Station wagons have lost considerable ground in popularity to minivans and SUVs. Most wagons, vans, and SUVs can carry two or three hunters and their gear, as well as a couple of dogs, in relative comfort. SUVs have the advantage of four-wheel drive. You'll need a big van or Suburban-sized SUV for more people, dogs, or a lot of gear, which hits your wallet harder both for initial cost and for poor fuel economy. You're also sharing breathing space with your dogs, and while we outdoor writers love to wax nostalgic about the aroma they emit, it gets old after a few days.

Pickups have separate space for hunters and dogs and can hold a lot of gear, but you do sacrifice people carrying capacity. My current vehicle is a small, extended cab pickup, which gives me room for two hunters and two or three dogs on a long trek. For shorter hops, I can handle a third hunter. Fuel economy is very good. My dogs ride in a double kennel under a topper with crank-open screen windows to give them ventilation and large side doors that give easy access to our gear.

I've never tried a dog trailer, but there are several very good ones on the market that will carry at least half a dozen dogs as well as some equipment. They would be a logical option for anyone who travels with lots of dogs, parties of four or five hunters, and all their attendant gear.

No matter what kind of vehicle you choose, your hunting rig should always include a few emergency items. I'm never without a set of jumper cables and an entrenching tool—one of the small, folding Army shovels. Unless you have had better luck than I with standard equipment lug wrenches, I'd suggest a four-way wrench in case of a flat. And if each of your wheels has one or more of those lug nuts designed to prevent theft and requiring a "special tool" to remove, I highly recommend that you replace them with standard nuts. From my own experience and that of several friends, I've found that theft-proof lug nuts are just as likely to keep you from mounting a spare tire as foiling a tire thief.

Appendix III
Equipment Checklists

Clothing

_____ Polypropylene underwear

_____ Inner socks

_____ Wool socks

_____ Long sleeve canvas/chamois shirts

_____ Pants, double-faced

_____ Hunting boots

_____ Billed hat

_____ Bandana

_____ Shooting gloves

_____ Shooting glasses

_____ Ear protectors

_____ Hunting vest/coat

_____ Down vest/coat

_____ Raingear

_____ Hip boots/waders
for waterfowl hunting

_____ Chaps

Dog Equipment Check List

In the Field

_____ Water

_____ Collapsible water bowl

_____ Honey

_____ Hemostat

_____ *Field Guide to Dog First Aid*

In the Truck

_____ Food

_____ Bowls

_____ Leads

_____ Check cords

_____ Dog First Aid Kit

_____ Dog boots, pad toughener

_____ Vaccination records

_____ Toenail clippers

_____ Training dummies

_____ Beeper Collars

_____ Extra whistle

_____ Extra collars

_____ Five gallons of water

_____ Water bottles

_____ Any prescription medications

Hunting Supplies

_____ *Wingshooter's Guide to Iowa*

_____ Shotgun/shells

_____ Cleaning kit

_____ Maps

_____ Knife

_____ Fanny pack

_____ Water bottle

_____ Camera, film

_____ Binoculars

_____ Game shears

_____ Ice chest

_____ Notebook, pen

_____ License

_____ Matches

_____ Axe, shovel

_____ Sunscreen

_____ Twine

_____ Decoys, decoy anchor

_____ Compass

_____ Flashlight

_____ Bird calls

_____ Spare choke tubes

_____ Magnifying glass for maps

Hunting Rig Check List

_____ Tool Kit

_____ Ax and Shovel

_____ Flares

_____ Jumper cables

_____ Tow rope

_____ Heavy duty jack and tire iron

_____ Spare tire

_____ Matches

_____ Magnifying glass

_____ Road maps

_____ Air gauge

_____ Flashlight

_____ Spare key

_____ Duct tape

_____ Chains

_____ Fuses

_____ Extra fuel

_____ Blankets

_____ Emergency food

Appendix IV
Preparing a Bird
for Mounting in the Field

by Web Parton, Taxidermist

The art of taxidermy has made considerable advances in recent years. This is especially true in the realm of bird taxidermy. How you take care of your birds in the field determines the finished quality of your mounts. This crucial step is out of the control of the taxidermist. However, with a modicum of preparation, you can proceed confidently when you are holding a freshly taken bird destined for the book shelf.

Start by putting together a small kit to be carried with you in the field. Use a small plastic container, such as a plastic traveler's soap box. Throw in some cotton balls, a few wooden toothpicks, a dozen or so folded sheets of toilet paper, and a pair of panty hose.

After shooting a bird, examine it closely. First, look for pin feathers. If there are any present, you will notice them on the head directly behind the beak or bill and on the main side coverts below the bird's wing. If there are even a few pinfeathers, the specimen may not be worth mounting. By all means, save it and let your taxidermist make the decision. However, it wouldn't hurt to examine additional birds to find one with better plumage. The taxidermist can always use extra birds for spare parts.

The next step is to check for any bleeding wounds in order to prevent the taxidermist from having to wash the bird before mounting. Plug any visible wounds with cotton. Use a toothpick as a probe to push the cotton into the holes. Now pack the mouth and nostrils, remembering that the body is a reservoir of fluids that can drain down the neck. Make a note or take a photo of any brightly colored soft tissue parts (unfeathered areas) for the taxidermist's reference later. Fold several sheets of toilet paper and lay them between the wings and the body. Should the body bleed, this will protect the undersides of the wings from being soiled. Slide the bird head first into the nylon stocking. Remember that the feathers lay like shingles: they slide forward into the stocking smoothly, but will ruffle if you pull the bird back out the same end. The taxidermist will remove it by cutting a hole in the material at the toe and sliding the bird forward. When the specimen is all the way down, knot the nylon behind its tail. Now you are ready to slide the next one in behind it.

Place the wrapped bird in an empty game vest pocket, allow it to cool, and protect it from getting wet. When you return to your vehicle, place the bird in a cool spot. At home, put it in a plastic bag to prevent freezer burn, and freeze it solid. You can safely wait several months before dropping it off at the taxidermist.

For the traveling hunter, there is the option of next-day air shipping. Provided that you can find a place to freeze the birds overnight, even a hunter on the other side of the nation can get birds to his taxidermist in good shape. Wrap the frozen birds, nylons and all, in disposable diapers. Line a shipping box with wadded newspapers. Place the birds in the middle with dry ice. Dry ice is available in some major supermarkets. Call your taxidermist to be sure someone will be there, and then ship the parcel next-day air. Be sure to contact them the next day so that a search can be instituted in the event that the parcel did not arrive.

Mounted birds are a beautiful memory of your days in the field. With just a little bit of advance preparation, you can be assured of a top-quality mount.

Appendix V
Field Preparation of Game
Birds for the Table

The two most important tools for preparing birds in the field for the table are game sheers and a knife with a gut hook.

During early season, when temperatures are in the 70° to 90° range, I draw my birds immediately or shortly after I leave the field. You can draw your birds by several methods. I make a cut with my sheers at the end of the breast, making a small entry hole into the body cavity. I then take my gut hook, insert it into the cavity and pull out the intestines and other body parts. The other method I use is to take my sheers and cut up the center of the bird's back, splitting the bird in two. Then I use my gut hook and knife to clean out the intestines and other body parts.

I like to place my birds in a cooler during the hot early season. When the temperatures are cooler (below 55°), I store my birds in either a burlap or net bag. This type of bag allows air to circulate around the birds.

I like to hang my birds before cleaning and freezing. I hang my birds in a room where the temperature is less than 60° F. I have found that two to three days hanging time is best for the smaller birds (i.e., huns, grouse, woodcock). I hang my larger birds (pheasants, ducks) from four to five days. Hanging birds is a matter of individual preference. My friend Datus Proper hangs his birds for a much longer period of time than I do. I suggest that you experiment and then pick a hanging time that suits your tastes.

When the temperature is over 60°F, I clean my birds and freeze them immediately. We wrap our birds in cling wrap, place them in a ziplock bag, and then mark the bag with the type of bird and the date.

Appendix VI
Information Sources

Maps

Farm & Home Publishers
P.O. Box 305
Belmond, IA 50421
800-685-7432
County plat directories. Also available at Recorder's Office in all county courthouses.

Iowa Department of Natural Resources Publications
Wallace State Office Building
Des Moines, IA 50319-0034
515-281-5145
Free maps of larger public hunting areas.

Iowa Department of Transportation
Office Supplies
800 Lincoln Way
Ames, IA 50010
515-239-1324
State transportation maps, county maps.

Iowa Atlas and Gazetteer
Topo maps with back roads and public areas, available through Wilderness
  Adventures

Other Sources of Information

Iowa Department of Economic Development
Division of Tourism
200 East Grand Avenue
Des Moines, IA 50309
515-242-4705

Statewide Road Information
515-288-1047—Winter road conditions (November 15–April 15) and detour information (April 16–November 14)

State Public Hunting Areas and Other Public Lands

The Iowa Department of Natural Resources manages 340 wildlife areas that total
more than 270,000 acres. Most of these are Public Hunting Areas. Varying in size
from under 100 to over several thousand acres and containing a variety of habitats

including wetland, grassland, timber and crop ground, these areas are scattered around the state. Contact the Iowa Department of Natural Resources for its free brochure, "Public Hunting Areas of Iowa", which lists the areas by county, and includes a description of the habitat and game species found on the area.

Iowa Department of Natural Resources
Wallace State Office Building
Des Moines, IA 50319-0034
515-281-5145
WWW.state.ia.us/dnr

Northwest District Office
611 252nd Avenue
Spirit Lake, IA 51360
712-336-1840

Southwest District Office
Cold Springs Park
Lewis, IA 51544
712-769-2587

Northeast District Office
RR#2 Box 269A
Manchester, IA 50257
319-927-3276

Southeast District Office
Lake Darling Station
Brighton, IA 52540
319-694-2430

County Lands

The conservation boards of Iowa's 99 counties control 1,464 areas totaling 133,885 acres. Many of the larger rural areas are open to hunting. All are listed in the Iowa Association of County Conservation Board's "Outdoor Adventure Guide." To obtain a copy, contact:

Iowa Association of County Conservation Boards
Box 79
Elkhart, IA 50073
515-367-4000

Appendix VII
Recommended Product Sources

Listed below are products and suppliers that I use and recommend:

Clothes

Orvis
Historic Route 7A
Manchester, VT 05254
1-800-548-9548

Patagonia
8550 White Fir Street
Reno, Nevada 89533
1-800-638-6464

Simms
101 Evergreen Drive
Bozeman, MT 59772
1-406-585-3557

Patagonia makes a heavy duty pant, called a "stand-up pant," that is my favorite late fall and winter hunting pant. I also use their fleece outer garments and their Capilene underwear. Simms makes an outstanding raincoat. They sell only through dealers; check with your local fly shop.

Eyewear

Sporting Optical Specialties
964 Reni Road
Fond du Lac, WI 54935
1-800-521-2239

Sporting Optical Specialties carries Ranger and Costa del Mar glasses. The owners, Jim McConnell and Rob Post, are opticians and can provide you with specialized service for your prescription lenses.

Dog Supplies

Purina Pro Club
P.O. Box 1004
Mascoutah, IL 62224
1-800-851-3148

The Pointing Dog Journal
The Retriever Journal
P.O. Box 968
Traverse City, MI 49685
1-800-272-3246

Purina makes healthful and dependable food for dogs. They have an excellent research lab and make products especially for the hunting dog. I've used Purina's Pro Plan food for 15 years. My dogs love it and perform well with this food. Purina supports hunters and has a special discount plan. *The Pointing Dog Journal* and *The Retriever Journal* are, in my opinion, the two best magazines for sporting dog enthusiasts. Their writers provide the latest news and tips on training and wingshooting.

Recommended Reading

American Game Birds of Field and Forest. Frank C. Edminster. New York: Castle Books, 1954.

American Wildlife & Plants: A Guide to Wildlife Food Habits. Alexander C. Martin, Herbert S. Zim, Arnold L. Nelson. New York: Dover Publishing, Inc., 1951.

• *Autumn Passages: A Ducks Unlimited Treasury of Waterfowling Classics.* Ducks Unlimited & Willow Creek Press, 1995. $27.50

• *Best Way to Train Your Gun Dog: The Delmar Smith Method.* Bill Tarrant. New York: David McKay Company, Inc., 1977. $20.00

• *Bill Tarrant's Gun Dog Book: A Treasury of Happy Tails.* Bill Tarrant. Honolulu: Sun Trails Publishing, 1980. A great collection of fireside dog stories. $25.00

• *Ducks, Geese & Swans of North America.* Frank C. Bellrose. Harrisburg, PA: Stackpole Books, 1976. $49.95

• *A Field Guide to Dog First Aid.* Randy Acker, D.V.M., and Jim Fergus. Gallatin Gateway, MT: Wilderness Adventures Press, 1994. An indispensible pocket guide. It could save your dog's life. $15.00

• *Fool Hen Blues: Retrievers, Shotguns, & the American West.* E. Donnall Thomas, Jr. Gallatin Gateway, MT: Wilderness Adventures Press, 1995. Don hunts sharptails, Huns, sage grouse, mountain grouse, pheasants, and waterfowl against the wild Montana sky. $29.00

Game Birds of North America. Leonard Lee Rue, III. New York: Harper & Row, 1973.

Game Management. Aldo Leopold. Madison, WI: University of Wisconsin Press, 1933.

• *Good Guns Again.* Steve Bodio. Gallatin Gateway, MT: Wilderness Adventures Press, 1994. A survey of fine shotguns by an avid gun collector and trader. $29.00

Grasslands. Lauren Brown. New York: Alfred A. Knopf, 1985.

Grouse and Quails of North America. Paul A. Johnsgard. Lincoln, NE: University of Nebraska Press, 1973.

• *Gun Dogs and Bird Guns: A Charlie Waterman Reader.* Charles F. Waterman. South Hamilton, MA: Gray's Sporting Journal Press, 1986.

• *Hey Pup, Fetch It Up: The Complete Retriever Training Book.* Bill Tarrant. Mechanicsburg, PA: Stackpole Books, 1979. $25.00

• *How to Hunt Birds with Gun Dogs.* Bill Tarrant, Mechanicsburg, PA: Stackpole Books, 1994. Bill covers all the birds, what dogs to use and how to hunt each game bird. $21.00

• *A Hunter's Road.* Jim Fergus. New York: Henry Holt and Co., 1992. A joyous journey with gun and dog across the American Uplands. A hunter's *Travels with Charlie.* $25.00

• *Hunting Upland Birds.* Charles F. Waterman. New York: Winchester Press, 1972.

• *Denotes book available from Wilderness Adventures, Inc.*

- *Kicking Up Trouble.* John Holt. Gallatin Gateway, MT: Wilderness Adventures Press, 1994. John takes you on a delightful bird hunting trip through Montana. $29.00
Life Histories of North American Gallinaceous Birds. Arthur Cleveland Bent. New York: Dover Publishing, Inc., 1963.
- *Meditations on Hunting.* José Ortega y Gasset. Gallatin Gateway, MT: Wilderness Adventures Press, 1995. The classic book on hunting. Special edition. $60.00
Peterson Field Guides: Western Birds. Roger Tory Peterson. Boston: Houghton Mifflin, 1990.
- *Pheasants of the Mind.* Datus C. Proper. Gallatin Gateway, MT: Wilderness Adventures Press, 1994. Simply the best book ever written on pheasants. $25.00
- *Problem Gun Dogs.* Bill Tarrant. Mechanicsburg, PA: Stackpole Books, 1995. $20.00
Prairie Ducks. Lyle K. Sowls. Lincoln, NE: University of Nebraska Press, 1978.
A Sand County Almanac. Aldo Leopold. New York: Oxford University Press, 1949.
- *Training the Versatile Retriever to Hunt Upland Birds.* Bill Tarrant. Gallatin Gateway, MT: Wilderness Adventures Press, 1996. $29.95
- *Waterfowl: An Identification Guide to the Ducks, Geese and Swans of the World.* Houghton Mifflin Co. $29.95
- *Waterfowling Horizons: Shooting Ducks and Geese in the 21st Century.* Christopher S. and Jason A. Smith. Gallatin Gateway, MT: Wilderness Adventures Press, September 1997. $39.95
Western Forests. Stephen Whitney. New York: Alfred A. Knopf, 1985.

- *Denotes book available from Wilderness Adventures, Inc.*

Index

NOTES

NOTES

NOTES

NOTES

NOTES

WILDERNESS ADVENTURES GUIDE SERIES

If you would like to order additional copies of this book or our other Wilderness Adventures Press guidebooks, please fill out the order form below or call **800-925-3339** or **fax 800-390-7558**. Visit our website for a listing of over 2500 sporting books—the largest online: **www.wildadv.com**

Mail to: Wilderness Adventures Press, P.O. Box 627, Gallatin Gateway, MT 59730

☐ **Please send me your quarterly catalog on hunting and fishing books.**

Ship to:
Name _____
Address _____
City _____ State _____ Zip _____
Home Phone _____ Work Phone _____

Payment: ☐ Check ☐ Visa ☐ Mastercard ☐ Discover ☐ American Express

Card Number _____ Expiration Date _____

Qty	Title of Book and Author	Price	Total
	Wingshooter's Guide to Kansas	$26.95	
	Wingshooter's Guide to Montana	$26.00	
	Wingshooter's Guide to South Dakota	$26.95	
	Wingshooter's Guide to North Dakota	$26.95	
	Wingshooter's Guide to Arizona	$26.95	
	Wingshooter's Guide to Idaho	$26.95	
	Flyfisher's Guide to Colorado	$26.95	
	Flyfisher's Guide to Idaho	$26.95	
	Flyfisher's Guide to Montana	$26.95	
	Flyfisher's Guide to Northern California	$26.95	
	Flyfisher's Guide to Wyoming	$26.95	
	Total Order + shipping & handling		

Shipping and handling: $4.00 for first book, $2.50 per additional book, up to $11.50 maximum